# LONDON'S
# BEST-KEPT
## SECRETS

# LONDON'S BEST-KEPT SECRETS

Mike Michaelson

**PASSPORT BOOKS**
a division of *NTC Publishing Group*
Lincolnwood, Illinois USA

**Editorial writers:** Michael Sweeney
Frank Sennett

**Editorial research
& production:** Glynis A. Steadman

**Type and layout:** MobiGraphics, Inc.


Published by Passport Books, a division of NTC
Publishing Group, 4255 West Touhy Avenue,
Lincolnwood (Chicago), Illinois 60646-1975.

Manufactured in the United States of America.

Library of Congress Catalog Card Number: 90-63161

1 2 3 4 5 6 7 8 9 ML 9 8 7 6 5 4 3 2 1

# CONTENTS

# INTRODUCTION

Do you know a spot in London that you can visit, but Queen Elizabeth can't? Or where you can find a cosy pub built by master architect Christopher Wren? Or a museum that exhibits the skeleton of Napoleon's horse? Or the shop that was the birthplace of the famous bowler hat, favoured by generations of upper-crust British businessmen?

This sampling of distinctive and intriguing attractions summarises what this book is all about—showing off all of the "bests" that London has to offer. Not just the classic things and places in this classic city (although, of course, they are included here, usually presented in a new way), but also the unique, the offbeat, and the irreverent—in short, a fascinating collection of things to do and places to see in and around London, including restaurants, pubs, hotels, shopping, entertainment, sports (to watch and participate in), museums, parks and gardens, cultural diversions, and much more.

This book will direct you to the finest and most elegant restaurants in London—as well as for takeaway fish and chips, the best jellied eels, traditional bangers and mash, and pub grub that breaks the mold of predictable ploughman's and soggy lasagne. We also visit casual eating spots, some of them hidden away in unexpected locations, and restaurants where you can sample the cuisine of Italy and India, California and Chicago, Japan and Jamaica. We'll take you to pubs frequented by Karl Marx and Charles Dickens, pubs mentioned in nursery rhymes and classic mysteries, and pubs located at the top of a high-rise hotel and beneath a train station. You'll read about halls offering top-flight classical music as well as venues for superstar jazz "jam sessions." We'll steer you to shops favoured by Princess Di (for some of the chic designer clothing she is known for wearing) and show you where you can haggle over bargains with a street vendor.

These contrasts—and many more!—are what make London such a vibrant and exciting travel destination. And this book shines its whimsical spotlight on all of the diverse facets of this sprawling, cosmopolitan world capital.

As you may have guessed, this is not your standard guidebook. Think of us as a well-informed friend—the kind you wish you had in every city you visited. Wouldn't it be great to have a friendly native Londoner to steer you to all the worthwhile (and even unusual) sites, while avoiding the travel cliches and the overrated or past-their-prime spots? Wouldn't it be fun to learn the real inside gossip and fascinating history about the sights you're seeing? Our aim has been to do just that—and more. Thorough chapter selections and a comprehensive index make this a practical book to use—but the innovative suggestions make it fun and (we think you'll come to agree) indispensable to use.

Looking for historic sights? You'll find the expected here, often examined in a new light...Buckingham Palace, the Tower of London, Big Ben...but we'll also introduce you to the unexpected. We'll tell you why Cleopatra's Needle is misnamed, show you where London's original tourists (the Romans) stayed, and warn you what you'll find at one of London's most famous addresses, 221b Baker Street (alas, not Holmes and Watson, but a friendly company that good-naturedly fields any calls they get for the super-sleuth, advising fans that he's out of the country on a pressing case).

For those with kids in tow, we direct you to an entire chapter of attractions keyed especially to families visiting London, from out of town or from out in the suburbs. Ditto for lovers—and honey-mooners—with the special selections in our "Romantic" chapter. And for those visiting London in pursuit of commerce—or for visitors mixing pleasure with business, there are special for suggestions for restaurants and other services of interest to the London-bound businessperson.

And for when you venture beyond Greater London? We've even got you covered there. Head for our "Environs" chapter for insights on some special places in the surrounding counties, such as: the most poetic little village in England; the homes and story settings for authors such as Dickens and Milton; a tranquil watering hole where you can take a trip on an authentic Thames sailing barge; and a fairy-tale castle described as perhaps the loveliest in the world.

This is a book to browse through, perhaps chuckling at some of the folly enclosed within (is it true that the person who purchased, dismantled, and relocated the London Bridge believed that he was buying the more famous and historic Tower Bridge?). But it is also a solid reference guide—we let you know not just what's out there, but why it's worth a visit. And, while this book strives to be a good, lively read, full of fun as well as fact, it is also a completely practical volume, providing addresses and phone numbers for attractions, so you'll have conveniently at hand all of the information you need for a delightful trip.

Our team of travel experts and expert travelers have prepared this book for the first-time visitor and the London resident alike. We help the first-timer find the unexpected treasures that can literally make a vacation. As for veteran travelers, we'd be hard-pressed to believe that anyone (even an immensely curious native Londoner) has journeyed to all of the 500-plus sites we've surveyed in this book. This means, of course, that we can help seasoned visitors get even more out of a trip to London by helping them discover hidden gems that may have escaped them on previous trips or by pointing out new worthwhile restaurants or attractions that have opened since they last visited.

Let's face it—it can be hard work having a great vacation, or even a stimulating weekend in the city or night out on the town. We've attempted to take some of the work out of your play time by tracking down everything you might want to do in and around London—including things that you didn't know you wanted to do, but *will* after reading about them!

So, what this book offers is both the famous and the should-be-famous...Both the expensive and the inexpensive (and even the free!). But, overall and most importantly, it offers a unique and entertaining perspective on one of the most popular vacation destinations in the world.

To say the least, our perspective (with equal touches of history and humour) is much like London itself: you are not likely to find anything like it anywhere else!

# LONDON BASICS

## Getting Around

As you might expect of a city with roots stretching back 2,000 years, London is a complex sprawl of tangled, often narrow, streets. It is a near-certainty that strangers will get lost at least once, so it's as well to make the best of it and soak up the colour and the scenery, secure in the knowledge that even native Londoners can get lost from time to time (except the cab drivers—more about whom later).

London streets rarely follow any pattern (much less something as constraining and non-imaginative as a grid), and often change names, direction, and numbering without any seeming rhyme or reason. Compounding the problem is the absence of identifying street signs on many intersections. So, the first and most important rule about getting around in London is to buy and use a detailed map. Not only will such a map help you navigate the maze of tiny, winding streets, mews, and cul-de-sacs, and direct you to the major sights, but it will also show you that (for example) Grosvenor Place is not Grosvenor Road is not Grosvenor Street!

In particular, should you stop to ask directions, you may find it easier (and more helpful) to ascertain exactly where you are (given the deficiency of street signs) and then rely on your map—rather than be directed to where you want to go. Although typically friendly, in general the average Londoner seems to be poorly informed on local geography and sometimes will cheerfully steer you wrong rather than admit this lack of knowledge. Stopping to ask directions, I have, on more than one occasion, been blithely pointed in totally opposite directions by different local experts within a block or two of each other. I have even been misdirected more than once by the famous friendly (but not necessarily geographically savvy) London bobbies—"Well, wots all this, then?"

A good way to get your bearings as you travel around central London is to look for an Underground station. London's public transport system is so comprehensive that, no matter in which direction you walk, chances are you'll soon come across a station. Then it's simply a matter of locating your position on a map—or hopping on a train!

London can be roughly divided into two unequal halves, with the River Thames as the divider. With the exception of a few attractions on the south bank, mostly clustered around the Waterloo Bridge, the southern half of London is generally considered to be of minor interest to tourists. While this book does suggest some worthy sites, attractions, restaurants, etc. in South London, for the most part, your adventures will be concentrated north of the Thames. And while its streets may be winding, London's topography is mostly flat, making it ideal for walking.

The "tourist's London" we will briefly describe here can be said to lie mostly west and southwest of the so-called "City of London," the square-mile financial district that was the site of the original Roman encampment of Londinium, founded in the First Century A.D. "The City," as this area is called, contains the Bank of England and the various financial and goods exchanges. It wasn't until the last 300-or-so years that London spread out from this nucleus. (It is important to remember that when Londoners refer to "the City," they are referring to this distinct area, rather than to Greater London as a whole. For a definition of Greater London, see "Government" below.)

Moving in a longish loop west and south from the City, visitors will first find Holborn (pronounced "HO-burn"), featuring areas of shopping and Fleet Street, the traditional home to London journalism (although all of the great dailies have now departed); next is Bloomsbury, site of the University of London and a variety of cultural attractions; spreading south is the main tourist/entertainment area known as the West End, home to a large number of theatres, restaurants, shops, and sightseeing attractions (and encompassing the smaller area of Soho, renowned for nightclubs and entertainment); further south, along the river, is Westminster, including the seat of government at Parliament, stately Westminster Abbey, and the royal residence of Buckingham Palace; turning west, you encounter the fashionable residences and international embassies of Knightsbridge and Belgravia; further west is chic Chelsea, in another era known for being "Bohemian," and still a bastion of fashion, music, and youth culture; north is the huge, green expanse of Hyde Park, the largest park in central London (and one of the largest urban parks in the world); and just northeast of the park (considered part of the West End, but individually notable) is Mayfair, boasting elegant, up-market shopping and equally high-toned residences.

As previously said, this represents just a small slice of Greater London. But, for the purposes of most visitors, the above-described areas will constitute most (if not all) of the region of immediate interest. (This book, however, does include sites and attractions for all portions of London and its environs. We trust that our reach will exceed your grasp!)

## Speaking English In England

(Being A Primer For Americans And Other Visitors Who Learned The Language Elsewhere)

Although English-speaking visitors to the U.K. may have little difficulty in communicating with the natives, occasional differences in language may seem an ocean apart. Not to worry, however—the English, reserved by nature, usually enjoy talking to Americans and other foreign visitors. In the conversations you are likely to have, you'll be pleasantly surprised at the depth the English will go to recommend a good pub, or to simply explain how to use the complicated (far more than it needs to be) phone system. Americans may rest assured that Londoners find their language (American English, that is) as fascinating (and as occasionally impenetrable) as Americans find theirs.

Often, the confusion that arises lies not only in words that are different, but also in words that are the same but have a different meaning in England. For example, in England, if you visited the local chemist, it wouldn't be to buy sulfuric acid—rather, chemist is the British equivalent of what is called a drug store, pharmacy, or apothecary in other places.

The following is a brief list of common words that American visitors may encounter as travellers to England—they'll find fun (and, probably confusion) as they add to it during their travels:

| **British** | **American** |
|---|---|
| bitter | bitter tasting ale (usually served warm) |
| bonnet | hood of car |
| boot | trunk compartment of car |
| car hire | car rental |
| car park | parking lot |
| chips | fried potatoes—french fries in American parlance (if you want potato chips, ask for "crisps") |
| cinema | movie theater |
| jumper | sweater |
| lift | elevator |
| loo | toilet, washroom |
| lorry | truck |
| mackintosh | rain coat |
| motorway | expressway |
| pavement | sidewalk |
| petrol | gasoline |
| queue | line (noun); to form a line (verb) |

| roundabout | continuous traffic ring (you won't find many stop signs in England) |
| sweet | dessert |
| surgery | doctor's office |
| ta | thanks |
| telly | television |
| underground | subway or underground trains (also "tube") |
| windscreen | windshield; thus, "windscreen wipers" |

## Transportation

Although not as decorative as the underground railways of some European cities, nor as clean as, for example, the subway in Toronto, London's Underground rail system is fast, frequent, and convenient. For Americans used to the often-dirty and generally-unappealing subways found in major U.S. cities, London's extensive Underground railway system can be a pleasant surprise. The Underground—the largest in the world and popularly called "the Tube" (rather than "subway," which means a below-ground pedestrian walkway in England)—also is a safe and relatively inexpensive way to get around. However, it can get quite crowded and hectic during morning and evening rush hours—approximately 7:30 a.m. to 9 a.m. and 4:30 p.m. to 6:30 p.m. During warm days—and contrary to popular misconception, Londoners do enjoy some—the subway cars, which lack air-conditioning, can become almost unbearably hot.

The Underground consists of 10 interconnected and colour-coded lines, serving 272 stations throughout Greater London and its suburbs. Of the system's approximately 250 miles of track, more than 100 miles are underground, running below the central part of London; the lines emerge to run above ground as they spread out into the outlying boroughs and suburbs. Fares are based on the distance traveled within the system's five zones; fares range from 60p to £4. Tickets are purchased from either a machine or a ticket window and are collected when you reach your destination (hold onto your tickets, as you may be asked to display them to an inspector on the train). Last trains run about midnight (depending on the line and station) and service resumes around 5:30 a.m. Overnight, limited bus service (on the "Night Buses") takes the place of the tube in some areas; all Night Bus routes stop at Trafalgar Square. The tube is closed on Christmas Day.

Buses—the traditional red double-decker model as well as smaller ones serving both central London and fanning out from it—are another way to get around town. The disadvantage is that surface routes can be complicated and can become hopelessly gridlocked during London's horrendous rush hours and during special events as well as in the event of emergencies great and small. If time is critical, these vagaries make the Underground a surer choice. But, for a leisurely sightseeing ride, the view from the upper deck of a bus, high above the hustle and bustle of traffic, is hard to beat.

To board a bus, the polite custom is to queue up (to form a line, single file). It has been said that so conditioned are the British to queuing up—particularly Britons who lived through the austerity years, following World War II—that when they see two or more people standing one behind the other, they automatically will tag on the end of the "queue." From this line, enter the bus, and, depending on the type of bus, either pay the driver or the conductor. Fares are based on distance traveled (and can range from 60p up to £3); tell the driver or conductor your desired destination, and he or she will tell you the fare. Route maps are free from transport information centres. A 24-hour information number handles inquiries about Underground or bus service: 071-222 1234.

To save time and, most likely, money, you can purchase 1- or 7-day Travelcards from London Transport (available at tube stations, news vendors and other locations). These are good on both the tube and the buses, and are priced depending on the zones in which you wish to use them. You'll need a photo ID, but this can be provided instantly and inexpensively behind the curtain of an automatic photo booth. An even better value (for those who can plan well ahead) is the Visitor's Travel Card, good for 3, 4, or 7 days of unlimited travel on the Underground and buses; these are only available through travel agents *outside* of the U.K.

British Rail (known popularly as "BritRail") runs trains from London to various regions of England. A money-saving BritRail Pass (again, available only before you arrive in England) is good for unlimited rail travel for a set period. (The popular Eurailpasses are not usable in Great Britain.)

Last, but far from least among your transportation options, are London's deservedly legendary taxis. No matter your budget or your inclination, a visit to London could hardly be considered complete without at least one journey by cab. Although the city's traditional "black cabs" can now also be found in other colours, they are still skillfully piloted by the same brand of always knowledgeable (due to extremely rigorous testing), usually friendly, and occasionally outspoken London cabbies. Once a cab stops for you, the cabbie will expect you to tell him your destination before you get in.

This is customary—and not because the driver hasn't decided if your destination is worth his while. Once a cab stops for you, it is required to take you to any location you want within six miles (for only the rate shown on the meter); the price for longer distances may be negotiated. You are also expected to pay for your ride after you get out of the cab; a tip of approximately 10%-15% will be appreciated.

## Currency

Before decimalisation was imposed upon the British monetary system (due to entry into the European Common Market), it was split into quaintly eccentric divisions of pounds, shillings, and pence—with half pennies ("ha'pennies") and farthings—there being 20 shillings in a pound, 12 pence in a shilling, and 2 ha'pennies and 4 farthings in a penny. To further complicate things, there was the guinea, not an actual coin or note, but an amount equal to one pound and one shilling (i.e., 21 shillings).

Today, the basic unit of British currency remains the pound (£) with only the pence (p)—colloquially referred to as "pea"—retained as a lower denomination. The decimal proportions are 100 pence to one pound. The units of currency consist of both metal coins and paper bills. The denomination of the coins are as follows: 1p, a copper-coloured round coin; 2p, a copper-coloured round coin; 5p, a silver-coloured round coin; 10p, a silver-coloured round coin; 20p, a silver-coloured seven-sided coin; 50p, a silver-coloured seven-sided coin; and a yellow-golden-coloured thick round £1 coin. The coins vary in size, with little correlation to value. Although the old system of pounds, shillings, and pence already is some 20 years into history, some coins remain in circulation and are still acceptable currency. The old six-penny coin, for example, now doubles as 5p.

Paper currency also varies in size and colour. The greenish £1 note has been phased out (replaced with the £1 coin), but occasionally pops up in odd change. Other currency denominations and colours are: the blue £5 note (referred to as a "fiver"); the brown £10 note (referred to as a "tenner"); the purple £20 note; and the green £50 note. Pounds are often referred to as "quid" in Cockney parlance.

As this was written, £1 was equal to approximately $1.75 US, $2 Canadian, 10 French francs, 2.90 German marks, and 244 Japanese yen. These rates vary; check with a bank or currency exchange for the exact rate available before you leave.

## City And National Government

London is a sprawling, amorphous giant. It has more in common with cities formed patchwork from incorporated pre-existing areas (such as the separate boroughs that make up New York City), than with steadily expanding cities of very definite areas.

Greater London spreads out for approximately 620 square miles; it was created in its present form in 1965 by combining the old County of London and parts of the surrounding "Home Counties." This huge area was then divided into 32 official Boroughs, each presided over by its own elected mayor and council. Until 1986, these boroughs were administrated by the Greater London Council (G.L.C.); that year, Parliament (the legislature of Great Britain—which consists of England, Scotland, and Wales—and Northern Ireland) dissolved the G.L.C. and split its controls between the individual county councils and various national government departments.

As mentioned above (in "Getting Around"), the phrase "the City of London" (or simply "the City") refers solely to the approximately square-mile of the financial district, located on the site of the original Roman encampment. The City is a separate county, governed by its own Corporation and Lord Mayor; it even has a separate police force.

The national government is headed by the Prime Minister. (The Queen is the official head of state; the PM is the head of the government.) The Prime Minister is chosen from and by the party with the majority (or the combined coalition to form a majority) in Parliament. The primary political entities are the Conservative Party—also called "the Tories"—and the socialist Labour Party. (A third party—with a small percentage of Parliament seats—is the Liberal Democrats or simply the Liberals.) Parliament consists of the House of Commons and the House of Lords. London is the national capital; Parliament meets in the Houses of Parliament along the River Thames, just south of Westminster Bridge.

## Public Holidays (known in England as "Bank Holidays")

In addition to several public holidays that are observed in many countries (such as Easter, Christmas, and New Year's Day), the British also celebrate May Day (May 1 or the first Monday in May), Spring Bank Holiday (last Monday in May), Summer Bank Holiday (last Monday in August) and Boxing Day (December 26).

Typically, you'll find that most establishments are closed on the day of a bank holiday. During the Christmas holiday season, many shops and work places are closed from Christmas Day to New Year's Day. Public transportation service is also scaled down to a minimum over the Christmas holiday season; the Underground shuts down completely on Christmas Day.

## Weather

Most of us have seen the old Sherlock Holmes movies depicting England's weather as being perpetually moist, uncomfortably cool, and eternally foggy. During the late 19th century of Holmes' time—and even into the first half of the 20th century—most homes were heated by coal-burning fires, air pollution ran rampant, and visibility-zero fogs were common. Today, an English fog is more likened to a clear consommé than a thick pea soup—if you even see a fog at all! (Laws prohibiting the burning of coal and other pollutants in central London are what cleared the air.) And, as for rain, you can generally expect more precipitation on the northern part of the European continent than on this supposedly soggy island. Why, even New York City has a higher annual average rainfall than London!

In spite of England's recently sporadic weather (with untypical sustained summer heat waves in some years), the island is generally temperate year around. However, the English did invent the raincoat (or mackintosh, if you prefer) and umbrella for good reason, so it's best to include these on your list of things to bring—especially if you're traveling during November through February, the rainiest months.

London's average mean temperatures are: 41°F (5°C) in winter (December-March); 52°F (11°C) in spring (March-June); 62°F (16°C) in summer (June-September); and 49°F (9°C) in fall (September-December).

## Tips On Tipping

Tipping does not have to be a very complex science—especially since London is not a particularly tip-conscience city (as compared, for example, to Paris, Brussels, and New York City, where tips are expected to be nothing shy of 20% and often are automatically added to the bill). Nevertheless, as a rule-of-thumb in London, you should tip 15% for waiters and waitresses (automatic gratuities are often added for large groups; read the bill carefully before giving what might be a gratuitous tip, so to speak), 10%-15% for bartenders and waitresses, and 10%-15% for cab drivers. In pubs, where you belly up to the bar to order your own round of drinks—or "call"—tips are usually not given, except perhaps to leave a few coins in bar change. Of course, you should tip according to your own perception of both expected and received service.

Speaking of service, London visitors should be forewarned about the service they might receive, which by some standards may seem below-par. Here a few examples of what not to expect: When dining out, don't expect a glass of water unless you ask for it (and, even then, unless you like warm water, clearly specify "with ice"); don't expect free coffee refills; don't expect a waiter or waitress to ask if everything is all right; and when visiting a clothing store or boutique, don't expect the sales staff to hover around you asking if you need assistance (this can actually be a blessing—who likes pushy sales people?).

All of this said, it must be noted that competition among various establishments is helping to increase service levels...So don't be surprised if you *do* encounter doting, occasionally pushy service.

## Calendar Of Events

(Dates/periods approximate and subject to change.)

Early January—January/post-Christmas sales (most London stores)

Early January—International Boat Show, Earls Court Exhibition Centre, Warwick Road, London SW5

Late January/early February—Chinese New Year parade and celebrations, Gerrard Street, London W1

Early February—Crufts Dog Show, Earls Court Exhibition Centre, Warwick Road, London SW5

March-January—Shakespeare Theatre Season, Royal Shakespeare Theatre, Stratford-upon-Avon

Late March—Spring Equinox Druid Ceremony, Tower Hill, London EC3 (also Summer Solstice Ceremony at Stonehenge and Autumn Equinox Ceremony at Primrose Hill, London NW3)

March or April—Oxford-Cambridge Boat Race, Putney to Mortlake, River Thames

Easter Sunday—Easter Sunday Parade, Battersea Park, London SW11

Easter Monday—London Harness Horse Parade, Regent's Park, London NW1

Late April—London Marathon

Late April/early May—FA Cup Final (soccer), Wembley Stadium, Wembley, Middlesex

Late April/early May—Rugby League Challenge Cup Final, Wembley Stadium, Wembley, Middlesex

Late May—Chelsea Flower Show, Royal Hospital grounds, Chelsea, London SW3

Early June—Derby Day, Epsom Racecourse, Surrey, Epsom

Early June-late August—Royal Academy of Arts Summer Exhibition, Royal Academy of Arts, Piccadilly, London W1

Saturday nearest June 11—Trooping the Colour, beginning at Buckingham Palace (elaborate parade to celebrate the Queen's official birthday)

June—Royal Ascot Races, Ascot

June/July—Lord's Test Match, Lord's Cricket Ground, St. John's Wood Road, London NW8

Late June/early July—All England Lawn Tennis Championships (better known simply as "Wimbledon"), All England Lawn Tennis & Croquet Club, Wimbledon, London SW19

Late June/early July—Henley Royal Regatta, Henley-on-Thames, Oxon

July-September—Henry Wood Promenade Concerts (the "Proms"), Royal Albert Hall, Kensington Gore, London SW7

Early September—London Rose Festival, New Horticultural Hall, Greycoat Street, London SW1

Early October—Horse of the Year Show, Wembley Stadium, Wembley, Middlesex

Early November—London to Brighton Veteran Car Run, beginning at Serpentine Road, Hyde Park, London W2 ("race" for cars built before 1905)

Early November—State Opening of Parliament, Houses of Parliament, Westminster, London SW1

Early November—Lord Mayor's Show, various sites in the City (parade and regalia accompanying the annual swearing-in of the City's official head)

Second Sunday in November—Remembrance Sunday, Cenotaph, Whitehall, London SW1

Late November-early January—Christmas Lights, Regent Street and Oxford Street, London W1

Mid-December-early January—Christmas Tree, Trafalgar Square, London WC2

December 31—New Year's Eve—Crowds gather at Trafalgar Square, London WC2, and Piccadilly Circus, London W1 (around Eros statue)

## Emergency

For police or ambulance, dial 999 from any phone. No coins are necessary.

**Hospital:** In the case of an emergency, you will receive treatment at any major hospital at no charge. However, we recommend that you purchase travel insurance prior to your trip, which covers medical expense should you become ill.

**Pharmacies:** Most pharmacies will dispense prescription drugs only if a doctor's receipt is presented. Most Boots (a chain of chemists) have pharmacy departments.

**Police Headquarters:** New Scotland Yard, Broadway Street, London SW1, 071-230 1212.

**Rape Crisis Line:** 24-hour crisis hotline, 071-930 0715.

**Embassies**: American Embassy, 103 Eaton Square, London SW1, 071-235 5422; Canadian High Commission, 12 Devonshire Street, London W1, 071-580 6392; French Embassy, 24 Rutland Gate, London SW7, 071-581 5292; German Embassy, 23 Belgrave Square, London SW1, 071-235 5033; Japanese Embassy, 46 Grosvenor Street, London W1, 071-493 6030.

**Driving Emergencies:** Car Breakdown—Call the AA (Automobile Association—0800 887766) or the RAC (Royal Automobile Club—071-839 7050); you can purchase a membership at the time of the service. Traffic Accident—In the event of an accident in which no one is seriously injured, simply exchange names and details of insurance carriers with the other party (calling the police is not required). Legal Aid/Release—If you are arrested you can call referral services for the name of a solicitor/lawyer (071-353 7411) or for assistance in obtaining release (bail) (071-377 5905).

## Driving And Parking

In two words, *don't bother.*

That said, we recognize that some visitors will still insist—perhaps of necessity—to attempt to drive in London. London traffic snarls can be dandies! Adding to navigational problems are the confusing nature of its tangled streets, the system of one-way streets that can thwart direct passage, and the general thoughtless driving of many British (English good manners seem to be forgotten once a motorist climbs behind a steering wheel). Also, parking spots are very hard to find in central London...And, of course, the English drive on the "wrong" side of the road (in the view of Americans)! If at all possible, when in London, better to avoid the confusion and rely on the fast, convenient, and safe combination of the Underground, buses, and cabs.

If you are braving the wilds of London driving— or, much better yet, setting out from London to outlying areas—keep these general driving rules in mind: Not only must you drive on the left, but you must pass ("overtake" in English parlance) only on the right; speed limits are 60-70 m.p.h. (approx. 100-115 kilometers per hour on bypasses and motorways, and 30 m.p.h. (approx. 50 kilometers per hour) on city, village, and town streets; pedestrians on white-striped crosswalks (called "zebra crossings") always have the right-of-way; and seatbelt use is mandatory. Also—English law is tough on drunk-driving offenders.

## Banking And Currency Exchange

In London, there are many places where the traveller can exchange currency. They include banks (Barclay's and National Westminster are Britain's largest banks with branches throughout London), bureau de change kiosks, hotels, restaurants, stores, and London post offices. Additionally, you'll find bank branches with extended hours at both Heathrow and Gatwick Airports. Normal banking hours are Monday through Friday, 9:30 a.m. to 3:30 p.m., with larger facilities offering limited service on Saturdays. Be warned that, although some banks do not charge service fees for exchanging currency, they typically offer lower exchange rates than can be found elsewhere—in other words, nothing is "free." *Caveat emptor.*

Your best bet for exchanging currency is at one the many bureau de change kiosks located throughout London. The kiosks will generally give you a better rate of exchange than banks, and often rates vary from kiosk to kiosk; comparing prices before changing any money is highly recommended. It is also a good idea to check a newspaper for the day's exchange rate—be an educated consumer! The most convenient spots to exchange money may be hotels, restaurants, or stores, but the rates given at these establishment will likely be the poorest.

It's a good idea to exchange a small amount of money before your trip. This means that when you arrive, you'll have currency to pay for immediate incidentals (such as cab, porter tips, etc.), and you won't be forced to change money at unfavourable airport-bank rates. Also, it's always a good idea to avoid carrying a lot of cash with you. Traveller's checks may be used for payment or cashed at most places.

Most major credit cards are accepted in London, but it's always a good idea to ask beforehand at any establishment at which you intend to make purchases. Americans should note that in England, Visa is also referred to as Barclay Card, and Mastercard as Access—but visitors typically will not have problems using the American versions.

To report lost credit cards: Visa/Barclay Card, 060-423 0230; Mastercard/Access, 070-235 2255; American Express, 027-369 6933; Diners Club, 025-251 6261.

## Telephone

Forget logic. Forget how you think the phone *should* work. Now you're ready to approach the muddle that is the British Telecom telephone system. Let's start with the prefix. If you're making a call to Central London from outside of Central London (that is, more than 4 miles in any direction from Charing Cross), it is necessary to use the prefix 071 before the number. If you're calling from Central London to within Greater London you will be required to use the prefix 081. For other calls from London to the rest of Britain, you will be required to use the appropriate regional prefix. When dialing within Central London to another Central London number, you only have to dial the regular seven-digit number (i.e., don't dial any prefix).

If you require assistance in making your call or are unsure of the correct prefix, dial 100 for operator assistance. If you need to find a number, dial 142 for directory enquiry (although this is a notoriously poor service; at times, it seems that you'd be better off trying to *guess* the number than relying on directory enquiry). In the case of an emergency, dial 999.

Another point of frustration for the traveller is the Telecom Phonecard pay telephone. You will find these smoke-grey cubicles throughout London. Often, travellers mistake these telephones for coin-operated phones boxes or credit card telephones. However, the Phonecard telephone works only with a pre-purchased Phonecard available in several denominations ranging from £1 to £20. Each time a call is made, the telephone debits the card until the purchase value is depleted. A digital display on the telephone shows the balance remaining on the card. Calls made on the Phonecard are 10p per unit. The Mercury Phonecard works basically the same as the Telecom Phonecard (but isn't part of the Telecom System). There aren't as many Mercury Phonecards around, but if you find one, you can expect lower rates.

Visitors to London expecting to catch a glimpse of the famous red call box may be in for a disappointment. Many of the boxes have been replaced by glass cubicals. When using the old call box, remember that they do not take your money until you're connected, and they don't make change. The newer version takes the money first and does provide change.

To save money (if not frustration), avoid making calls from your hotel room. Many hotels add a substantial surcharge to your bill. Instead, use a public phone—*if* you can find one...And *if* it works...And *if* the operator or enquiry assistance ever bothers to answer. British Telecom *has* been making some improvements to this rickety system—but they have been slow in coming.

## Sightseeing Companies

London is a great city for exploring on foot. With the help of the Underground, you can conveniently travel to virtually anywhere in the city fast, safe, and inexpensively. However, you may want to enlist the services of a professional tour company to provide insight to the places you visit.

The following is a partial listing of companies offering sightseeing tours of London's major attractions and the surrounding areas: London Transport Sightseeing Tour (bus tours of London using traditional red double-decker buses), 071-227 3456; City Walks of London (guided walking tours of London's attractions), 071-937 4281; Tower Pier (trips to Greenwich and Westminster by boat), 071-488 0344; Harrods (upscale, guided bus tours run by the famous department store), 071-581 3603.

For more information, you can also contact the London Tourist Information Center at 071-730 3488.

## Safety Tips

Like any cosmopolitan big city, London has its share of crime—although, by any measure, especially compared to most large U.S. cities, it is relatively safe.

To minimize your chances of being victimized by criminal activities, you need to use basic common sense and an awareness of where you are. In your hotel, use lockboxes to store valuables, never leave your key unattended at the front desk, and don't announce your room number to anyone as you go out. On the streets, carry wallets in inside jacket or front trouser pockets, not hip pockets (better yet, use a money belt or another hidden, zippered compartment). Carry purses close to your body, preferably with the strap across your body. Don't carry large amounts of cash or traveller's checks with you—leave these instead in your hotel lockbox. Also, keep a copy of your traveller's check receipts and your passports in your hotel room or lockbox.

Central streets are universally safe during the day (although pickpockets and purse-snatchers, while not prevalent, have been known to work any area at any time), and most are well-lit and safe at night (the City is mostly abandoned at night—but also has no real attractions to lead you there after dark). In general, be alert when entering a street that seems less-well-lit than the one you are on. On the tube, be watchful for people jostling you from the front or rear as you get on or off a train; they may be trying to distract you while an accomplice tries to pick your pocket or snatch your purse. If waiting for a train after dark, stand on the platform near the other people.

Of course, in the unfortunate event of being threatened with force (whether a weapon is visible or not—and *especially* if one *is*), stay calm, give them the wallet, purse, or jewelry that they want, and don't cause a commotion. After they have fled, immediately contact the police (see "Emergency" above).

In general, stay alert and be smart—maximized preparation can help minimize the chances of trouble.

# LONDON'S
# BEST-KEPT
# SECRETS

# DINING

## Best French Food Without Crossing The Channel

L'Arlequin

In a somewhat unexpected setting—on a dark and slighty run-down street—is this restaurant, offering some of the finest French cuisine in town. Established chef Christian Delteil and his wife Genevieve run an attractive room, decorated in soft pastel colours, highlighted by flower arrangements. There are inventive, artfully presented daily specials, as well as regular chicken and seafood dishes. Added touches such as delicate asparagus mousse, delightful between-course sorbets, and terrific desserts—the favourite is Grand Marnier soufflé—round out the satisfying meals at L'Arlequin. A bit expensive, but regarded as worth it; the £16 set lunch menu is a (relative) bargain. It's a little out of the way (south of the river), but worth a trip for some of the best nouvelle cuisine in London.

L'Arlequin, 123 Queenstown Rd, London SW8, 071-622 0555. Mon-Fri 12:30-2 pm, 7:30-10 pm, Sat 7:30-11 pm.

## Best Bit Of Paris In Soho

Soho Brasserie

This brasserie-style restaurant with a bar in front

that, in summer, opens up onto the street, is a pleasant island in the mainstream of Soho. Relax over a coffee and croissant or a salad and glass of wine after shopping and sightseeing expeditions, or before or after the theatre. If you don't mind the somewhat trendy clientèle (although, hopefully, they'll move on to the *latest* trendy brasserie), this is a relaxed, informal spot if you want to linger, or, if you're in a hurry, a civilised alternative to fast-food emporia. Fish is fresh and reliable, and choices often include brill, turbot, and hake—or choose a good seafood salad. The eclectic menu ranges from sautéed clams, rissotto, steak tartare, and a particularly rich and flavourful fish soup, to fluffy omelettes, smoked chicken salad, and beef and lamb steaks.

Soho Brasserie, 23-25 Old Compton St, London W1, 071-439 9301. Mon-Sat 10 am-11 pm.

## Best Brasserie For Bordeaux
Café Bordeaux

Showcasing the food and drink of Bordeaux, this is one of a trio of restaurants specialising in French regional cuisine (the Café Loire and Café Burgundy are similarly themed). Having moved to premises a short walk from Shaftesbury Avenue, the friendly café occupies two floors and resembles a French brasserie. Handy to the theatre district (the restaurant is close to the Shaftesbury Theatre), Café Bordeaux is a good spot for a pre-curtain or after-the-show meal. Starters include spinach tart with cream cheese topping, smoked haddock marinated in lime juice, and coarse country pâté with garlic croutons. Main courses feature such traditional favourites as grilled duck breast with a sweet red currant sauce and fillet of lamb and chopped mushrooms in puff pastry. Desserts run to apple and lemon tarts, mousse, soufflé, and assorted French cheeses. House wines are, of course, red and white bordeaux—from a list of two dozen or so bordeaux and burgundies.

Café Bordeaux, 24 Coptic St, London W1, 071-580 3422. Mon-Sat noon-11 pm.

## Classiest Créperie
Bar Créperie

*Parlez-vous Suzette?* Lighter-than-air, French-accented crépes are the main draw on the menu at this very popular Covent Garden Market restaurant. The Bar Créperie offers more than three dozen different varieties of entrée or dessert crépes—including chicken, several vegetarian varieties, and cheese on the savoury side, with strawberry, blueberry, banana, and other fruit varieties among the sweet versions. Bar Créperie also features a light menu of other entrées, including hamburgers, pasta, salads, and soup. If you choose, you can enjoy this light meal out of doors—the restaurant offers alfresco dining, usually with a view of a lively crowd of passersby.

Bar Créperie, 21 Southhall, Covent Garden Market, London WC2, 071-836 2137. Daily 11 am-11:30 pm.

## Best Restaurant You May Not Be Able To Get Into

Le Caprice

May not be able to get into? Why? A snooty maitre d'? A month-long reservation list? No, it's just that this fashionable restaurant is very small—and it does attract large crowds. Located on the ground floor of an office-and-apartment building, this is a stylish place, offering modern European fare. Popular menu choices include steak tartare, rack of lamb, and salmon and other seafood dishes, accompanied by a nice selection of French, Italian, and American wines. Le Caprice draws a well-heeled crowd of media professionals, and has been known to attract the occasional Royal or rock star. This restaurant is not as expensive as its size or reputation might suggest (dinner for two can run from £30-£50); also offers a highly regarded Sunday brunch, perhaps the best in town. Jazz piano accompanies dinner.

Le Caprice, Arlington House, Arlington St, London SW1, 071-629 2239. Daily noon-3 pm, 6 pm-midnight.

## Best Places To Rub Shoulders With London's Jet-Set, Celebrities, And All-Around "Beautiful People"

Bill Bentley's and San Lorenzo

These two restaurants, on the same block of Beauchamp Place, combine to make already-fashionable Knightsbridge *the* place to wine and dine among actors, models, rock stars, writers, socialites, and other figures of the London elite. Bentley's is an attractive restaurant, offering a variety of seafood specialities and French dishes. It offers a dark, atmospheric wine bar on the main floor, with as many as 30 wines by the glass and a well-regarded oyster bar; and a quietly bustling restaurant upstairs. Bentley's has several other locations, but this is the one that attracts a crowd that is often sprinkled with famous figures. San Lorenzo offers a pleasant garden-like decor, including a "convertible" room in back with a glass roof that is opened when the weather is favourable. Its menu of Italian specialities changes daily, and features such items as minestrone soup, homemade fettucine, spaghetti, and other pastas, and veal and chicken dishes, complemented by a good house red. These are served by a casually attired wait staff (whose service, alas, has been known to be as casual as their outfits—unless, of course, you're a recognizable luminary!). Celebs and other notables also favour toney Langan's Brasserie; actor Michael Caine is a part-owner of that restaurant (see separate listing).

Bill Bentley's, 31 Beauchamp Pl, London SW3, 071-589 5080, Mon-Sat 11:30 am-3 pm, 5:30-11 pm. San Lorenzo, 22 Beauchamp Pl, London SW3, 071-584 1074, Mon-Sat 12:30 pm-3 pm, 7:30-11:30 pm.

## Best Restaurant With A Famous Actor As Part-Owner
Langan's Brasserie

Although its boisterous, high-living namesake Peter Langan is dead, this favoured spot still brings in the trendy crowds; partly because of the attraction of actor Michael Caine as a partner, and partly because of the inventive, bistro-type French-English menu of Richard Shepherd, the longtime head chef. Langan's is a bit pricey, and some detractors feel it offers less than top-of-the-line service and food, but it is still very popular as a place to see and be seen. (And it definitely has its fans and defenders, who say the food—especially the salads, spinach soufflé, veal and lamb dishes, and inventive homemade desserts—is excellent.) The restaurant is nicely lit, spacious, and appointed with modern art; tasteful live music accompanies dining every evening. There are two levels—upstairs is more cozy and proper-seeming than the casual downstairs room, but the menu and prices are the same. (The recognizable faces from stage and screen that contribute to Langan's hip aura are often ensconced upstairs). Reservations are essential here, especially for lunch (dinner usually is slightly less hectic).

Langan's Brasserie, Stratton St, London W1, 071-493 6437. Mon-Fri 12:30 pm-1 am, Sat 8 pm-1 am.

## Best Restaurant By A Cookbook Author
Leith's

There are not too many restaurants where you can

enjoy a signal dining experience and recreate it faithfully back home. Cookbook author and consultant Pru Leith has just such a restaurant. And, while it is not news (it opened to wide acclaim in the 1960s), the good news is that it remains on top. Start with a selection from its celebrated appetizer cart—perhaps pastry-encased artichokes or delicate smoked salmon wrapped around smoked trout pâté. Stilton soup defines the genre, while entrées include duckling, roast quail, and deliciously prepared lamb cutlet, seasoned with thyme and charcoal-grilled. Desserts, also served from a trolley, include blackberry and strawberry tarts and standout ginger syllabub. A Victorian house, with understated, elegant decor, provides a perfect setting for well-executed (and pricey) British cooking. Don't forget to purchase a cookbook (autographed, of course!) to take home.

Leith's, 92 Kensington Park Rd, London W11, 071-229 4481. Daily 7:30-11:30 pm.

## Trendiest Anglo-French Restaurant Not To Tire Of

Bibendum

This is an Anglo-French marriage that works! Coexisting nicely are traditional grilled beef and roast lamb with mint sauce and *tête de veau*. Certainly, one would be hard-pressed to find more attractive surroundings than this stylish restaurant in London's now-fashionable Brompton Cross. It occupies part of the refurbished 1911 headquarters of the Michelin Tyre Co., with its art nouveau theme, mosaic floors, and decorative tiles depicting racing cars. Designed by Sir Terence Conran, the restaurant has high ceilings, a soft grey-and-blue colour scheme, roly-poly Michelin Men in stained glass, spacious, comfortable seating, and the colourful splash of fresh flowers. Start with tomato or mushroom soup, a delicate cold curried apple soup, or a combination of sausages and lentils. Move on to grilled rabbit with mustard sauce, a basic, fluffy omelette, calves' liver, or halibut with fresh mussels. Choose a simple fruit tart for dessert. For expense-account meals, there is an extensive and pricey wine list; for luncheons on a budget, good house wine is available by the glass. A downstairs oyster bar offers a limited seafood menu.

Bibendum, Michelin House, 81 Fulham Rd, London SW3, 071-581 5817. Daily 12:30-11 pm.

## Best Vietnamese Vittles

Saigon

Well-versed with Mandarin, Szechwan, and Hunan Chinese cuisines? Tried Korean and Thai? Then perhaps this Soho restaurant, offering the latest food import from southeast Asia, may be for you. In general, Vietnamese cooking has elements and dishes in common with other Oriental cuisine—such as egg rolls, spring rolls, and other appetizers—but it also tends to be spicier than some other Oriental choices. Top at Saigon are the seafood specialities—including entrées featuring prawns, shrimp, crab, and red snapper—as well as spicy beef-and-vegetable and grilled chicken dishes. The decor is comfortable, with touches of the proprietors' Vietnamese heritage, including photos, artwork, and decorative items.

Saigon, 45 Frith St, London W1, 071-437 7109. Mon-Sat noon-11:30 pm.

## Best Bet For Borscht

Luba's Bistro

*Glasnost* comes to London! This friendly, affordable restaurant offers large portions of hearty Russian cooking. It's a cozy and crowded place—all the better for sharing long tables with fellow diners (you can make friends fast here, if you desire). The bill of fare includes excellent borscht, other soups, dumplings, savoury fish or meat pies, rich and authentic Beef Stroganoff, blintzes, and other exports from mother Russia. Luba's gets busy as the night creeps on—go early for the quickest service and the shortest wait. This restaurant isn't licensed to serve alcoholic beverages, but you can bring your own wine—or, even better, an iced bottle of vodka—to accompany the dining choices offered.

Luba's Bistro, 6 Yeoman's Row, London SW3, 071-589 2950. Mon-Sat 6 pm-midnight.

## Best Bet For Veggie Lovers

Cranks

Because it isn't only nut cutlets and tofu, even basic carnivores seem to enjoy this attractive cafeteria-style restaurant that was a health-food pioneer in London. Particularly popular at lunch time, it serves good crisp vegetable salads, fresh-fruit salads, minestrone and other robust vegetable soups, quiche, wholemeal pancakes, stone-ground bread and rolls, and a variety of other hot and cold vegetable dishes such as vegetable-and-tofu lasagne, as well as wholefood snacks. Desserts run to delicious carrot cake, cheesecake, honey cake, nut bars, and gingerbread. Beverages include a variety of juices, a tasty blend of yogurt, milk, and honey, and a number of English country wines. The decor features plain wooden tables, wicker-basket lamps, and appealing pottery dishes. There is an adjoining health-food shop and branches of the restaurant in Covent Garden Market (11 Central Avenue) and Bloomsbury (9-11 Tottenham Street).

Cranks, 8 Marshall St, London W2, 071-437 9431. Mon-Fri 8 am-10:30 pm, Sat 9 am-10:30 pm.

## Best Breakfast For Veggie Lovers
Food For Thought

Before a morning spent exploring the lanes around Covent Garden and browsing the stalls in the market, stop for a healthful breakfast at this popular vegetarian restaurant. This family business is housed in an 18th-century building that once was a banana warehouse; intimate seating alcoves have been created in an area where fruit once hung to ripen. Breakfast choices include freshly-squeezed orange juice, plus apple, peach, apricot, and other juices, butter croissants, fresh-baked bagels (plain, onion, or poppyseed), homemade scones and wholewheat bread, and fresh fruit salad topped with yogurt. There are whole-earth jams, vegetable pâté, and cereals that include muesli, granola, and bran flakes. For lunch or dinner you can sample such items as lasagne with fresh tomato and basil sauce, Thai curry, goat's cheese and spinach filo, and a noodle hot-pot with spiced peanut sauce. On Fridays, a special ethnic menu focuses on the cuisine of a chosen country— one week Japan, another Mexico, Poland, etc. This restaurant is a good spot to eat on the cheap; a three-course meal can come in at well under £10.

Food For Thought, 31 Neal St, London WC2, 071-836 0239. Mon-Fri 8:30 am-8 pm.

## Best Bet For Breakfast Bangers
Fox And Anchor

Wiry Smithfield porters and natty city gents congregate for morning vittles at this handsome Victorian pub that is virtually on the doorstep of both London's meat-packing and financial headquarters. The pub actually dates back to the 16th century. It opens at 6 a.m. (those porters are early risers!) and serves up hearty English-style breakfasts between 7-10:30 a.m. Trenchermen go for the "full house," consisting of fried mushrooms, eggs, bacon, sausage, black pudding, and beans—or steak and eggs served with chips and fried tomatoes. The pub's lunch menu also includes such popular British stodge as steak-and-kidney pie, and a delectably sweet fruit pie for dessert. Beer is available with breakfast; the more adventurous opt for a Black Velvet (Guinness mixed with champagne) or a Buck's Fizz (orange juice and champagne).

Fox and Anchor, 115 Charterhouse St, London EC1, 071-253 4838. Mon-Fri 6 am-3 pm.

## Tastiest Taramasalata
Kalamaras (Micro & Mega)

These two Greek *tavernas* on the same block offer excellent Greek dining in a festive atmosphere. The Micro branch lives up to its appellation—it's small and so (relatively) are its tabs (and it doesn't serve liquor). The Mega branch is bigger, slightly more formal and expensive, and is licensed to serve alcohol. Unlike many Greek restaurants in London, these restaurants offer cuisine from mainland Greece, rather than from the Greek-Turkish island of Cyprus. Start with some of the acclaimed appetizers—especially the restaurants' namesake, squid, spicy Greek sausages, and taramasalata, the creamy fish-roe dish served with a crusty round of bread. Suggested entrées include grilled lamb, Greek salads, spinach pie, and excellent seafood dishes. A bouzouki band provides lively Greek music on some evenings.

Kalamaras, 66 Inverness Mews (Micro) & 76-78 Inverness (Mega), London W2, 071-727 9122. Mon-Sat 7pm-midnight.

## Best Restaurant To Shout "Opaa!"
Anemos

At Soho's busy north end, this lively Cypriot-Greek restaurant offers typical *taverna* food (moussaka, kebabs, taramasalata, hummus, lamb, etc). And, when your waiter isn't busy delivering a tempting tray full of this mid Eastern fare, he's likely to be joyously singing, dancing, and smashing plates—or demonstratively encouraging patrons to do likewise! This extravaganza is great for parties and large groups and is not for the shy (unless they want to be pulled out of their shells by the restaurant's resident Greek revellers!). This six-nights-a-week party spills out onto the sidewalk in fair weather (Anemos offers outdoor dining seasonally) and is popular year-around, so be sure to make reservations. It's a good bargain, too—around £15 for two, including Greek wine and strong coffee.

Anemos, 32-34 Charlotte St, London W1, 071-636 2289. Mon-Sat noon-2:45 pm, 6 pm-midnight.

## Best Turkish Kebabs Cooked At Your Table

Efes Kebab House

If you're an inveterate amateur chef—of the kitchen or ordinary garden variety—you may feel compelled to provide some "backseat" cooking advice to the chef preparing your kebabs tableside at this restaurant...But, unless you've got experience with Turkish cuisine, just relax and leave the cooking to them. Considered perhaps the top Turkish restaurant in London, Efes is often packed. Reserve ahead and you can watch your chosen type of kebabs being charcoal-cooked to order at your table. The different varieties of kebabs to choose from include beef, lamb, and chicken. Vegetable dishes and desserts (prepared in the kitchen) accompany the kebabs; strong Turkish coffee is a perfect finish to a meal here.

Efes Kebab House, 80 Great Titchfield St, London W1, 071-836 1953. Mon-Sat noon-11:30 pm.

## Best Restaurant In Theatreland

Sheekeys

Need to get to a theatre from this restaurant? Sheekeys gladly will give you a map showing no fewer than 35 theatres within a few minutes' walk. Looking for a restaurant appropriate for a pre- or post-theatre meal? Sheekeys is one of the top choices of theatregoers and theatre *players*. Colourful theatre posters look across St. Martin's Court to Sheekeys, where portraits of past generations of actors and actresses gaze down on contemporary players who frequent the restaurant, which also is popular with publishers, impresarios, and assorted media people. Established in 1896 and now operated by the Scott restaurant group, Sheekeys specialises in good English cooking and is particularly known for its excellent fish. Lobsters, oysters, crab, and such fresh finfish selections as turbot and trout, sole and salmon, are mainstays of the menu. Attractive private dining rooms include the intimate Venetian room, decorated with rows of Venetian carnival masks, and the larger Art Nouveau room with elegant mirrors and painted tiles.

Sheekeys, 28-32 St. Martin's Ct, London WC2, 071-240 2565. Mon-Sat 12:30-11:30 pm.

# Theatregoers' Favourite Greek Restaurant

## Beotys

Its name is Greek for "welcome"–and patrons are definitely made to feel as if they are at this comfortable restaurant favoured by theatregoers since just after World War II. It features mostly Cypriot cuisine, but also offers non-Greek menu choices (such as duck, filet of sole, and beef dishes). But the best selections are the great Greek specialties–lamb, chicken, moussaka, souvlaki, and kalamarakia (squid cooked in its ink and red wine). Beotys is also known for its desserts–sticky sweet baklava, nutty halva, etc., plus complementary boxes of Turkish Delights to take with you. As is expected in lively Greek/Cypriot eateries, the service is fast and friendly.

Beotys, 79 St. Martins Ln, London WC2, 071-836 8768. Mon-Sat 6-11:30 pm.

# Theatregoers' Favourite French-Provincial Restaurant

## Chez Solange

This restaurant is found among Covent Garden's charming warren of streets, nestled amid the area's beloved used and rare bookshops. This is one of the oldest French restaurants in this neighbourhood—and one of the few traditional French restaurants (rather than those offering nouvelle— or *beyond*—cuisine) in London. Near Charing Cross Road and St. Martins Lane, Chez Solange is known for its pre-theatre dining, starting at 5:30 p.m. on weeknights; it offers prix fixe pre-theatre (and lunch) menus for £13.50. Among the restaurant's dining choices are indoor and outdoor dining and a downstairs wine bar. Chez Solange's kitchen is open late—past midnight—making this one of the best bets in town for an above-average late-night bite.

Chez Solange, 35 Cranbourn St, London WC2, 071-836 0542. Mon-Sat noon-2 am.

# Most Elegant After-Theatre Supper

## Waltons

Glitterati-gazers enjoy this celebrity-frequented upmarket restaurant in the heart of Chelsea (within walking distance from Knightsbridge). Intimate and luxurious, it has well-spaced tables, primrose and grey silk walls, mirrored ceilings, and floral decorations. Specialities include terrine of truffled foie gras, whole roast lobster with coriander and ginger, and *mille-feuille* of bitter chocolate and orange mousse on a white chocolate sauce. The "Simply Waltons" three-course lunch is a good value at £13.75, while the "After Theatre Supper" served from 10 p.m. onward offers three courses with coffee for £19.50. Starters for this late supper include hot and chilled soups, saffron-flavoured winter salad (with artichoke, white radish, and mushrooms), and cheese favours (filo pastry parcels stuffed with English Bonchester and baked until crisp). Main-course selections include 18th-century saffron chicken (nuggets of chicken breast simmered in cream with saffron and tomato and served with a "ragoo" of cucumber) and salmon lattice (stuffed with fish mousse, wrapped in spinach, and held in a web of pastry). Suppertime desserts might include pudding, treacle tart, or homemade ice cream. An extensive wine list offers a range of clarets, red and white burgundies, champagne, and rare vintage cognac and port.

Waltons, 121 Walton St, London SW3, 071-584 0204. Mon-Sat 12:30-11:30 pm, Sun 12:30-10:30 pm.

## Artsiest Restaurant

Tate Gallery Restaurant

Plan a lunch at this pretty restaurant because of the wine, the art, and the food—in that order! Of course, if you are more of an art lover than an oenophile, you might reverse the order of the first two. Food is relegated to third place because of the restaurant's obsession with historical cooking—the likes of Umbles Paste (pâté) and Hindle Wakes (chicken and prunes)—some of which should have remained buried in the recesses of history. The kitchen does an okay job with more recognizable traditions, such as steak-kidney-and-mushroom pie, meat roasts, and desserts such as fruit tart. It also offers some good English cheeses. So, enjoy your delicious roast sirloin and accompany it with a bordeaux or burgundy from a superior wine list at prices that might make you want to consider a second bottle. A selection of wines is available by the glass and you'll find connoisseurs raving over both the bouquet and the bargains. As for the art, a celebrated Rex Whistler mural adorns the walls of this semi-basement restaurant.

Tate Gallery Restaurant, Millbank, London SW1, 071-834 6754. Mon-Sat noon-3 pm.

## Jazziest Fern Bar/Restaurant

Palookaville

This strangely named restaurant is one of Covent

Garden's recent success stories. Housed in the
basement of an office block (the basement was
once a fruit warehouse), it's a new place, but looks
as though it has been there forever, down to the
worn collection of posters, paintings, and photos
found on its brick walls. Run by the son of the
proprietress of Chez Solange (which offers perhaps
London's finest nouvelle cuisine—see separate listing), Palookaville offers an inventive menu of
mixed choices, such as Oriental-style openers,
ribs, and light duck, chicken, and fish entrées.
Offers live jazz accompanying dining or drinking
(in a raised bar area); very popular among a young
crowd.

Palookaville, 13a James St, London WC2, 071-240
5857. Mon-Sat 6 pm-midnight.

## London's Oldest Restaurant

Rules

In 1798, the year Napoleon opened his campaign
in Egypt, Thomas Rule opened an oyster bar in
Covent Garden. While Bonaparte's empire eventually crumbled, Rule's continues to thrive as (it
calls itself), "The most English of Restaurant Insti-
tutions." And so it is, with steak, kidney, and
mushroom pie and pudding, Aberdeen Angus beef,
and game of all kinds. If it walks, swims, or flies
around the fields and streams of Britain, you'll
find it here—grouse, ptarmigan, partridge, wild
duck, pheasant, woodcock, teal, snipe, salmon,
sea trout, boar, and venison. (You can even bag
your own game by joining a shooting party on
Rule's keepered estate!) Wonderful starters include
mussel and saffron soup, scrambled egg with
smoked salmon and fresh basil, and wild rabbit
and pigeon smoked and potted with orange. Traditional British desserts include sherry trifle, treacle
sponge pudding with custard, and steamed chocolate sponge pudding with rum. The walls are covered with hundreds of drawings, paintings, and
cartoons; literary, theatrical, and royal associations abound. This was the haunt of Thackeray,
Galsworthy, Wells, Greene, and Dickens (see playbills presented to the restaurant by Dickens), and
of Barrymore, Chaplin, Laughton, and Gable. On
the first floor by a lattice window is perhaps the
most celebrated "table for two" in London, a
favourite of the Prince of Wales (later Edward VII)
and actress Lillie Langtry.

Rules, 35 Maiden Ln, London WC2, 071-836 5314.
Mon-Sat noon-midnight.

## Best Hot From The Oven
Baker & Oven

When it comes to comfort food, the English, with their love of crusty pies—as appetizers, as the entrée, for dessert, and as savoury snacks—probably define the genre. This restaurant does an excellent job with pies and other classical English dishes, which it serves in an unusual but wonderfully appropriate setting. The restaurant is housed in a turn-of-the-century bakery and its patrons are seated at tables installed in converted brick-lined ovens. Onion soup, rich and flavourful, is a good starter, as is coarse, country-style pâté. English favourites such as chops and roasts are handled simply but well, and specialities such as jugged hare, pheasant, and Aylesbury duckling are worthwhile. Desserts run to traditional steamed puddings and pies, with hot apple pie drenched with thick Devonshire cream a standout.

Baker & Oven, 10 Paddington St, London W1, 071-935 5072. Mon-Fri noon-10:30 pm, Sat 6:30-11 pm.

## Best Baronial Setting For Roast Beef And Yorkshire Pudding
Baron of Beef

This City restaurant, popular for expense-account lunches and with visiting Japanese (a menu is available printed in Japanese), specialises in basic British fare in general and beef in particular. Pride of this club-like restaurant, with hunting prints, comfortable banquettes, and sparkling white napery and glittering heavy cutlery, is a silver trolley bearing roast sirloin of prime Scotch beef. The joint is carved tableside with standard accompaniments of puffy, crisp-crusted Yorkshire pudding, roast potatoes, and horseradish sauce. Starters include hot or cold vichyssoise, cockle and mussel chowder, duck terrine, cod roe, and smoked salmon. Alternatives to the beef entrée include grilled salmon, plaice, Dover sole, fish pie, liver and bacon, chicken pie, breast of duck in raspberry sauce, and traditional steak, kidney, and mushroom pie. Side dishes include fresh asparagus (for which this establishment is known) and a version of that popular British recipe for using up Sunday's leftovers, bubble and squeak (fried potatoes and cabbage). Desserts include traditional puddings, fresh fruit assortments, and a good cheese board served with celery and walnuts.

Baron of Beef, Gutter Ln, London EC2, 071-606 6961. Mon-Fri noon-9 pm.

# Best Bet For All-You-Can-Eat Beef

Carvery Restaurant

The carvery-restaurant concept has become extremely popular in England—particularly among trenchermen, since seconds and thirds are *de rigueur* at these carve-the-joint-to-your-own-specs joints. Another reason is that they offer good value on quality roasts of beef, lamb, and pork. For one all-inclusive price you can build yourself a substantial traditional British meal with Yorkshire pudding and horseradish sauce to accompany the prime rib of beef *au jus*, mint sauce and redcurrant jelly to pair with roast spring lamb, and a spicy bread dressing to go with roast pork and cracklings. Vegetables include customary roast potatoes, green peas, carrots, cauliflower, and brussels sprouts. This particular Carvery in the Tower Thistle Hotel (see separate listing) has big picture windows overlooking the now-revitalized St. Katharine's docks, where sleek yachts bob at their moorings. Meals include soup or appetizer and selections from the dessert trolley, which offers puddings, pastries, trifle, and fruit salad and cream.

Carvery Restaurant, Tower Thistle Hotel, St. Katherine's Way, London E1, 071-481 2525. Daily noon-midnight.

# Best American-Cut Beef

The Rib Room

International power brokers are in their element at this plush, club-like Knightsbridge restaurant that would be equally in *its* element amid the canyons of Manhattan or slowly revolving atop a Dallas high-rise. Located in the elegant Hyatt Carlton Tower (see separate listing), it is at once warm and austere, with subdued lighting, mahogany panelling, flowers and artworks (such as Topolski drawings and a sculpture of a Texas longhorn steer), comfortable club chairs, and tables with gleaming white napery and glistening silver and glassware. This truly is a bovine-fancier's kind of place, renowned for its thick American cuts of the finest ribs of Scotch beef. Carnivores go for a slab of prime rib or a thick steak, but those who prefer to steer clear (so to speak) of red meat will find a new menu with good selections of finfish and shellfish, including Dover sole and fresh oysters. The lively Rib Room bar with a resident virtuoso at a grand piano is a popular meeting spot.

The Rib Room, Hyatt Carlton Tower, Cadogan Pl, London SW1, 071-235 5411. Mon-Sat noon-10:45 pm, Sun noon-10 pm.

# Best Restaurant That's An English Institution

Simpson's-in-the-Strand

This longstanding establishment is perhaps considered as much a part of the "London experience" as is the Changing of the Guard, the British Museum, or Westminster Abbey. Simpson's has been serving excellent roasts since its founding in 1828; the current site opened in 1904 and its atmosphere is not unlike that of an Edwardian club, complete with Adam panelling and white-gloved service. The main draw is the perfectly roasted joints of beef, which are carved tableside from rolling carts with great flourish, and served with crispy Yorkshire pudding. Simpson's also offers solid choices of appetizers, such as pâté, prawn cocktails, smoked salmon, and oxtail soup; a variety of other entrées, including lamb, veal, venison, roast duck, Dover sole, and steak, kidney, and mushroom pie; and well-rendered desserts, most notably apple pie, treacle roll, and fresh fruits (in season) with cream. Additionally, there are good selections of after-meal cheeses and an impressive wine list (which includes vintage port by the glass). Simpson's is definitely formal (jackets and ties are required) and expensive, but it *is* worth it—and to save money and still partake here, opt for the prix fixe lunch and pre-theatre menus—still a bit pricey, but a relative bargain at around £17. (P.S. Proving that man does not live by ale alone, as might have been suggested by his frequent appearances in London's 19th-century pubs, Charles Dickens was known to have dined here—perhaps he was giving his liver a break on those nights!)

Simpson's-in-the-Strand, 100 The Strand, London WC2, 071-836 9112. Mon-Sat noon-3 pm, 6-10 pm.

# Best Bet For Olde English

The Lindsay House

In the heart of Soho, just off Shaftesbury Avenue, a once-badly-neglected building has been recreated into the fine 19th-century townhouse it once was. You gain admittance by discreetly ringing the bell. Inside, you'll find striking rich colours and fabrics, interesting and beautiful antiques, oil paintings of traditional hunting scenes, pretty porcelain lamps, stunning arrangements of fresh flowers, and working fireplaces. Classical British dishes such as collops of Southdown lamb with a rich red wine sauce, guineafowl with summer fruits, and roast breast of duckling with a sauce of orange-and-lime marmalade are interspersed with unusual dishes created from centuries-old recipes—Brye favours (baked parcels of blue cheese in paper-thin pastry) and wild-mushroom tartlet with a cream Madeira sauce. Firm favourites are burnt orange cream and summer pudding (which is served year around). Other popular entrées include baked salmon filet with a parsley crust and basil sauce and stuffed chicken breast with prawns. Desserts include red-berry pudding served with chilled clotted cream and homemade ice creams.

The Lindsay House, 21 Romilly St, London W1, 071-439 0450. Mon-Sat 12:30-midnight, Sun 12:30-10 pm.

## Best Dining In An English Mansion

The English House

In a beautiful setting that is reminiscent of an elegant private house, TV chef and food historian Michael Smith works magic with 18th-century recipes. The rich, warm ambience features fine polished mahogany furniture, gleaming copper and brass, fresh flowers, open fireplaces, and the soft glow of tall candlesticks. Blues and terracotta predominate, and the walls are clad in a printed cotton with a traditional English design of autumn leaves and blackcurrants. Food selections are unabashedly British, with many old-time recipes updated and refined. You'll find such selections as gelatine of guinea fowl with blackcurrant preserve, warm scallop-and-orange salad, chicken-and-leek pie, grilled lamb cutlets with redcurrant glaze, individual beef-and-Guinness pie, veal-and-hare terrine served with apple jelly, and home-made pork-and-sage sausages served with spiced fruit chutney and creamed potato. Finish with an 18th-century chocolate pie (a rich chocolate mousse served in a crisp almond crust), peach parcels with brandy syrup, chocolate sandwich cake, or hot Stilton cheese.

The English House, 3 Milner St, London SW3, 071-584 3002. Mon-Sat 12:30-11:30 pm, Sun 12:30-10:30 pm.

## Best Dining In An English Garden

The English Garden

Flowers are the theme here—real flowers, fresh and dried, and flowers printed on draperies, upholstery, and wall coverings. The Garden Room on the ground floor features white-washed brick and stark white curtains contrasted with pelmets in vivid floral colours. Completing the pretty picture are domed conservatory roofs, banks of plants, Gothic rattan chairs, and pink tablecloths. An upstairs apartment for private parties has antique furniture and a carved wooden fireplace. Interesting dishes include roast rack of lamb with almond and parmesan cheese crust, salmon-egg-and-parsley pie, homemade sausages with black-currant sauce, and poached breast of chicken with pickled walnut stuffing and madeira cream sauce. Creative starters might include Arbroath smokie fishcakes with tomato-and-basil chutney and home-smoked saddle of venison served in a gin-and-juniper-berry sauce. Traditional desserts include saffron cake, adapted from an old West Country recipe and served with honey custard, treacle tart with butterscotch custard, and plum-and-cinnamon ice cream served with cinnamon shortbread.

The English Garden, 10 Lincoln St, London SW3, 071-584 7272. Daily 12:30-10 pm.

## Best Bet For The Best Of British Cooking
Connaught Hotel Restaurant

Traditionalists who stay at the posh Connaught Hotel can order such breakfast staples as kippers, kedgeree, and finnan haddie. If you visit this bastion of British cooking for lunch or dinner, you'll find other splendid examples of plain native fare done well. Master chef Michael Bourdin has created an Anglo-French menu that includes such dishes as pastry-encrusted rack of lamb stuffed with artichoke-and-mushroom mousseline, and Connaught's signature *terrine de foie gras* garnished with port jelly and truffles. The kitchen does an admirable job with basic roast beef and lamb chops, as well as with game, langoustines, mixed grill, kidneys and bacon, and such dishes as *filet de boeuf en croute* and haddock quenelles. Service, as is to be expected at what might be London's grandest hotel, is impeccable. The decor includes dark wood panelling, cut-glass screens, vases of fresh flowers, elegant place settings, and crisp napery.

Connaught Hotel Restaurant, 16 Carlos Pl, London W1, 071-499 7070. Daily 12:30-10:15 pm.

## Best British Stodge
Porters English Restaurant

Porters is the name, pies are the game—but this popular Covent Garden spot may appeal mostly to visitors to England—or Britons who miss home cooking (the cynical might say stodge). There are British standards such as toad in the hole, salmon fish cakes, roast beef and Yorkshire pudding, and bubble and squeak. For dessert there are spotted dick, fruit crumbles, treacle tart, and bread-and-butter pudding. But the speciality is pies—and they are good, well-rendered in individual dishes with light puff pastry and filling combinations that include steak and mushrooms, chicken and asparagus, lamb and apricots, turkey and chestnuts, and, of course, steak and kidney. There also are fish pie and a vegetarian pie. (Inexplicably, steak-and-kidney pudding is served for weekday lunches only during months with an "r"). Porters is a little hokey, with ornaments that include Fry's chocolate signs and a bus stop, and jokes on the menu, but the food is surprisingly good.

Porters English Restaurant, 17 Henrietta St, London WC2, 071-836 6466. Mon-Sat noon-11:30 pm, Sun noon-10:30 pm.

## Best Indian Cuisine On A Budget

Khan's

Indian restaurants are not especially known for being expensive (although some very upmarket Indian restaurants can be found throughout London). And this popular Bayswater Indian eatery is perhaps the king of excellent Indian dining on a budget, providing a sizable menu of affordable traditional favourites (such as curries, tandooris, and kebabs—try the house speciality of curried meatballs in a spicy cream sauce) for a tab that runs well under £10 per person. This is a large restaurant—it seats around 300—and it is very popular, attracting a generally lively crowd, making it an excellent spot for a group outing. Khan's offers its large portions for (relatively) small cost in takeaways, too.

Khan's, 13-15 Westbourne Grove, London W2, 071-727 5420. Daily noon-3 pm, 6 pm-midnight.

## Best Indian Restaurant With Bonnie (But Not Clyde!)

Bombay Brasserie

Indian restaurants tend to spring up in London like rice in a paddy. Many of them are good, most of them are inexpensive. This one, adjoining Bailey's Hotel in Kensington, is among the best, and it *is* expensive. Its opulent style, with ceiling fans, wicker chairs, regal chandeliers, historic photographs of the Imperial days, and a plant-filled conservatory is reminiscent of the Raj, while its wide-ranging menu provides a culinary voyage across the sub-continent. Ambience and food combine to draw a fashionable crowd and a number of celebrities—its name-dropping menu suggests that the featured Kashmiri-style hot-curry dishes are much-admired by actress Faye Dunaway. Regional specialities include Goan fish dishes, the food of the Punjab and the Moghul Empire, tandoori cooking with traditional mint chutney, the spicy-hot cuisine of central India, and the melting-pot dishes that are pure Bombay. Any Englishman who grew up eating mulligatawny at least once a month at school or in the service, should give it another chance here. Indian beer—perhaps a Taj Mahal lager—is a perfect accompaniment.

Bombay Brasserie, Courtfield Cl, London SW7, 071-370 4040. Daily 12:30-midnight.

## Most Varied Indian Cuisine
Jamdani

This is the latest—and, according to avid restaurant-goers who flock here, the best—in restaurateur Amin Ali's small group of Indian restaurants in London. Its stylish and austere decor (created by renowned restaurant designers Fitch & Company) is highlighted by namesake jamdanis, traditional hand-woven prints, hanging on the walls. An eclectic menu features cuisine from various regions of India (with a concentration on the area surrounding Bangladesh), offering conventional favourites such as tandoori-style entrées, but also other dishes that may be less familiar, such as fish tikka, prawn masala, lamb with nutmeats, and rabbit cooked in a thick, spicy vinegar sauce. In general, the long, varied menu includes as many seafood and vegetarian choices as it does meat and chicken entrées. Jamdani is also known for an inventive wine list, and a great Sunday buffet lunch (offering selections from the week's menu) for only £10. Jamdani has quickly become fashionable and popular; reservations are recommended.

Jamdani, 34 Charlotte St, London W1, 071-636 1178. Mon-Sat noon-2:30 pm, 6-11:30 pm; Sun 12:30-3 pm.

## Best Formal Indian Restaurant
The Veeraswamy

This is said to be the oldest Indian restaurant in London (it opened in 1927), and it boasts an atmosphere not unlike a formal, private club—with an inscrutable turbanned doorman out front and traditionally attired waiters inside, serving customers swiftly and unobtrusively. The menu is fairly typical—curries, tandooris, and other cuisines, mostly North Indian in origin—set off by the restaurant's proper, upmarket ambience. For a generous bargain sampling, try the lunchtime buffet, offering all-you-can-eat fish, chicken, veggies, and meat dishes for just over £10. The Veeraswamy *does* feel a bit like a club—and the good food and nicely attentive service will likely make you feel like a treasured member.

The Veeraswamy, 99-101 Regent St, London W1, 071-734 1401. Mon-Sat noon-2:30 pm, 6-11:30 pm; Sun noon-2:30 pm, 7-10:30 pm.

## Best Pakistani Restaurant
Salloos

Indian cuisine is well-established in London, but this longtime Pakistani restaurant is one of few in town offering the cuisine of this northwestern region of the subcontinent. Presided over by patriarch "Salloo" Salahuddin, this family-owned and -operated restaurant is elegant and comfortable, with a casual bar downstairs and the dining room upstairs. The authentic, spicy cooking includes traditional beef, lamb, and seafood kebabs and a variety of tandoori dishes (which are prepared in a clay oven). These dishes are coloured with interesting continental touches—such as quail tandoori, and delicate vegetables accompanying spicy roasted meats. Salloos attracts a dedicated core of followers—reservations are recommended.

Salloos, 62 Kinnerton St, London SW1, 071-235 4444. Mon-Sat noon-2:30 pm, 7-11:30 pm.

## Choosiest California Cuisine
Clarke's

Although chef-owner Sally Clarke received some of her training in California restaurants, the cuisine here is nouveau Anglo-French, with some influence from Italy and the United States. The wine list is predominantly French, although there are some interesting selections from California. The simple, bright dining rooms feature fresh flowers and crisp white napery. The food is excellent, but you won't have to agonise over selections, since the menu is set, determined a week or so ahead. Appetizers include such selections as buttered herb pasta ribbons tossed with chicken livers and prosciutto ham, black-bean cake served with salmon eggs, spiced soured cream, and lime, and duck-breast salad accompanied by rocket (mustard), deep-fried corn bread, Belgian endive, and blood-orange dressing. Main courses are just as imaginatively prepared and range from guinea fowl, swordfish, and lamb, to halibut and grilled breasts of pigeon. Desserts might include chocolate tart with clotted cream, rich chocolate cake with coffee ice cream, and pear, apple, and orange zest strudel. Breads and rolls arrive freshly made from the restaurant's bakery next door.

Clarke's, 124 Kensington Church St, London W8, 071-221 9225. Mon-Fri 12:30-10 pm.

## Best American-Style Deli

Widow Applebaum's

Although the upmarket calm of South Molton Street in Mayfair will never be mistaken for the grimy ambience of New York's Seventh Avenue (home of that city's famous Carnegie and Stage delicatessens), this establishment will definitely fill the bill for those who want a taste of authentic N.Y.-style deli delicacies. Decorated with atmospheric photos of 1920s-1930s-era New York, this restaurant offers piled-high pastrami, salt beef, and B.L.T. (bacon, lettuce, and tomato) sandwiches, with requisite sides of chicken soup, matzos, and cole slaw. Top these off with a seltzer water or an ice cream soda. This is a good stop for lunch after shopping nearby Bond or Oxford Streets, and, during summer, it also offers pleasant outdoor seating. But a question remains that differentiates Widow Applebaum's from its Big Apple progenitors: What's a deli without Brooklyn-accented *kibitzing*?

Widow Applebaum's, 46 South Molton St, London W1, 071-629 4649. Mon-Fri 11:30 am-9 pm, Sat 11:30 am-2:30 pm.

## Best Bite Of The Big Apple In London

Joe Allen

The bright lights of a different big city don't seem as far away at this restaurant, which is a branch of a New York-based eatery that strives to replicate the Big Apple dining experience of its original outlet. Located in a large basement room of a converted warehouse, it features a nightly menu chalked on a board, theatre posters on walls, and a lively and noisy crowd. The Manhattan-style choices here include hearty steaks, seafood, ribs, huge salads, excellent hamburgers, crab cakes, and spicy Cajun-style chicken, with such typical offerings as fresh cheesecake and carrot cake for dessert. The original Joe Allen is near Broadway in New York, and often attracts celebrated figures; this branch is also popular with a loyal crowd of "see-and-be-seen-ers," including local actors, writers, artists, photographers, models, and the like. Joe Allen stays open late, making it a good choice for post-theatre dining; the restaurant is close to Drury

Lane, the Royal Opera House, and the theatres along The Strand (Savoy, Adelphi, etc.). Reservations are strongly recommended.

Joe Allen, 13 Exeter St, London WC2, 071-836 0651. Mon-Sat noon-12:45 am, Sun noon-11:45 pm.

## Creamiest Milkshake Made With Real Milk
Ed's Easy Diner

Greasers and Teddy Boys, Mods and Rockers—these are the colourful character types of the '50s and '60s that you'd expect to find at this recreated diner in Soho. Inspired by Chicago's hugely popular Ed Debevic's diner (but not associated with it), Ed's features picture-perfect decor: Counter stools, gum-snapping waitresses, gleaming chrome fixtures, miniature juke boxes in the booths (to play your favourite '50s hits—perhaps Elvis Presley for the Yanks and Cliff Richard for the Brits). Popular offerings include burgers, fries, chili, club sandwiches, tempting homemade slices of pies, and thick, generous, nearly-impossible-to-draw-up-a-straw shakes and malts made with plenty of real ice cream. Ed's provides friendly, fun, wisecracking service by young wait staff in period uniforms. But this is not a place to linger—"eat up and get out" is its unofficial motto. (P.S. Check out the last digits of the phone number—it pinpoints the diner's main year of reference.)

Ed's Easy Diner, 12 Moor St, London W1, 071-439 1955. Sun-Thu 11:30 am-midnight, Fri & Sat 11:30 am-1 am.

## Best All-American Food
Windy City Bar And Grill

When it comes to American food in London, Chicagoan Bob Payton is the acknowledged king. However, it is somewhat ironic that Payton is not that well-known (except among fellow restaurateurs and frequent London visitors) back in his stateside hometown. In fact, Chicagoans are much more familiar with *another* Payton, a former U.S.-football-playing chap named Walter! This large and beckoning Payton place follows the form of his other eateries (such as the Chicago Pizza Pie Factory and the Chicago Rib Shack—see separate listings), featuring a loud, lively atmosphere enlivened by a collection of Chicago memorabilia (photos, posters, signs, sports insignias, etc.). The menu is as American as apple pie, including meaty burgers, char-grilled steaks, crispy broiled chicken, piled-high beef sandwiches, barbecued baby back ribs, pasta dishes, huge salads, bar-food-type appetizers, and a piece of you-know-what à la mode for dessert. Wash it all down with a Budweiser or other U.S. beer. And, if Mr. Payton is in residence, be sure not to make the mistake of telling him you enjoyed the way he played for the Chicago Bears!

Windy City Bar And Grill, 163 Knightsbridge, London SW7, 071-589 7077. Daily 11:30 am-11:30 pm.

## Best Tex-Mex Restaurant
Los Locos

It may be something of an oxymoron to consider that the cuisine at this pair of restaurants was voted by the *Evening Standard* "the best Tex-Mex this side of the Atlantic." Still, the chili probably is as authentic as you'll find in London, the grilled food is cooked over mesquite wood, the drinks of choice are tequilla, mescal, and Mexican and American brews, and these two eateries *are* owned and run by Texans. In early evening, the atmosphere is that of a quiet cantina where you can sip a Dos Equis or Corona beer—or an exotic mixed drink such as a Snakebite (Jack Daniels and peppermint schnapps) or potent Texas Tea (vodka, gin, rum, tequila, sour mix, and cola), and munch on nachos, guacamole, and deep-fried alligator meat. The menu also features fajitas, steaks, hamburgers, grilled prawns stuffed with hot peppers and cheese and wrapped in bacon, and such Tex-Mex favourites as chimichangas, enchiladas, and quesadillas. A small section of desserts includes chocolate fudge cake, margarita pie, deep-fried ice cream, and a confection called "Death by Chocolate." At 11 p.m. the dining area is cleared away and the place becomes a hot dance joint until around 3 a.m.

Los Locos, 24 Russell St, London WC2, 071-379 0220; 14 Soho St, London W1, 071-287 0005. Mon-Sat 6 pm-3 am.

## Closest Thing To South Of The Border
Down Mexico Way

It probably is impossible to find a decent slice of Melton Mowbray in Mexico City and equally difficult to encounter a steaming steak-and-kidney pudding or a carton of jellied eels in Los Angeles and environs. One shouldn't be surprised, then, at how difficult it is to find decent chile rellenos and queso fundido in London. This former Spanish restaurant in (of all places!) the heart of Piccadilly comes closest, with decent flour tortillas, tacos,

and enchiladas. Certainly, the chilis and spicy sea-
sonings used in many of the dishes add authenticity, as does the use of mesquite for grilling some of
the meat-and-vegetable combinations. If you are a
fan of Mexican fare, order up a pitcher of margaritas, kick back and admire the ornate ceramic tiles
and bubbling fountain—and think fondly about
that 12-seat storefront Mexican joint you once
found not five miles from LAX. Note: The first line
in the song—South of the Border—was appropriated by an Indonesian restaurant south of the
Thames!

Down Mexico Way, 25 Swallow St, London W1, 071-
437 9895. Mon-Sat noon-11:45 pm.


## Best Chicago-Style Ribs

Chicago Rib Shack

Expatriated Chicagoan Bob Payton has struck
again! And, although rib-fanciers in Kansas City
and Texas might take umbrage at Chicago's barbeque boasts, you'll find here, from whatever origin, some pretty good barbequed baby back ribs.
In fact, before he introduced the genre to London
in 1982, Payton embarked on a barbeque
odyssey—a 10-day trip through the United States,
sampling ribs at 85 restaurants in 10 cities. Along
with the ribs, you'll find barbecued chicken, barbecued beef sandwiches, thick loaves of onion
rings, and potato skins stuffed with cheese, sour-
cream, and spring onions, plus cheesecake, pecan
pie, and ice cream. The decor could best be
described as "Victorian Architectural Salvage,"
including a 45-foot-long mahogany and mirrored
bar from a pub in Glasgow, and stained-glass windows from a chapel in Lancashire. As the restaurant punningly declares on the giant bibs in which
it wraps its rib-eating customers, "Bone Appetit!"

Chicago Rib Shack, 1 Raphael St, London SW7, 071-
581 5595. Mon-Sat 11:45 am-11:30 pm, Sun noon-11
pm.


## Best Chicago-Style Pizza

Chicago Pizza Pie Factory

At Chicago's O'Hare Airport, one frequently spots
homebound visitors toting unique items of carry-
on luggage—cartons of deep-dish pizza. Bob Payton, a former Chicago advertising executive, has
taken a step further the exportation of the Windy
City's most famous culinary creation. He opened a
Chicago-style pizzeria in the heart of Mayfair. This
large, warehouse-style basement restaurant is full
of Chicago memorabilia—street signs, autographed

pictures of mayors, music from a Chicago radio station, and videos of Bears football and Cubs baseball games. Deep-dish pizza comes in small and large sizes with cheese and a choice of sausage, pepperoni, mushrooms, green peppers, onions, and anchovies. Sides include stuffed mushrooms and killer garlic bread. Dessert choices include ice cream, chocolate cheesecake, and carrot cake with honeyed whipped cream. Wash down your thick, crusty pizza with a Budweiser or an enormous theme cocktail. Patrons have included the Duchess of Kent and ladies-in-waiting to the Queen (the restaurant's original location was close to Buckingham Palace).

Chicago Pizza Pie Factory, 17 Hanover Sq, London W1, 071-629 2669. Mon-Sat 11:45 am-11:30 pm, Sun noon-10:30 pm.

## Fanciest Pizza Parlour

Kettners

Eating at this incongruous-seeming restaurant might be akin to being invited to a grand country house and watching your blue-blooded hosts consume an anchovy and onion pizza! What long was the home of a succession of famous, classy restaurants (occupying this site since the mid-19th century) is today perhaps the most elegant pizza parlour in the world. Kettners' surprisingly plush Victorian interior provides a strange counterpoint to its contemporary eat-and-run menu of pizza, burgers, salads, and pasta dishes. But, somehow, the pairing works (perhaps because the affordable fare is of a higher level than that found at mos t pizza or other fast food restaurants). Compounding the unexpected, the restaurant also offers a champagne bar and piano bar (often featuring performances by the restaurant's singing maitre d'). There is additional seating in a room with modern decor (tiled walls and bright lighting)–avoid seating there, if possible, in favour of the classic, original room. Owned by the Pizza Express chain (see separate listing).

Kettners, 29 Romilly St, London W1, 071-437 6437. Daily 11 am-midnight.

## Best Restaurant For An Around-The-World Trip

Pomegranates

You wonder about a Welshman named Gwynn-Jones operating a restaurant with such an eclectic international menu. And then you learn that he sailed the world in the merchant marine, and it all makes sense. Along with Welsh salt duck with white onion sauce and English game pie, you'll find West Indian peppered filet of beef and curried goat with plantain, New Orleans-style jambalaya, Mauritian spicy "Raçon" soup flavoured with tamarind and curry, Jamaican red mullet broth with rum, Mexican enchiladas with frijoles, steak stuffed with oysters from an Australian recipe, and a variety of French and Oriental dishes. You can finish your meal with cheese and port, or with a traditional comfort-type dessert such as treacle tart with cream. Restaurateur Gwynn-Jones likes to refer to his offerings as "peasant food," although what may be prosaic dishes in their homelands are elevated here. The ambience of this basement restaurant is warm and inviting, from the moment you enter through its handsome oak door, to the moment you're ready to leave comfortable seating in a burgundy banquette or bentwood chair. Wines on an extensive list are as well-travelled as recipes on the menu. Prix fixe meals include crudités.

Pomegranates, 94 Grosvenor Rd, London SW1, 071-828 6560. Mon-Fri 12:30-11:15 pm, Sat 7:30-11:15 pm.

## Best Restaurant To Conduct Business Over Lunch

Le Poulbot

Whether you're looking to close that big deal or just to have a brisk, but satisfying lunch in the midst of a busy business day, this lunch-only restaurant on one of the City's most famous streets is a good bet. Le Poulbot has been one of the City's favourite spots for business lunches for more than 20 years. The restaurant consists of two levels: A brasserie on the ground floor offers steaks, chops, and a changing variety of à la carte specials (this attracts large crowds and accepts no reservations); the basement room features a prix fixe menu–for £28.50, it includes choices of such appetizers as foie gras, soups, and salad (especially niçoise), and such entrées as calves' livers, lamb, beef, and fish (salmon and sole are popular). Le Poulbot also is known for its good selection of cheeses and its attentive, accommodating, and rapid service. In general, the brasserie upstairs is busier and noisier than the basement, but both are good places to talk figures and contracts over a well-prepared and -presented lunch.

Le Poulbot, 45 Cheapside, London EC2, 071-236 4379. Mon-Fri noon-3 pm.

# Best Restaurant To Conduct Business Over Dinner

Harvey's

This out-of-the-way, but worth-the-trip restaurant is a good choice for business dining, because of its exquisite French cuisine and for the fact that it isn't a common business-district hang-out. (Visiting businesspeople can score a coup by taking London clients or associates to such a well-regarded but not-commonly-considered restaurant for a post-meeting meal.) Located about a half-hour's ride south of the West End, this restaurant is the domain of Marco Pierre White, a young chef who already has made a name for himself among London's elite chefs. In the classy surroundings of a cosy, tastefully decorated all-white room, patrons can enjoy fine à la carte or prix fixe (lunch from £22, dinner from £42) menus. Acclaimed dishes include excellent seafood entrées (especially those featuring salmon, prawns, and scallops), tender saddle of lamb with basil, roast rabbit with mushrooms, and some fabulous stuffed pigs' feet (the recipe for which is credited to White's friend, Pierre Koffmann, of La Tante Claire—see separate listing). There is also a good (but expensive) selection of wines, and a tempting menu of homemade desserts. A note of warning: If traveling to Harvey's by cab, it's probably best to order your return cab when you arrive; this neighbourhood is off the beaten track to begin with, and cabs are notoriously hard to come by here later in the evening.

Harvey's, 2 Bellevue Rd, London SW17, 081-672 0114. Mon-Sat 12:30-2:30 pm, 7:30-11:30 pm.

# Best Spot When Cost Is Of No Concern

La Tante Claire

There is no "Auntie Claire" behind the sublime French cuisine at this celebrated restaurant— rather, there is an Uncle Pierre. Chef/owner Pierre Koffmann is considered one of the top three chefs in London (with La Gavroche's Albert Roux and Chez Nico's Nico Ladenis—see separate listings), and he uses his small, but constantly changing menu much like an artist uses a palette of colours—touches of seafood here, highlights of fresh vegetables there. The results are decidedly artistic. For starters, try the archetypal rendering of pâté foie gras, or an imaginative ravioli filled with sea bass, frog meat, or sweetbreads. Entrées vary, but usually include such choices as seafood (especially inventive dishes featuring mullet, scallops, and salmon), field-fresh game (such as squab, venison, and duck), and even a twist on classic English roast beef (zestily flavoured with bacon and mushrooms). Accompanying these are a terrific selection of classic wines; the house wines also are very good. The restaurant is elegant, its tastefully small room enlivened by a collection of splashily colourful paintings; the service is excellent and efficient. Of course, this lofty level of dining comes with a commensurately high price tag: Dinner for two (with a moderately priced wine) will run from £125-£150; for a taste of this cuisine for less of a bite, try the set-price lunch, a comparative bargain at £21.50. There usually is a long waiting list—inquire up to three weeks ahead for reservations.

La Tante Claire, 68 Royal Hospital Rd, London SW3, 071-352 6045. Mon-Fri 12:30-2 pm, 7-11 pm.

## Most Elegant Afternoon Tea
Ritz Palm Court

Since the 1920s, the Ritz has been the place to be seen taking afternoon tea—and, for a good many of the intervening years, this mid-afternoon ritual has been presided over with style and panache by Michael Twomey, who joined the hotel more than 40 years ago. Setting for this afternoon repast is the lovely Palm Court, with rose-coloured light filtering through a skylight and with marble columns, a magnificently ornate ceiling, elaborate chandeliers, and sculptured fountain. Place settings are elegant, with fine china and fresh flowers, and the offerings are traditional—finger sandwiches, scones with jam and cream, pastries, cream cakes, rich fruit cake, and, of course, a variety of the finest teas. Service (strictly white-glove!) is between 3 p.m. and 4:30 p.m., cost is £12.50 per person, and it is necessary to book well in advance. Dress is formal—definitely no jeans or sneakers. (On Fridays and Saturdays post-theatre supper is served in the Palm Court from 10 p.m. to 1 a.m., with dancing to the big-band sounds of the twenties, thirties, and forties.) The Ritz, opened in 1906, is, of course, one of London's most famous and fashionable hotels (see separate listing).

Palm Court, The Ritz Hotel, Piccadilly, London W1, 071-493 8181. Daily 3-5:30 pm.

## Best Devon Cream Tea
Palm Court Lounge

With today's hectic lifestyles, the traditional break for formal afternoon tea has become more of a luxury than a necessity for working Londoners. But this does not mean that the tradition has vanished—it still makes a perfect occasional break for residents and can be a delightful treat for visitors (who should be careful not to call it "high tea," which means more of a special meal than the conventional afternoon tea). The Palm Court Lounge (in the Park Lane Hotel) is a good spot to partake in this relaxed, enjoyable custom. The hotel was built in 1927, and this opulent room was recently restored by noted interior designer John Siddeley to reflect its original grandeur. Under a domed glass ceiling, surrounded by the lounge's namesake potted palm trees, you can enjoy an aromatic pot of tea, crumbly scones (accompanied by thick Devonshire cream and strawberry jam), a choice of cucumber and other finger sandwiches, and sweet cakes. Offered daily from 3-6 p.m., this tea runs around £7, and is a good fortifier before a night of theatre (with dinner after).

Palm Court Lounge, Park Lane Hotel, Piccadilly, London W1, 071-499 6321. Tea daily 3-6 pm.

## Best Afternoon Tea In An Old-Fashioned Tea Shop
The Muffin Man

Many of London's most prestigious hotels are famous for their ultra-elegant afternoon teas, served with great panache by white-gloved waiters, with piano or harp music providing a proper background for the polite chink of fine bone china and low conversations. In contrast, The Muffin Man is a traditional English tea room, one of the few remaining in London. When you are ready to be revivified at the appropriate afternoon hour, you'll find pots of strong tea, rich gateaux, toasted teacakes, hot buttered scones, and plates of petite finger sandwiches. Of course, many afternoon teatakers go for the Devon cream tea with its fresh scones, fruit-rich preserves, and thick clotted cream. This pretty, two-story Kensington tea shop also offers substantial breakfasts (and simple fresh croissants and coffee), and lunchtime salads, soups, and sandwiches. It tends to get crowded during the tourist season, having been discovered by Americans staying at the nearby Kensington Close and London Tara hotels.

The Muffin Man, 12 Wrights Ln, London W8, 071-937 6652. Mon-Fri 8:15 am-5:45 pm, Sat 8:45 am-4:45 pm.

## Most Unpassable Bakery
Patisserie Valerie

The window of this Soho bakery and café beckons

temptingly, full of creamy cakes, freshly made biscuits and muffins, and other baked goods. And if the sight doesn't get you, the rich, wafting aroma may just lure you in! This Belgian patisserie is not only known for its pastries and cakes—it also contains a café, which is especially popular with actors, models, and various "wannabes" of the local entertainment scene. They favour the atmosphere of the cozy café, which more resembles a café in the heart of a romantic little Paris or Brussels neighbourhood than a bake shop in the middle of busy Soho. This is a nice, leisurely spot for breakfast or a light lunch of a sandwich, salad, or soup, or perhaps a fresh-baked dessert.

Patisserie Valerie, 44 Old Compton St, London W1, 071-437 3466. Mon-Sat 8 am-7 pm, Sun 10 am-6 pm.

## Best Nouvelle Cuisine

Inigo Jones

This romantic restaurant, a fixture in Covent Garden for 25 years or so, is appropriately named after Inigo Jones, the father of English classical architecture who was involved in the early planning of Covent Garden. With exposed brick walls, picture windows, and comfortable peach-coloured seating, the restaurant occupies a former Victorian stained-glass studio and workshop and has become a temple of nouvelle cuisine. Imaginative creations from Paul Gayler's kitchen change frequently and might include such selections as duck confit with lentils, quail in tangerine sauce, scallop tart with champagne butter, and roast lamb with rosemary and garlic. There is a good selection of cheese, and inventive desserts that include pear-and-walnut burnt cream. There are fixed-priced lunches and pre-theatre dinner, a pricey wine list, and a decent house wine.

Inigo Jones, 14 Garrick St, London WC2, 071-836 6456. Mon-Fri 12:30-11:30 pm, Sat 6-11:30 pm.

## Best Restaurant With A Virtuoso (But Temperamental) Chef

Chez Nico

Nico Ladenis, a self-taught master of inventive cuisine, is one of the most respected chefs in London—and also the one most likely to be described as a megalomaniac. Nico is very demanding when it comes to the quality of everything in his restaurant—the food, the service, even the diners, if one is to give credence to the perhaps-apocryphal story of him ejecting an unappreciative customer (for loudly demanding his dish be prepared contrary to the menu's description). However, this single-mindedness has its merits. Some of Nico's regulars, well-versed in his whimsical ways, leave their dining choices to chance and let the master himself choose their meals, depending upon what he fancies presenting them with that evening. (Nico seems to delight in these sort of gastronomic missions, perhaps sometimes giving diners who make this request a higher level of personal attention.) What might he choose? Perhaps saddle of lamb; ragout of fin- and shellfish, redolent with saffron; duck, prepared any of several excellent and accomplished ways; or maybe a daily fresh fish special—the common denominator of these are Nico's inventive and appealing combinations of ingredients. To accompany these dishes, there is also an exceptional wine list and a very good after-dinner selection of cheeses. Of course, this level of dining is expensive—dinner usually goes for around £100 for two (with wine); lunchtime is a comparative bargain, with a terrific set-price menu for £25. Reservations are an absolute must—book at least two weeks ahead.

Chez Nico, 35 Great Portland St, London W1, 071-436 8846. Mon-Fri 12:15-2 pm, 7-11:15 pm.

## Best Of The Best Most Memorable Meals

### Le Gavroche

When you visit the restaurant of the first chef in Britain to receive three stars from Michelin, you're prepared to expect extravagant cuisine with prices to match. This Mayfair restaurant of the celebrated Albert Roux lives up to both expectations. Dinners can run to £100 or more if ordered à la carte; a set-price luncheon is a relative bargain at under £30. Service is attentive and knowledgeable, the food prepared with intricate attention to detail and served with a flourish on domed silver platters. Mousseline of lobster usually draws rave notices, and the soufflés are ambrosial. The raspberry soufflé is a standout at a restaurant known for exquisite desserts that include a renowned grapefruit-and-orange gateaux and excellent poached fruit and fruit tarts. Other notable dishes include cream of crayfish soup enhanced with caviar, prawns in an herbed tomato-and-brandy sauce, chicken casserole with lentils and thyme, and lamb and veal stews that define the genre. The basement restaurant is decorated in understated neutral colours; enjoy an aperitif and canapes upstairs as you peruse the menu before being shown to your table. The wine list is extensive—and expensive, with a big mark-up—and features a wide range of bordeaux and burgundies.

Le Gavroche, 43 Upper Brook St, London W1, 071-408 0881. Mon-Fri noon-11 pm.

## Restaurant Where The Decor Gets Better Reviews Than The Food

Criterion Brasserie

The food here isn't bad—average-to-above-average brasserie fare—but the decor is so outstanding as to overshadow the menu's offerings. What has become one of the most beautiful restaurants in all of London was once the city's most popular 19th-century Turkish bathhouse! A restoration uncovered and enhanced its neo-Byzantine splendour and added attractive art deco touches. Today, a gold-and-jewel-encrusted mosaic perches breathtakingly above the restaurant's attractively appointed dining room; there are sparkling touches of glass and mirrors scattered throughout, as well as floor plants smartly accenting the comfortable seating. When you're finished taking in the gorgeous effects, place your order—there's brasserie-style light dining up front and modern French dining in the rest of the large restaurant; fish and lamb are regarded as the best dishes. Criterion Brasserie is a popular spot for pre-theatre dining (or even post-theatre dining, for some early shows). But don't be surprised if the decor here is more dramatic and engaging than the evening's theatrical presentation!

Criterion Brasserie, 222 Piccadilly, London W1, 071-839 7133. Mon-Sat noon-3 pm, 6-11 pm; Sun 6-11 pm.

## Best Instant Trip To The Caribbean

Beewees and Caribbean Sunkissed

When the day is grey and rainy, with no hope of the mercury rising above 5°C, there are two ways to escape: 1. Head for Heathrow and jump on a jet for the islands, or 2. Try either of these friendly restaurants for a taste of the islands. Beewees specialises in the cuisine of Trinidad, offering more than three dozen dishes. Try a spicy goat curry or rice and peas (actually a beans-and-rice mixture, laced with coconut milk and spices). Beewees also offers a great variety of non-alcoholic juices (as well as fruity rum drinks) and take-aways. Caribbean Sunkissed boasts a staff direct from the Caribbean island of St. Lucia, and offers a good choice of spicy, flavourful fish dishes and other specialities such as pork simmered in lime juice, rum, and garlic. Adding to the island atmosphere, there is usually a lilting reggae or calypso tape playing at Caribbean Sunkissed.

Beewees West Indian Restaurant, 96 Stroud Green Rd, London N4, 071-263 4004. Mon 6-11 pm, Tue-Sat 12:15-11 pm, Sun 5-10 pm. The Caribbean Sunkissed Restaurant, 49 Chippenham Rd, London W9, 071-286 3741. Mon-Sat noon-3 pm, 6 pm-midnight.

## Best Pierogi Purveyor
Lowiczanka Restaurant and Café

Pierogis? Those ubiquitous Polish delicacies (of dumplings stuffed with meat or cheese) can be found wherever Poles congregate, from Krakow to Chicago. And, of course, also in London—most notably at this large restaurant and café located in the POSK (Polish Social and Cultural Centre) Building. The restaurant (on the first floor) serves up a variety of international dishes and Polish specialities—including pierogis, *bigos* (a sausage, meat, and sauerkraut stew), traditional kielbasa sausages, and homemade desserts, especially sweet thick cakes. The restaurant also offers music and dancing on weekend nights. Downstairs is the café—which is smaller, more informal, and cheaper. Open Wednesday-Monday 10:30 a.m.-10 p.m., it is a nice, casual spot for tea and dessert. The Polish Social and Cultural Centre promotes Polish cultural and artistic achievements—it shows films, offers music, opera, dance, and dramatic performances, and houses a large library of Polish-language and Polish-subject books.

Lowiczanka Restaurant and Café, 238-246 King St, London W6, 081-741 3225. Daily noon-4 pm, 6-11 pm.

## Best Fish And Chips To Go
Rock Sole Plaice

In a quiet backwater, virtually within range of a drunken yobbo's yell from the noisy throngs of Covent Garden, this fish-and-chip shop is almost a throwback to the days when this English staple came wrapped in newsprint. Order your fish and chips to take away—or to eat at this tiny, pleasant cafe, with half-a-dozen tables inside and a like number of picnic benches on the pavement. It was late and quiet the evening I visited, and they deep-fried my large portion of fresh cod while I waited, sipping a cup of strong tea. (They also offer coffee and soft drinks and customers are invited to bring beer or wine.) In addition to the standard fish-and-chip offerings of cod, haddock, plaice, etc., you can order deep-fried cod roe. Not in the mood for fish?

Try deep-fried batter-dipped sausages. A saveloy (the ready-cooked, spicy sausage that is a London institution) makes a good starter.

Rock Sole Plaice, 47 Endell St, London WC2, 071-836 3785.

## Best Fish & Chips To Stay

### Geale's

Basic fish and chips—but better than you'll find on High Street—is the attraction of this restaurant tucked away on a side street across from Notting Hill Gate tube station. It's housed in a corner, painted-brick storefront with tiny, attractive window panes and potted plants on the pavement. Football star George Best is a patron, as are (according to the framed photographs) actors Jeremy Brett and Edward Hardwoode, respectively television's most recent incarnations of Sherlock Holmes and Dr. Watson. There's a small waiting bar upstairs and a dining room that looks as though it belongs in a tea shop. As you wait, you can study the blackboard menu, featuring such daily specials as crab soup and deep-fried clams, and admire the framed Player's cigarette cards featuring, of course, fish. Fresh fish arrives daily, so the selections vary (but include such standards as cod, plaice, and sole). Fish is well prepared and accompanied by good chips. There are wines by the glass and traditional puddings for dessert.

Geale's, 2-4 Farmer St, London W8, 071-727 7969. Tue-Sat noon-11 pm.

## Best Fish And Chips, Sit-Down Elegant

### Sea-Shell

This restaurant started life as a simple fish-and-chip shop...But, as its reputation spread and it attracted a more well-heeled clientèle, it expanded into a 150-seat restaurant—which still happens to offer some of the best and most elegant fish and chips in town. Sea-Shell serves generous portions of traditional fried fish (haddock, cod, plaice, etc.); these choices are dock-fresh, so menu selections vary day-to-day, according to what's available. This restaurant also offers good desserts (the apple pie is an acclaimed favourite), and has been recently licensed to serve alcohol. All-in-all, a nice, mid-level fish restaurant with friendly, attentive service. Its location near Lord's makes it a popular dining spot with fans after snoozing through an afternoon of cricket.

Sea-Shell, 51-53 Lisson Grove, London NW1, 071-723 8703. Tue-Sat noon-10:30 pm.

# Best Spot For Cockles And Whelks (Outside Of Southend)

Tubby Isaacs

For generations, this seafood stall (at the corner of Goulston Street and Middlesex Street) has been a fixture at the Aldgate end of the Petticoat Lane Sunday street market (see separate listing), as much at home as the barrow boys and buskers, tipsters and tie salesmen. Jellied eels are the speciality—basically, eels in aspic, spooned out of cartons. If you're not up to this traditional East London delicacy, you may wish to try a paper cup filled with cockles or whelks (the latter tend to be a little more rubbery, but do have their following). Drizzled with malt vinegar and sprinkled with white pepper, these mollusks are perfect finger food. There also are prawns, crabs, and oysters in season. This family business was started in 1919 by the original Tubby Isaacs, who always wanted to go to America. Eventually, he fulfilled his dream and lived in New York. He loved the country and stayed there until his death.

Tubby Isaacs, corner of Goulston and Middlesex St, London E1. Daily 11 am-11 pm.

# Most Authentic Pie-And-Eel Shop

F. Cooke & Sons

Admittedly, it's not for the squeamish. Out front is a tank of live eels; inside you can buy them steamed or jellied. But, even if you're not up to trying eels, a trip to this long-established business in working-class East London is worthwhile. The restaurant's other speciality is meat pies, filled with minced steak and kidney, served with scoops of mashed potato, and topped with a parsley sauce known in pie-and-eel-shop parlance as "liquor." Many patrons who have moved away yearn for this basic East London fare; tacked on the wall is a collection of letters and cards from aficionados in New Zealand, Canada, and other far-flung outposts of the Commonwealth. The ambience is traditional, with marble tables and wooden benches, and tiled walls with insets picturing fishing scenes of long ago. Fruit pies and custard are offered for dessert. (It is *de rigueur* to eat pie and mash with a fork and *spoon.)*

F. Cooke & Sons, 41 Kingsland High St, London E8, 071-254 2878.

# Savviest Seafood Restaurant

Scotts

If it swims—or otherwise resides in the fresh or

briny deep!—you'll find it here. The menu at Scotts does offer some other choices (such as a good selection of game birds, for example), but this restaurant is primarily known for its seafood. The oysters, lobster, and caviar to be found here have been widely acclaimed as the best in London—and as some of the best anywhere in the entire world! Other choices include excellent lobster bisque and grilled Dover sole (in fact, Dover sole prepared in any fashion is one of the restaurant's top specialities). The bill of fare varies with the availability of fresh ingredients, but generally includes a variety of other fin- and shellfish, including salmon, turbot, plaice, halibut, shrimp, and crab. For starters—or just a bite—try the restaurant's individual caviar and oyster bars. Scotts is located in Mayfair, and reflects it: Comfortable, upmarket, and expensive—perhaps £50 per person, not including wine—and offering good, attentive service. Scotts has been known for entertaining royalty and celebrities since its founding in the mid-19th century.

Scotts, 20 Mount St, London W1, 071-629 5248. Mon-Sat 12:30-3 pm, 6-11 pm; Sun 7-10 pm.

# Best Upmarket Seafood Restaurant

Bentley's Restaurants

Premium seafood of all kinds, and oysters in particular (from Bentley's own beds in Northern Ireland), have been the speciality here since William Fitzherbert Bentley opened his original restaurant in 1916 (bombed during World War II and reopened at the present Swallow Street location). Here, two elegant dining rooms feature handsome wooden booths and walls covered with paintings and framed historical prints. A new location serving the City lunch crowd gleams with a wealth of mahogany and brass. Start with gravlax, mussels in white wine and cream sauce, devilled whitebait (sprinkled with cayenne pepper and deep fried), or salmon-and-scallop quennelles. Your entrée might be a simple fish dish, such as poached halibut, trout, or Scotch salmon or grilled Dover sole or sea bass. Or you might opt for a house speciality, such as turbot prepared with a white wine, tomato, and parsley sauce, steamed brill served with mint and mustard seed sauce, or lobster roasted with fresh basil. Both restaurants have a good complementary wine list and both locations offer connected oyster bars (see separate listing).

Bentley's Restaurants, 11-15 Swallow St, London W1, 071-734 4756. Mon-Sat noon-10:45 pm; 11 Queen Victoria St, London EC4, 071-248 5145. Mon-Fri noon-3 pm.

## Best Bet For Bivalves (West End And City)

Bentley's Oyster Bars

When all you're looking for is a light lunch—perhaps a glass of chablis and half dozen oysters, or maybe a fresh lobster salad or a simple plate of Scottish smoked salmon served with brown bread and lemon—this well-regarded oyster bar may fit the bill. Doubly so, in fact, since the popular West End location recently was joined by a Bentley's champagne and oyster bar in the heart of the City, featuring a 24-foot marble top bar and additional seating in four booths. The original location is clublike with subdued lighting from wall sconces illuminating comfortably upholstered booths; it also offers seating at a marble counter. Other selections might include crab cocktail, fresh prawns on avocado, and such hot dishes as salmon fish cakes, baked prawns with ginger, oysters Rockerfeller (with cream spinach and Pernod sauce), and oysters Kilpatrick (cooked in tomato sauce with spring onion and chopped bacon). A rich bisque of lobster, crab, and prawns is a popular soup course. Bentley's oysters, harvested from its own beds in Northern Ireland, also are available at a retail outlet (see separate listing). At each location a seafood restaurant (see separate listing) offers a full à la carte menu plus daily specials.

Bentley's Oyster Bar, 11-15 Swallow St, London W2, 071-734 4756. Mon-Sat noon-10:45 pm. Bentley's Champagne & Oyster Bar, 11 Queen Victoria St, London EC4, 071-248 5145. Mon-Fri 11 am-10 pm.

## Best Bet for Bivalves (Victoria)

Overton's Oyster Bar & Restaurants

If you've just gotten off the train or bus (or boat train) and you've a craving for oysters, slip into this popular Victoria oyster bar for a half dozen or so fresh, plump bivalves. Upstairs is a full service restaurant serving oysters hot and cold, rich lobster bisque, smoked Scotch salmon, platters of prawns, dressed crab, scampi, smoked eel, lobster, sole, turbot, brill, trout, fish cakes, and fish pies, as well as a variety of game such as young grouse and partridge. A more sedate branch is located at St. James's—close enough to be viewed by the scarlet-coated guardsmen at the Palace, were they permitted to turn their heads a fraction. This branch has political prints covering more than two centuries lining Jacobean-style panelling behind tables spread with snowy Irish linen.

Overton's Oyster Bar & Restaurant, 4-6 Victoria Bldgs, Terminus Pl, London SW1, 071-834 3774. Mon-

Fri noon-11:30 pm, Sat 5:30-11:30 pm; Overton's Restaurant, 5 St. James's St, London SW1, 071-839 3774. Mon-Fri noon-10:45 pm, Sat 5:30-10:45 pm.

## Best Budget Sushi

Ajimura

It may seem that most Japanese restaurants in London are inordinately expensive, making them suitable primarily for patrons on expense accounts. This attractive, but casual restaurant is the most notable exception. The prices for all of its menu choices are reasonable...but it truly reaches budget status with its inexpensive prix fixe menus offering good bargains for lunch and pre-theatre diners. The around-£10 menus start with an appetizer such as marinated fish or fried bean curd, and also include sashimi (raw fish in a soy-based sauce) and a flavourful teriyaki dish, accompanied by soup, rice, and dessert. Ajimura also offers crispy deep-fried tempura dishes and a good sushi bar—considered one of the best in London. You won't have any trouble making your choices known—the restaurant's Japanese staff speaks English (many are second- or third-generation Londoners).

Ajimura, 51-53 Shelton St, London W1, 071-240 0178. Mon-Fri noon-3 pm, 6-11 pm; Sat 6-11 pm.

## Best Upscale Sushi

Masako

Near the prime shopping of Oxford and Bond Streets, is this, one of the pioneering Japanese restaurants in London. And—forewarned is forearmed—with its longstanding reputation comes a concomitant high price tag. In its spare, private dining rooms (which are served by courteous, kimino-clad waitresses), patrons can enjoy fine renderings of all the favourites of Japanese cuisine—including teriyaki, sashimi, tempura, and sukiyaki dishes. Masako is also known for its selection of sushi, in which fluke, tuna, flounder, and other traditional raw fin- and shellfish is attractively and inventively presented. (P.S. A way to lessen the potentially high cost of dining here— a little bit, anyway—is by ordering the fine set tempura and sukiyaki dinners, the price of which is fixed around £25.)

Masako, 6-8 St. Christopher's Pl, London W1, 071-935 1579. Mon-Sat noon-10 pm.

# Best Chinese Restaurant

Memories of China

The memories offered here—in edible form—are those of the restaurant's founder and major domo, Ken Lo, prolific food writer (having written or contributed to more than 30 books on Chinese cooking and dining) and onetime tennis champion from Hong Kong. And it seems as though his memories (and imagination) run true—this Belgravia restaurant offers what arguably may be London's best Chinese cuisine. The menu rotates every few months, reflecting whatever happens to be Mr. Lo's current proclivity. Typical dishes include shredded chicken in a garlic sauce, barbecued lamb, crispy and hot Szechwan beef, and crab or other seafood in a classic black-bean sauce. For what is labelled a "gastronomic tour" of China, try the £22 set menu, offering dishes from a variety of regional Chinese cuisines. Memories of China offers a good wine list, and, as might be expected, is fairly expensive—but reasonable bargains can be had on à la carte Dim Sum items for lunch. Don't be surprised to find out that the large group at the next table (enjoying themselves quietly) are visiting dignitaries from China—Lo's reputation is not only high, it has also travelled far. Reservations are a must.

Memories of China, 67-69 Ebury St, London SW1, 071-730 7734. Mon-Fri noon-2:15 pm, 7-10:45 pm; Sat 7-10:45 pm.

# Most Legendary Chinese Restaurant

Mr. Kong

In Chinatown, Mr. Kong is king! Located in the heart of this noisy, crowded neighbourhood, this longtime establishment attracts visitors and residents alike. Both of these groups visit this large restaurant (situated on three brightly decorated floors, seating around 150) for Mr. Kong's good bargains on good food. The regular menu offers excellent versions of Peking duck and Emperor chicken, and well-executed dishes featuring prawns, scallops, and other seafood. A list of daily specials offers some inventive choices, such as English game meats (pheasant, rabbit, etc.) prepared with Cantonese-style sauces and vegetables, or roasted chicken heavily spiced with salt and ginger (from a regional cuisine called Hakka, which is a variation of Cantonese cooking). Unlike too many Chinatown establishments, Mr. Kong offers noticeably attentive, patient, and helpful service. It doesn't accept reservations, so there may be a wait. Night owls take note: this restaurant serves its adept Chinese cooking well past midnight, seven days a week.

Mr. Kong, 21 Lisle St, London WC2, 071-437 7341.
Daily noon-2 am.


## Best Dim Sum

Joy King Lau

For those who enjoy sharing food, this is the place
to head with a large, hungry group. This attractive,
friendly restaurant (housed on four levels) offers a
variety of Cantonese dishes, especially those featuring seafood (lobster with garlic and ginger is a
favourite)...But the primary attraction is satisfying
and fun Dim Sum dining. For the uninitiated, Dim
Sum dining consists of sampling from a variety of
appetizer-sized portions of light Chinese food.
These little dishes are wheeled to your table on a
cart, and you choose what you wish from each
pass. The dishes can vary day to day, but typically
include small stuffed pastries and dumplings,
steaming spring rolls, prawns prepared several
ways, spare ribs, and sweet buns and cookies for
dessert. Joy King Lau also offers set meals (from
around £8), but let your curiosity and appetite
wander through the Dim Sum offerings wheeled to
your table; this will likely set you back about £20
per couple. The Dim Sum offerings are available
from 11 a.m.-5:30 p.m., making it a perfect quick
lunch or pre-theatre meal.

Joy King Lau, 3 Leicester St, London WC2, 071-437
1132. Mon-Sat 11 am-11:30 pm, Sun 11 am-10:30
pm.


## Best Place For Italian

Orso's

This basement restaurant was opened only in
1986 (by Joe Allen, known for his namesake
restaurant—see separate listing), but has already
become regarded as one of London's best Italian
restaurants, if not *the* best. In the impeccable, yet
casual style of its proprietor's other eatery, Orso's
is exceptionally fashionable. It is stylishly decorated in white, and features an open kitchen and
solid racks of wine on display (Orso's is, after all, a
below-ground restaurant, meaning the restaurant's dining room is also its wine cellar!). Menu
choices include varied "antipasti" assortments of
meats, cheeses, and vegetables; small custom-
ordered thin-crust pizzas; a rotating selection of
pastas (in side order- or entrée-sized portions);
well-regarded fish dishes; and a special wood-
grilled chicken with vegetables and spices. Many of
the fresh ingredients—such as cheeses and

spices—are flown in weekly from Italy. Orso's also offers an excellent list of Italian wines including decent (and very affordable) house wines. Open every day until midnight, this is a popular restaurant for both pre- and post-theatre dinners.

Orso's, 27 Wellington St, London WC2, 071-240 5269. Daily noon-midnight.

## Best Place For Multiple-Choice Italian Dining
Café Italien

When you're ready for Italian food and can't decide between restaurants offering casual, light cuisine, solid Italian favourites, or more classic dining, head for this Italian eatery that really is three restaurants in one. The atmosphere and the fare get more formal—and the prices get higher!—the farther back you go. Up front is a pleasant, airy wine bar, featuring top-notch and moderate wines by the glass, and light dining choices, such as salads, pasta dishes, and antipasto plates. This is a good spot for a quick lunch or a pre-theatre bite. Next, in the middle of the restaurant, is Café Italien's brasserie, offering a variety of Italian and Continental entrées, including steak, meal-sized portions of freshly made pasta, veal, chicken, and a favoured calves' liver dish. Café Italien is housed in a location where the respected Bertorelli's restaurant once was; in the rear is the formal Bertorelli Room, where a menu of classic Italian favourites is featured, including such choices as spaghetti Bolognese, veal scaloppine, and saltimbocca. Reservations are required for this popular room. The prices range from well under £10 per person in the wine bar to around £25-£30 apiece in the Bertorelli Room.

Café Italien, 19-23 Charlotte St, London W1, 071-636 4174. Mon-Sat noon-11:30 pm.

## Most Affordable Italian Cuisine
The Spaghetti House Restaurant

Not every dependable Italian eatery need be some long-established *ristorante* or trendy *trattoria*. A prime example is this busy, friendly chain of Italian restaurants scattered throughout London (which also includes the Vecchia Milano, Zia Teresa, and Villa Carlotta restaurants). While you may not find Renaissance antiques among the decor nor international film stars among the clientèle, you will find good food and dependable service at affordable prices. The typical fare at this chain includes a terrific minestrone soup, a variety of fresh pastas, veal entrées (saltimbocca is popular and well-executed), and good Italian meat and fish/seafood dishes. There are also Italian pastries and ice creams for dessert, and a good selection of wine—mostly Italian offerings, as you might expect. The Spaghetti Houses (and their related restaurants) are notably inexpensive—a dinner for two, with wine, can usually be had for about £10-£15.

The Spaghetti House Restaurant, 77 Knightsbridge, London SW1, 071-235 8141. Mon-Sat noon-11 pm. (And other locations.) Also: Vecchio Milano, 74 Welbeck St, London W1, 071-935 2371; Zia Teresa, 6 Hans Rd, London SW3, 071-589 7634; Villa Carlotta, 33-37 Charlotte St, London W1, 071-636 6011.

## Loveliest Lebanese Lamb

Al Hamra

Lebanese food is a grazer's delight! There is variety enough to allow you to order from the appetizer menu without ever having recourse to the entrées. Starters are called *meze*, and you can wind your way through a list of 60 or so, hot and cold. In addition to the predictable *hummus* (chickpea spread) and various yogurt combinations, the list includes zucchini stuffed with a mixture of lamb and rice, Armenian sausages, ground-beef-stuffed pita with an eggplant dip, cheese salad, a Lebanese version of the Greek fish-roe spread *taramasalata*, and little envelopes of pastry filled with a savoury mix of lamb, onions, and pine nuts and deep fried. Along with the hors d'oeuvres you can nibble at a good green salad (of course, with plenty of olives and cucumber). If you do make it to the main course, a variety of grilled lamb kebabs are a good bet, along with a zesty trout dish, and ground lamb wrapped in grapevine leaves. Delicious bread is baked on the premises and the dessert cart features a number of honey-and-nut confections. In warm weather you can dine alfresco.

Al Hamra, 31-33 Shepherd Mkt, London W1, 071-493 1954. Daily noon-midnight.

## Winningest Spot To Dine With Winnie

Winston's Restaurant & Wine Bar

Whenever I stop at the wine bar in this Bloomsbury restaurant, I am reminded of a friend who is perhaps an even greater admirer of Churchillian humour than I am. He loved to quote Winnie's acerbic commentary on Labour leader Clement Attlee's well-developed sense of self-importance: "There, but for the grace of God, goes God." For

Churchill fans and trenchermen alike, this restaurant combines an array of memorabilia relating to the wartime Prime Minister, along with well-prepared traditional cooking, such as beef Wellington, grilled salmon steak, pastry-encrusted fried Brie, fillet of pork with apricot dressing, and excellent puddings, apple pie, and treacle tart (with orange and walnuts). The downstairs wine bar in this 18th-century house has a good wine list, while the upstairs Edwardian-style dining room has a distinguished, clubby look and is decorated with portraits of the Tory leader and a profusion of press clippings chronicling his exploits.

Winston's Restaurant & Wine Bar, 24 Coptic St, London WC1, 071-580 3422. Mon-Fri 11 am-11:15 pm, Sat 5:30-11:15 pm.

## Happiest Haven For Hungry Hungarians

Gay Hussar

This intimate Soho restaurant offers some of the best and most authentic Hungarian cuisine that you'll find this side of Budapest (even if it is located on Greek Street). Its most celebrated dish is a starter—wonderful chilled wild cherry soup. Come here for excellent renditions of dishes you'd expect to find on a Hungarian menu—creamy veal goulash with egg dumplings, chicken paprika, stuffed cabbage, and roast duck and goose. But also be experimental and sample roast saddle of carp, pike with beetroot sauce, and smoked white baked beans. Standout desserts include lemon-cheese pancakes, rich tortes, and simple berries with whipped cream. Hungarian wines are available by the bottle and the carafe. Although this restaurant is known as a socialist haunt (union meetings once were held upstairs), it is a surprisingly sophisticated and romantic spot with lots of mirrors, plush red seating, a genial host, and attentive old-world waiters.

Gay Hussar, 2 Greek St, London W1, 071-437 0973. Mon-Sat 12:30-11 pm.

## Niftiest Noshing

Bloom's

Waiters wisecrack with studied surliness, the cabbage borscht is thick and wholesome—a good way to start a meal—and an oil painting of founder, Morris Bloom, looks down forbiddingly on the diners. It was back in 1920 that Bloom opened this East End restaurant. Since then, it has become London's most famous Kosher noshery, with a second, smaller branch now purveying gefilte fish, chopped liver, and matzos in Golders Green. Sunday mornings are particularly busy at this bustling restaurant, when it attracts hungry shoppers from the nearby Petticoat Lane street market (see separate listing). Unquestionably, the best-known and most-requested menu item is Bloom's salt-beef sandwich, with which it also does a big take-away business. Recommended also are the chicken blinzes, latkes, and kreplach soup, with apple strudel for dessert and, perhaps, a glass of Israeli wine. Up front, is a busy delicatessen counter.

Bloom's, 90 Whitechapel St, London E1, 071-247 6001. Sun-Thu 11:30 am-10 pm, Fri 11:30 am-3 pm.

## Best Taste Out Of Africa
Calabash Restaurant

It's a culinary jungle in here! This restaurant, a stone's throw from Covent Garden and the Royal Opera House, offers good, authentic African cuisine in an atmosphere of native art and music. The casual decor includes African weavings and carvings on the walls; taped music, heavy with rolling drumbeats and lilting vocals, plays in the background. The menu offers dishes from across the African continent, including *egusi* from Nigeria (a piquant stew of meat, thick white seeds, and vegetables), East African *dorowot* (chicken in hot pepper sauce), beef with fried green bananas and coconut cream, and a variety of well-regarded fish entrées. These flavourful (and often spicy) dishes are best washed down with a North African wine or beer—perhaps a Tusker lager. The service here is usually helpful, but can be most charitably described as *relaxed* when it comes to speed. Open since 1964, Calabash is located in the basement of the Africa Centre, which houses a bookshop and art gallery, and presents regular series of lectures, dance and drama performances, and live African music (on Friday and Saturday nights).

Calabash Restaurant, The Africa Centre, 38 King St, London WC2, 071-836 1976. Mon-Fri 12:30-3 pm, 6-10:30 pm; Sat 6-10:30 pm.

## Best Bet When You're Fit To be Thaied
Blue Elephant

Put aside preconceived notions that Thai restaurants are found only in drab storefront premises— even in mundane Fulham. This London sister of the acclaimed L'Eléphant Bleu in Brussels is the Disneyland of southeast Asian eateries, with lush hothouse foliage, waterfalls, orchids, Buddhas, bamboo, rattan, and a background of taped Thai folk music. *Sattays* (skewered chicken, beef, or lamb) are accompanied by a munchy peanut sauce, and curries and stir-fries are well executed. Try prawn curry, Tandoori-style roasted curried duck, stir-fried scallops with a medley of vegetables and a piquant oyster sauce, and *massaman* (lamb in coconut sauce). Shellfish is predominant on the menu—start with "floating market," sort of a Thai bouillabaisse. Some dishes employ fiery chilis, but with plenty of alternatives for those whose tastes run to less spicy fare. Traditional accompaniments are cucumber salad and rice—try a rice dish flecked with tasty pieces of shrimp. Forsake the pricey wine list in favour of imported Thai beer.

Blue Elephant, 4-5 Fulham Broadway, London SW6, 071-385 6595. Mon-Fri noon-11:30 pm, Sat 7-11:30 pm, Sun noon-10:30 pm.

## Cheapest Eastern European Eats

Daquise

Even when *glasnost* and the post-Berlin Wall era was practically unimaginable, this friendly little restaurant was doing its best to show that things from behind the Iron Curtain didn't necessarily have to be evil or the work of "Communist plots." And, anyway, as plots go, what could be so insidious about filling us up with good, substantial, and cheap food? Daquise serves up prodigious portions of Eastern European cuisine (with a heavy Polish accent) to an appreciative crowd of mostly regulars, many of whom are students trying to squeeze the most out of limited budgets. The satisfying homestyle fare tends toward pierogis, borscht, thick goulash, sausages, and excellent homemade pastries. This is a good spot for a breakfast of coffee or tea and a sweet bite. The main floor offers casual dining in a room decorated with '50s memorabilia (posters, advertising signs, and photos of the era); Daquise also features more formal (but still inexpensive) dining in a quiet basement room.

Daquise, 20 Thurloe St, London SW7, 071-589 6117. Daily 9 am-11 pm.

## Tastiest Tapas Tasting

Bar Escoba

Every year British holidaymakers stream to Spain by the tens of thousands, lured by the sun and sand. They return with snapshots, cheap souvenirs, and in many cases a taste for Spanish food and wine. Especially popular are *tapas*, those appetizer-sized portions of food that are perfect for sampling and sharing. Here, you'll find *tapas* at their best. They are often spicy (but not necessarily so) combinations of manchego cheeses, air-dried hams, squid, olives, anchovies, chorizo, cold veal, mushrooms, marinated chicken, sun-dried tomatoes, and a variety of other tempting ingredients creatively mixed and matched into bite-sized portions. Also outstanding is the *paella*, golden and delicately saffron flavoured, full of quality pieces of mussels, shrimp, and chicken. Bone-dry fino sherry is the perfect aperitif. You'll also find excellent wines from Rioja and Navarra along with other Spanish and Latin-American wines, beers, and spirits. The informal atmosphere of this often-crowded *tapas* bar/restaurant features red tablecloths, wrought-iron sconces, a stylish surrealist decor, and rousing flamenco dancers.

Bar Escoba, 102 Old Compton Rd, London SW7, 071-373 2403. Mon-Sat 11 am-11 pm, Sun 11 am-10 pm.

# Best Late-Night (Or Is It "Early Morning?") Spot

Up All Night

True 'round-the-clock dining, as is common in U.S. big cities (in a variety of diners and so-called "family restaurants"), is difficult to find in London. A handful of small, usually family-run ethnic restaurants—particularly in Chinatown—stay open on sometimes-erratic, but often 24-hour schedules...These, however, can be somewhat of a mixed bag. Up All Night is an aptly named noon-6 a.m. joint, more akin to a U.S. late-night restaurant. It offers a simple, but solid menu, featuring eye-opening rations of burgers, steaks, egg dishes, chili, bar-food-type snacks (jacket potatoes, nachos, deep-fried veggies), pastas, and desserts, plus lots of tea and coffee. If your eyes are weary from a night of pub crawling or jazzing it up in a smoky spot, they won't be further irritated by Up All Night's pleasant decor of art deco fixtures, soft lighting, and ferns. (And, for reliable 24-hour ethnic dining, your best bet probably is the Chinese fare of Canton, at 11 Newport Place in Chinatown.)

Up All Night, 325 Fulham Rd, London SW10, 071-352 1996. Daily noon-6 am.

# ACCOMMODATION

## Best Original Ritzy Hotel

The Ritz Hotel

Around the turn of the century, hotelier César Ritz dreamed of creating "the most fashionable hotel in the most fashionable city in the world." Nearly 90 years later, it remains apparent that he succeeded. The Ritz is smallish in size (116 rooms, 14 suites), but enormous in stature; its elegance is credited with being the inspiration for the term "ritzy." This hotel is located in the heart of toney Mayfair, overlooking Green Park (across the park from Buckingham Palace), near some of the city's finest shopping, museums, dining, and sights. Interiors are meticulously crafted and stunning in appearance, especially the Long Gallery, an ornate corridor, replete with arches, statuary, and plants, running the length of the hotel. The meeting rooms and banquet halls also are opulent; the most famous of these is the Marie Antoinette Suite (a replica of a room at the Palace of Versailles), which once hosted a meeting of Churchill, Eisenhower, and de Gaulle during WWII. Each exactingly elegant room includes a stocked mini-bar, direct-dial telephone, and satellite-hookup TV. For dining choices, guests need look no further than the Ritz Restaurant for fine dining, the Ritz Bar for cocktails, or the Palm Court for traditional afternoon tea (see separate listing). Definitely an extravagance, but worth the price.

The Ritz Hotel, Piccadilly London W1, 071-493 8181.

## Best Hotel Fit For A Queen

Claridge's

Many hotels have Victorian roots and Victorian architecture; Claridge's claims the distinction of having hosted the royal personage herself. (Back in 1860 Queen Victoria visited guest Empress Eugénie of France.) Since that time, this solid, old-fashioned Mayfair hotel (opened in 1838) has offered quiet luxury, lavish hospitality and, above all else, discreet service to crowned heads, princes and politicians, and assorted statesmen and celebrities. Among its charms are art deco styling, suites with log-burning fireplaces, liveried staff, spacious bathrooms with dressing rooms and majestic fittings, and a dining room featuring a string quartet. Dining choices include the hotel restaurant, high-ceilinged and formal, done in pastel colours—try the roast lamb or the *filet de boeuf aux truffes*. The more intimate Causerie is known for its luncheon smörgåsbord and for after-theatre dining.

Claridge's, Brook St, London W1, 071-629 8860.

## Classiest Big Hotel

The Savoy

This stylish hotel was created in 1889 by Richard D'Oyly Carte, the famed theatrical impresario known for presenting Gilbert and Sullivan operettas at the Savoy Theatre. After achieving success with his then-ultra-modern theatre, D'Oyly Carte built his grand vision of a hotel next to the theatre and gave it the same name. Today, the Savoy attracts a clientèle of royalty, celebrities, aristocrats, and top-level international business travellers. No two of its 152 rooms and 48 suites are the same: Some are decorated in classic Edwardian style, others are art deco, while still others are completely modern-looking (each are redecorated every three years). Top-of-the-line lodging can be found at the Savoy in a number of deluxe suites, each offering exquisite views of the Thames (considered perhaps the best hotel-room views in all of London). The hotel offers lunch or dinner at The Savoy Grill, classic cocktails at the American Bar, and seafood and other light fare at Upstairs. In general, the hotel's high level of service reflects D'Oyly Carte's oft-repeated personal slogan: "Never compromise." (In a bit of trivia, César Ritz was once manager here, before setting off on his own and establishing the Ritz—see separate listing; Ritz hired as chef the legendary

Auguste Escoffier—many of his creative dishes live on in The Savoy Grill.)

The Savoy, The Strand, London WC2, 071-836 4343.

## Best Traditional English Hotel

The Chesterfield

This graceful, traditional Mayfair hotel is located on the site of the Earl of Chesterfield's 18th-century home. It offers refined surroundings that the cultured Earl (renowned as the author of *Letters To His Son*, a collection of missives on the nature and responsibilities of a dignified, educated man) likely would have appreciated. From its elegant lobby—replete with artworks and chandeliers—to its briskly bustling and polite help, the Chesterfield offers a level of accommodation that can be likened to staying in a comfortable and sophisticated private home. The hotel offers 114 lavishly appointed rooms, all with private bath and modern amenities. There also is a quiet, pleasant lounge (the perfect spot for relaxing with a book or for conversation over drinks) and top-notch dining in the hotel's Regency-style-decorated restaurant (which features a well-regarded selection of European cuisine). Overall, the Chesterfield is a charming small hotel, offering attentive, friendly service.

The Chesterfield, 35 Charles St, London W1, 071-491 2622.

## Top-Of-The-Line Traditional London Hotel

The Dorchester

More than a few celebrities and other notables found themselves in a quandary when they discovered that their favourite London hostelry had temporarily closed. However, their chagrin was short-lived, since the widely beloved Dorchester reopened in 1990 after undergoing an extensive refurbishment (which is estimated to have cost more than £70 million). Originally opened in 1931, this hotel has long attracted an array of famous guests—General Eisenhower, Elizabeth Taylor, Somerset Maugham, Charlton Heston, James Mason; Prince Philip, a regular speaker and guest of honour here, helped commemorate the reopening of the hotel with a plaque and a speech. The hotel's 252 guestrooms are furnished and decorated in traditional English Country House style, including many antique pieces. Accommodations include four exquisite roof garden suites with landscaped terraces affording magnificent views of London. Guests can avail themselves of the Dorchester Health Club, which offers weight machines, fitness classes, Jacuzzis, saunas, and massages. A variety of cuisines are available at the formal Terrace restaurant, the Oriental Restaurant, and the more casual Grill Room. The Dorchester lavishes attention and service on its guests—its staff-to-room ratio of three-to-one is one of the highest in the hospitality industry.

The Dorchester, Park Ln, London W1, 071-629 8888.

## Best Hotel Near Airport (Gatwick)
London Gatwick Airport Hilton

If this 552-room hotel was any closer to Gatwick Airport, it'd be a hangar! Access to the South Terminal is via covered walkway, to the North Terminal via rapid transit system. Sound-proofed rooms with standard Hilton amenities such as climate control and minibars, plus flight information on TV, make this the ideal hotel of first and last resort for the air traveller. You can work off travel weariness with a swim in a 15-metre heated indoor pool, relieve tensions in a Jacuzzi/sauna/steam room, and work out in a well-equipped gym. You can lounge in the atrium lobby beneath a suspended full-scale replica of a De Havilland Gypsy Moth "Jason," commemorating Amy Johnson's solo flight from nearby Croydon to Sydney, Australia, in 1930. Or you can stop for a libation at the Jockey Bar, sleek with chrome, mirrors, and framed racing prints. There are shops and banking facilities, 24-hour food, beverage, room, and business services and dining options that range from snacks and pub food to the more-upscale Garden Restaurant (open for breakfast at 7 a.m.).

London Gatwick Airport Hilton, West Sussex RH6 OLL, 0293 518080.

## Best Hotel Near Airport (Heathrow)
Edwardian International

During its heyday in the early 1960s, The Skyway at Heathrow, first on "The Strip," hosted Liz Taylor, the Beatles, and Jimmy Stewart. Then it fell into a decline and eventually was purchased by the Edwardian group, massively renovated, and reopened early in 1991 as the Edwardian International. The object was to transform the hotel into an elegant country-home-style property, complete with marble lobby, open fireplaces, wood-panelled walls, suites with whirlpool tubs and four-poster beds, English chintz fabrics, hand-woven deep-pile carpeting imported from the Orient, and hand-painted Edwardian-style furniture. A health club with a swimming pool and fully equipped gymnasium allows travellers to unwind before or after a long flight. Other touches designed to please travellers include international time-zone clocks in rooms, duvets rather than sheets in some guestrooms, foreign-language TV channels and in-house videos, and sophisticated business and convention services. The hotel includes first-class restaurants, the Drawing Room for afternoon tea or cocktails, and the intimate Polo Lounge Bar.

Edwardian International, Bath Rd, Hayes, Middlesex UB3 58W, 081-759 6311.

## Best Luxury Hotel To Remind You Of A Country Estate

The Connaught

With doormen in top hats and white gloves, twice-a-day maid service, kedgeree, kippers, and kidneys on the breakfast menu, and a high ratio of employees to guests, this upper-crust hotel ranks with London's best. Although it is in the heart of Mayfair, close to storied Berkeley and Grosvenor squares, it has a quiet, subdued elegance that brings to mind an aristocratic country estate. With high French windows, a grand staircase, lots of mahogany panelling to show off tasteful antiques and exquisite reproductions, and fresh flowers throughout, this hotel exudes discreet Edwardian opulence. The dining room ranks among the best in London for classical British cuisine, and the panelled bar and other public areas are the sort of places where men would feel uncomfortable (and probably be frowned upon) if not wearing jacket and tie and where you might run into some of the celebrities who make this relatively small (little more than 100 guestrooms) Savoy-group hotel their choice in London. If you want the best and don't mind paying for it, look no further—but do book well in advance.

The Connaught, 16 Carlos Pl, London W1, 071-499 7070.

## Best Hotel Overlooking Kensington Gardens

Hospitality Inn On The Park

If staying near the park—or just finding a spot to park—is important to you, this basic hotel will appeal. Housed in a modern-looking block on Bayswater Road, it offers good rates and an excellent location: The hotel overlooks the green contiguous expanses of Kensington Gardens and Hyde Park. (The park and gardens are the home of the

Serpentine lake, the Rotten Row horse path, Speakers' Corner, and a Peter Pan statue that is a popular spot for children—see separate listings.) The hotel's 175 comfortable rooms all offer air conditioning, private bath, TV, radio, phone, and mini-bar; for those driving their own or rented cars, the hotel offers a free car park—a rare amenity for hotels of any size in central London. The Hospitality Inn On The Park is part of the Mount Charlotte Hotel chain, the second-largest in the U.K.

Hospitality Inn On The Park, 104 Bayswater Rd, London W2, 071-262 4461.

## Best Hotel To Sleuth Out

Sherlock Holmes Hotel

If you've already visited the famous 221b Baker Street address (only to find the offices of the Abbey National Building Society—see separate listing) and hoisted a pint or two at the Sherlock Holmes pub (once frequented by Conan Doyle—see separate listing), where else can you go to be reminded of the world's most famous (and favourite) fictional detective? Try this 126-room hotel, also located on the street on which Holmes was supposed to live. Part of the Hilton National chain, the Sherlock Holmes is comfortable and convenient, and is decorated with a variety of Holmes memorabilia. You can relax in the Watson or Moriarty public rooms, and, if you get the desire to reacquaint yourself with Holmes' adventures, there are copies of Conan Doyle's classic books on sale here. But, no, the hotel's snack bar doesn't serve red herrings...

Sherlock Holmes Hotel, Baker St, London W1, 071-486 6161.

## Most Uncommon Hotel Near Wimbledon Common

Cannizaro House

You get the best of all worlds when you stay at this luxury hotel: lodgings in a Georgian mansion on a beautiful country estate adjacent to Wimbledon Common that is within easy access of London's attractions, convenient to both airports, and ideal for Wimbledon tennis. Originally built in 1705 by a wealthy London merchant, the house was leased in 1785 by Henry Dundas (later Viscount Melville), a leading member of the government. During this time Prime Minister William Pitt was a regular house guest and King George III came for breakfast after military reviews on the common. As is appropriate in a country house, life revolves around an elegant central room where flames flicker on polished wood, fresh-cut flowers give off their sweet perfume, and a long-case clock ticks steadily. Rooms offer canopied four-poster beds, exquisite marbled bathrooms, and tall windows overlooking the grounds with their sunken gardens, Gothic aviary, ornamental lake, and sweeping lawns. You can go riding on the common, enjoy a game of golf, and stroll through unspoiled woods. Or stay "home" and enjoy such treats as breakfasts with home-baked breads and home-made jams and relaxed afternoon teas. Dinners might include such creative offering as red-cabbage-and-Stilton soup, sautéed pigeon breast with avocado salad, and fillets of red mullet garnished with mussels and cream of chablis sauce.

Cannizaro House, West Side, Wimbledon Common, London SW19, 081-879 1464.

## Best Hotel Where You Might Expect To Meet A Flapper
The Pastoria

Decades later, the heady times of the Roaring '20s are still fascinating. After the devastation and deprivation of the First World War, society seemed to burst at its seams—collectively flaunting convention and embarking on gay adventures that lasted until the Great Depression. Those "Jazz Age" times are remembered at this small, pleasant hotel located on the south side of Leicester Square, close to many sights and theatres. Its decor reflects a genteel 1920s and early 1930s style, complete with period pictures and fixtures. You almost expect to run into Scott and Zelda Fitzgerald in the cosy parlour! The Pastoria's 58 rooms have been recently refurbished to reflect the same era, with the added modern conveniences of private bathrooms, TV, radio, direct-dial phones, and hair dryers; the hotel also offers a bar and restaurant.

The Pastoria, 3-6 St. Martins St, London WC2, 071-930 8641.

## Best Hotel To Bump Into Diplomats
Hyatt Lowndes

If you don't spot a foreign diplomat at this hotel—perhaps from Finland, Luxembourg, or Peru—you'll have fun guessing who's who (even when the Portuguese ambassador at the next table turns out to be a manufacturer's rep from Manchester). Set on a quiet residential street close to "embassy row" in the heart of Belgravia, this small hotel (75 rooms and five suites) is frequented by the diplomatic community. With its stylish Adam theme, it offers a pleasant alternative for travellers who prefer intimate lodgings to train-station-size lobbies and mass-feeding eateries. Its small neo-classical lobby has black-and-white marble floors and an ornate ceiling hung with glittering chandeliers. The Adam theme continues in the Chippendale Bar and the elegant Adam restaurant. Tastefully decorated guest rooms are equipped with such amenities as hair dryers, trousers' press, minibar, and in-room movies. In warm weather the Terrace Café provides alfresco dining, with tables covered with blue-and-white checkered tablecloths and shaded by pretty matching floral umbrellas, and geraniums spilling from sleek white planters.

Hyatt Lowndes, Lowndes St, London SW1, 071-235 6020.

## Best Hotel To Bump Into A Ghost

Langham Hilton

Opened in 1865 by the Prince of Wales (later Edward VII), London's first great luxury hotel was the essence of Victorian chic, equipped with such wonders as air conditioning and hydraulic lifts. It played host to Toscanini, Mark Twain, Oscar Wilde, Emperor Louis Napoleon III of France, and, in room 333, allegedly the ghost of a lovesick German prince who threw himself from the fourth floor. The hotel closed in 1940 after war damage and reopened in 1991, restored to its former grandeur. The 410 rooms and suites are luxurious, amenities are state-of-the-art, and the public areas are splendid, from the marble floors and pillars of the lobby to the Palm Court, destined to again become a fashionable meeting place—particularly at tea time, with a piano tinkling in the background. The Chukka Bar has a polo theme and specialises in gin drinks; Tsar's, done in rich green and gold, offers an array of vodkas and caviar served with buckwheat blinis and cream. The restored dining room, Memories of the Empire, offers traditional English and Commonwealth fare such as Devonshire lamb and Aylesbury duck, plus drunken shrimp and beggar's chicken from Hong Kong, Shanghai dumplings, and Peking duck. Guests can drop their postcards into an original 1865 post box.

Langham Hilton, 1 Portland Pl, London W1, 071-636 1000.

## Hotel Mrs. Worthington Would Have Approved Of

The Berkeley

Noel Coward was not one to scrimp on comfort—

he frequently chided friend Ian Fleming about *his* Spartan lifestyle. While the Berkeley that Noel Coward admired has long since gone, its successor (in a new location) carries on the tradition of lavish accommodations and cosseting service. Unquestionably, this is a hotel that falls into the deluxe category. Rooms are spacious and individually decorated, while the suites are sumptuous with huge bathrooms. Public areas are full of handsome marble, antique panelling, glittering crystal, and exquisite chandeliers. The Berkeley Hotel Restaurant is first-rate, noted for its fresh fish and excellent game; the more informal Buttery is an attractive spot for an excellent—but economical—buffet lunch; Le Perroquet bar is low-key and elegant. Excellent amenities include an opulent rooftop swimming pool and sauna, a fitness centre, beauty salon, and small cinema.

The Berkeley Hotel, Wilton Pl, London SW1, 071-235 6000.

# Best Hotel For Nosmo King
Scandic Crown Hotel Victoria

Music-hall performer Nosmo King (who took his name from "No Smoking" signs), would have loved it here! Housed in a recently constructed glass and concrete building next door to Victoria Station, this modern hotel is the place to head if you smolder about smoking. Nearly half of its 205 rooms are designated as non-smoking rooms—perhaps the highest percentage of such rooms to be found at any hotel of this size (or larger) in London! All rooms (smokeless and otherwise) offer air conditioning, TV (with in-house feature films), mini-bar, hair dryer, trouser press, and tea/coffee-making facilities. Additionally, there are top-of-the-line lodgings in five elegant, roomy penthouse suites (which include in-suite Jacuzzis). Part of the Scandinavian Scandic hotel chain, the Scandic Crown Hotel Victoria also offers a large fitness centre (including an indoor pool, sauna, massage, and other health facilities), a restaurant, a piano bar, and a coffee shop.

Scandic Crown Hotel Victoria, 2 Bridge Pl, London SW1, 071-834 8123.

# Suite-est Hotel
Hotel Conrad Chelsea Harbor

In the United States, the concept of "all-suite" hotels have proven very popular, especially with business and family travellers. That lodging concept has spread to the U.K., with this all-suite hotel—the first of its kind in England (indeed, in all of Western Europe). This hotel offers 160 suites, including seven luxurious (and exclusive) penthouse suites. Each suite consists of a bedroom, full bathroom, and living room (unlike many U.S. suite hotels, there are no kitchens or kitchenettes). These suites are packed with plenty of appealing amenities: The baths are stocked with comfy robes, plenty of fluffy towels, and an assortment of Crabtree and Evelyn toiletries, and have separate bathtubs and showers; there are three dual-line phones and a fully stocked mini-bar in each suite. Additional on-site facilities include restaurants and bars, a fitness centre (with an indoor swimming pool, weight equipment, and sauna), and available business services (such as computers, fax machines, and temporary secretaries). The hotel is situated overlooking a marina on the Thames, affording great river views from many suites. There is a handy water-taxi service to the City and various sightseeing spots.

Hotel Conrad Chelsea Harbor, Chelsea Harbor, London SW10, 071-823 3000.

## Best Hotel Near Buckingham Palace

St. James Court Hotel

For lodging neighbours, it's hard to improve upon royalty! So, if staying in the general vicinity of Elizabeth and Philip appeals, this gracious hotel is a good bet. Built at the turn of the century (originally as flats for politicians, aristocrats, and royalty), the St. James Court is housed in a true late Victorian/Edwardian edifice—made of red brick, with terraces, balconies, turrets, and inset columns sprawling throughout eight connected buildings. It offers 400 hotel rooms and 100 longer-stay apartments, a fully equipped business centre (including private offices, meeting rooms, a reference library, word processors, fax and telex machines, and secretarial staff), the Olympian Health Club (offering Universal weight machines, saunas, steam rooms, massages, and a health food bar), and a pair of restaurants—Auberge de Provence (for French Provincial cuisine) and Inn of Happiness (considered one of London's leading Chinese Szechwan restaurants). A tranquil courtyard at the center of the hotel is full of flowers and trees and includes a period fountain (believed to have been a gift from Queen Victoria) and an elaborate terra cotta frieze (claimed to be the longest in the world) depicting scenes and characters from Shakespearean plays. This courtyard is a nice spot for small receptions or parties, or simply some casual alfresco relaxing.

St. James Court Hotel, Buckingham Gate, London SW1, 071-834 6655.

# Best Small Hotel Near Buckingham Palace

The Stafford

From the antique clock on its Adam fireplace, to an engaging dining room with starchy napery, a stunning chandelier, and a wine list presided over by a sommelier, this small hotel (62 guestrooms including seven suites) is more like a private club. Although it now is part of the Cunard group, this hotel remains discreet and luxurious to a fault, the kind of establishment where management and staff recognize and acknowledge frequent guests. It offers superb food and wine, and its St. James's location is ideally situated for viewing London's regal sights. Each of the renovated rooms is individually decorated to maintain the hotel's 19th-century charm while delivering all of the amenities expected by today's international travellers. The American Bar, decorated with ties, caps, and pennants, opens onto a terrace. Fitting, perhaps, for a hotel so properly English, the building it occupies was at one time the quarters of the Public Schools Club.

The Stafford, 16 St. James's Pl, London SW1, 071-493 0111.

# Best Family-Owned Small Hotel Near Buckingham Palace

The Goring Hotel

For three generations this superb, privately owned hotel around the corner from Buckingham Palace has been fastidiously cossetting guests with British hospitality. "When your name is above the door," says George Goring, whose grandfather started the hotel in 1910, "you try much harder!" When it opened, this was the first hotel in the world with a private bathroom and central heating in every bedroom. Among its charms is a garden, surprisingly large for central London, with manicured lawns, neatly-trimmed shrubbery, formal flower beds, and flagstone walkways. Inside, the furnishings are elegant, befitting diplomatic guests who frequently stay here while visiting the Palace. Although many hotels claim that every room is individually decorated, at the Goring each of its 86 guestrooms is distinctive, with such flourishes as brass "cartwheel" bedsteads, satin bedspreads, thick carpeting, and handsome writing desks. Many rooms offer garden views (be sure to request one); some have pretty balconies overlooking the garden, ideal for alfresco breakfasts. You can take coffee in the Garden Lounge, featuring an ornate fireplace and plenty of fresh flowers, and dine in the richly appointed restaurant on such English specialities as saddle of hare and steak-and-kidney pie. The Garden Bar, with big picture windows, is a pleasant spot for an aperitif.

The Goring Hotel, Beeston Pl, Grosvenor Gardens, London SW1, 071-834 8211.

## Most Secluded Hotel Near Buckingham Palace

Dukes Hotel

Arriving at this small luxury hotel is like being ferried back in time to an earlier, quieter age. The charming Edwardian hotel, first opened in 1908, is tucked away on a picturesque flower-filled courtyard where gaslamps are lit by hand every evening. Part of the Cunard group (which also operates the Ritz), Dukes offers only 36 bedrooms and 26 suites, with no two alike. All feature classic furnishings, direct-dial telephones, colour televisions, and handsome marble bathrooms equipped with hair dryers, plush towels, bathrobes, and exceptional toiletries. Deluxe double rooms all have four-poster beds; suites have comfortable sitting rooms with fireplaces. The hotel's intimate restaurant is noted for its excellent English cooking; the bar resembles a gentlemen's club with its soft red leather chairs. The sitting room with its open fireplace is a cozy spot for morning coffee, afternoon tea, or cocktails. From Dukes' tranquil location, you can set out to explore nearby Royal residences and parks, fashionable shops, restaurants, theatres, art galleries, and auction houses—with help, if needed, from a knowledgeable concierge.

Dukes Hotel, St. James's Pl, London SW1, 071-491 4840.

## Best Hotel That's Not A Palace

Hyde Park Hotel

It would not be surprising if foreign visitors were to mistake this hotel for a palace, and perhaps even for *the* palace. Standing castle-like on the edge of Hyde Park, this imposing Victorian red-brick hotel offers 180 spacious and well-appointed guestrooms, frequently occupied by members of England's fashionable society in town from their country estates. Possibly, as management claims, the hotel is "patronised by international royalty." Certainly, it exudes style and grace, with handsome high ceilings in public rooms, Edwardian-styled guestrooms with soothing views of the park, and the gracious tradition of afternoon tea. Unlike the fine dining rooms of many deluxe hotels, the speciality of the Park Room, elegant with its Louis XV chairs and picture windows looking out onto Hyde Park, is Italian cuisine, imaginatively prepared. The buffet in the Grill Room is a good choice for lunch, with a table d'hôte that features the likes of lamb chops, grilled sole, and roast beef.

Hyde Park Hotel, Knightsbridge, London SW1, 071-235 2000.

## Best French-Style Hotel
Le Méridien

Located steps from Piccadilly Circus, this hotel once was the glamourous Piccadilly Hotel (built in 1908)—but the years took their toll, and the early 1980s found it looking rather worn down. What followed was a £15 million restoration, a sale to the French Société des Hotels Méridien (a division of Air France) in 1986, some further sprucing up, a new name, and, *voilà!*, the end result is a luxurious French-style hotel in the heart of London. Its Edwardian, neoclassical exterior is complemented by an attractive French-country-style interior. Its 284 rooms (including 30 luxury suites) each feature such amenities as TV (with satellite channels), radio, and air conditioning. The hotel also incorporates Champney's health club (with weight equipment, sauna, pool, billiard tables, and more), a disco and cocktail lounge, and two highly regarded, very pleasant restaurants. The classic Oak Room offers elegant French dining in a chic, stylish atmosphere; the Terrace Garden is a bright, airy glass-enclosed restaurant hung with plants, featuring light dining.

Le Méridien, 21 Piccadilly, London W1, 071-734 8000.

## Best English-Style Hotel With French Name
The Montcalm

Although it's named after an 18th-century French general, the Marquis de Montcalm, this small, club-like hotel is very much an English institution. In a delightful townhouse tucked away on a quiet tree-lined Georgian crescent, it is just steps away from Marble Arch, Oxford Street, and the West End. It offers 116 bedrooms and suites plus 12 duplex apartments and two penthouse suites. Guestrooms are air conditioned and equipped with direct-dial telephones with bathroom extensions, televisions with free feature films, mini-bars, hair dryers, and bathrobes. The hotel's handsome restaurant, Les Célébrités, is decorated in warm tones of pink and burgundy and offers Anglo-French cuisine, including standards such as veal piccata, rack of lamb, Dover sole, and pan-fried calves' liver with tomato, sage, and sherry. The restaurant also serves a hearty English-style breakfast. An adjoining bar is decorated in sophisticated earth tones. The hotel can arrange horseback riding in Hyde Park, boat trips on the Thames, and Turkish baths at the nearby Porchester Centre, as well as sightseeing, concerts, theatre, and opera.

The Montcalm, Great Cumberland Pl, London W1, 071-402 4288.

## Best Large Hotel In The Theatre District
Strand Palace

Although by no means elegant, this big, old hotel (777 rooms, built in the early part of this century) offers good value and an excellent location for theatre-going, sightseeing, and browsing nearby Covent Garden. It also is the home of an original Carvery, the now-proliferated restaurants specialising in carved roast beef, pork, and lamb in serve-yourself, all-you-can-eat portions with all the trimmings. Rooms, redecorated in pastel colours, are uninspiring—but comfortable enough—with facilities for making tea and coffee. The public areas are busy, with shops, lots of tourists, and varied opportunities for eating and drinking, including an American-style bar and an Italian restaurant.

Strand Palace, The Strand, London WC2, 071-836 8080.

## Top Spot Near The Tower
The Tower Thistle Hotel

Most of the promotional pictures of this hotel dwell on its interior and upon its neighbours. And well they should. Unprepossessing on the outside, this modernistic concrete slab houses a surprisingly attractive interior and offers a spectacular location—across from the Tower of London (viewable from some rooms), close to the Tower bridge, and alongside St. Katharine's boat harbor with its yachts, shops, walkways, and bridges. All of the more than 800 rooms have air conditioning, remote-controlled television, in-room feature films, trousers press, and hair dryer. Several executive floors have their own dedicated check-out desk and pamper guests with extras such as bathrobes, mini-bars, and complimentary newspapers. Guests have a choice of three restaurants. The

Carvery features traditional roast joints (see separate listing), the Princess Room, with an adjoining cocktail lounge, has international cuisine and dramatic views of the Thames and the Tower Bridge, and the Which Way West is an airy café, full of greenery, which also offers sensational views of the bridge and river through its conservatory-style windows and roof.

The Tower Thistle Hotel, St. Katharine's Way, London E1, 071-481 2575.

## Best Hotel With A River View

Howard Hotel

A large number of the 137 rooms at this elegant riverside hotel offer sweeping views of the Thames, making it a rarity among London hostelries. Located close to the embankment on the periphery of the City, this contemporary hotel is convenient to centres of commerce and to the courts and law offices. As a result, it is well-equipped with amenities and services designed for business travellers. Grand on a small scale, its public rooms are formidably ornate with gleaming marble, Oriental carpets, pillars and arches with intricate mouldings, and a stunning centrepiece crystal chandelier. An intimate restaurant looks out onto a garden. Well-appointed guestrooms feature stylish French marquetry furniture and bathrooms done in marble.

Howard Hotel, Temple Pl, The Strand, London WC2, 071-836 3555.

## Best Small Hotel On A Grand Scale

Halcyon Hotel

This "baby grand" of hotels is an elegant townhouse created from two adjoining 19th-century stucco mansions restored in the Belle Epoque style of early Victorian architecture. Each of the 44 oversized rooms—large enough to be called suites—has been individually decorated with beautiful furnishings and fabrics and has a private bathroom finished with Italian marble tiling. Many have four-poster beds; some have Jacuzzis. Some of the antique-filled rooms feature traditional chintz and taffeta, others are lacy and romantic— one room, with swathes of boldly striped fabric, brings to mind a sultan's tent. Amenities include lavish robes and towels, fine toiletries, hair dryers, fresh flowers, and such conveniences as 24-hour room service, fax, secretarial, translation, and other business services, and free daily membership at nearby health clubs. The hotel restaurant serves international cuisine and has French windows opening onto a ornamental garden and paved patio. There's a pleasant bar to relax with an aperitif or an after-dinner drink, and an airy conservatory decorated with wicker furniture, potted palms, and colourful umbrellas suspended from the ceiling. Among the famous said to have signed the guest register here are Yoko Ono, William Hurt, and Mick Jagger.

Halcyon Hotel, 81 Holland Park, London W11, 071-727 7288.

# Best Hotel Started By A Gentleman's Gentleman

Brown's Hotel

James Brown, who was Lord Byron's valet, opened this hotel in 1837 to provide city comforts for country gentlefolk. Although it now is part of the massive Trust House Forte group, this sprawling hotel maintains its tradition of country-house comforts, with antique furnishings, liveried doormen attending guests beneath stately white columns and huge Union Jack, panelled lounges, and a general club-like ambience. Afternoon teas are a tradition, served in the Albermarle Room, where waiters in tails produce delicate sandwiches filled with potted meat, cream cheese, and, of course, cucumber. Over the years, the guest register has been signed by the likes of Rudyard Kipling, Theodore Roosevelt, and Queen Wilhelmina of Holland. The 134 guestrooms have been modernised to provide today's standards of comfort but have been allowed to retain some of their antique flavour and fixtures—and do tend to be on the small side.

Brown's Hotel, Albermarle & Dover Sts, London W1, 071-493 6020.

# Best Edwardian Best Western

Best Western Coburg Hotel

Travelers who are familiar with this independent, moderately priced lodging chain will find a unique property across from Kensington Palace and Hyde Park. Built in 1905, the Coburg has been extensively renovated and restored. This landmark Edwardian hotel was one of London's first "purpose built" hotels—designed specifically as a hotel, rather than as an existing structure converted to a hotel. There are 119 rooms and suites, all redecorated, and guest amenities that include hospitality trays, satellite televisions, in-room safes, minibars, complimentary newspapers, and a full buffet-style

English breakfast. The Spice Merchant restaurant features a blend of Indian and East African cuisines and highlights delicately spiced barbecued meats and vegetables.

Best Western Coburg Hotel, 129 Bayswater Rd, London W2, 071-229 3654.

# Best Small Georgian Hotel
## Durrants Hotel

With white pillars in front and hanging baskets of flowers, this hotel, built in 1789, blends well-preserved Georgian architecture with modern amenities. The decor, with knotty-pine panelling, pretty floral draperies, writing desks, and tufted leather sofas, is that of a country inn—which it was in the late 18th century. The hotel also is something of a chameleon; step into the George Bar and Pump Room, with its fine paintings and antiques, and you get the feeling of a private London club of the 19th century. The rooms, however, are designed strictly for the 20th-century traveller, with remote-controlled televisions and spacious bathrooms with built-in hair dryers. The hotel dining room serves continental and hearty English breakfasts as well as luncheon and dinner for which the kitchen produces such dishes as beef Wellington, baked gammon with pineapple sauce, steak-and-kidney pie, salmon en croute, and game in season. Situated in the heart of the West End, this pleasant small hotel is within easy reach of the Royal Parks and the theatre district.

Durrants Hotel, George St, London W1, 071-935 8131.

# Best Hotel For Workouts
## Hyatt Carlton Tower

Yes, that trim gent doing aerobics is Olympic champion runner Sebastian Coe. He is a founding member of The Peak Health Club, two floors of glass constructed on the roof of the east wing of this hotel at a cost of £2 million. It has computerized Lifecycles, Liferower, and Stairmaster equipment, a programmable treadmill, plus weight equipment, a fitness assessment unit, and a studio for aerobic and yoga classes. There are steam rooms, saunas, sunbeds, massage, nutritional counseling, and a beauty salon run by DeCleor of Paris offering facial, body, and slimming treatments for men and women. A members' restaurant and bar (hotel guests receive free temporary membership) provide a nice overview of the city. This 233-room hotel is decidedly upmarket in the Park

Hyatt style, with a harpist at teatime, and fresh flowers, perfumed soaps, and thick towelling bathrobes in guestrooms. The Rib Room (see separate listing) is known for its thick slabs of Scotch beef, while the Chelsea Room, with fine art, fresh flowers, and oversized conservatory windows overlooking the gardens of Cadogan Place, has received international recognition for its classical French cuisine.

Hyatt Carlton Tower, 2 Cadogan Pl, London SW1, 071-235 5411.

## Hotel With The Most Attractive Health Club

Rembrandt Hotel

This hotel, named after the famous Dutch artist, can help you turn your body into a work of art! The centerpiece of the hotel is its stunning Aquilla Health Club, a large fitness centre, complete with weight machines, saunas, workout classes, and an indoor swimming pool. The club is very attractive, appearing somewhat like an art deco-ish, stylized version of a luxurious Roman bath and spa—with gleaming marble, mosaic tiles, shiny fixtures, and recessed lighting. Even if you're not interested in working up a sweat, the Rembrandt can provide nice lodgings—it boasts a quiet, homey atmosphere, not unlike a country hotel (although it's located in Knightsbridge, across from the Victoria & Albert Museum and near Harrods). The hotel's 190 rooms offer full amenities; on-site are a lounge and a branch of the popular Carvery restaurant chain (with all-you-can-eat, buffet-style dining).

Rembrandt Hotel, Thurloe Pl, London SW7, 071-589 8100.

## Best Hotel For Good Sports

Kensington Close

You can keep both your body and your wallet in good shape at this Trusthouse Forte hotel in the heart of Kensington. Its comfortable, but by no means opulent, guestrooms have a mid-range price tag and its amenities include a wide range of fitness facilities. Converted from a former block of flats, the 529-room hotel presents an unprepossessing, dreary exterior that conceals a fine range of guest amenities which includes a cocktail bar, two restaurants, an indoor swimming pool, solarium, a pair of squash courts, sauna, a well-equipped gymnasium, and a garden terrace with ornamental ponds and tables set out when weather permits. It is centrally located close to the stores of Kensington High Street and convenient for performances at the Royal Albert Hall and shows at the exhibition centres at Earl's Court and Olympia.

Kensington Close, Wrights Ln, London W1, 071-937 8170.

## Best Hotel With No Name

### 11 Cadogan Gardens Hotel

Unobtrusive and understated are the keynotes of this small hotel in a Chelsea backwater. It has no sign and no name, just an anonymous number over the door of its Edwardian facade. Four fashionable houses have been joined together to create this delightful 50-room hotel. It is filled with antique furnishings, has cheery fireplaces and a private garden, and offers the hired services of a chauffeur-driven Rolls Royce. Each room has its own character and charm; all have bathrooms, many with extra-deep tubs, some with showers. Niceties include Devonshire cream teas and snacks of pâté and toast served in the drawing room and a sumptuous traditional-style breakfast.

11 Cadogan Gardens Hotel, 11 Cadogan Gardens, London SW3, 071-730 3426.

## Best Small Business Hotel With No Name

### 22 Jermyn Street

Designed with the business traveller in mind, this hotel has a great address—on the street which (along with neighbouring Savile Row) is acknowledged as the preeminent centre in London for quality gentlemen's clothing. In the heart of St. James's, it is also convenient to West End theatres and Bond Street shops, and has easy access to the City. Re-opened in 1990, this small (only 13 suites and five studios), private hotel is like coming home to a London pied-a-terre. With a fine eye for detail, owners Henry and Suzanne Togna (an interior decorator) have created a luxurious ambience with mahogany armoires, antique writing desks, Oriental porcelain lamps, four-poster beds, luxury fabrics, architectural prints, plants and fresh flowers, a well-stocked private bar, bathrooms supplied with fine toiletries and thick towels and robes, and around-the-clock room service. This hotel is a perfect spot to relax in quiet luxury, but for those whose purpose is commerce, the sitting rooms of suites are ideal for meetings, and every room is equipped with two telephone lines, with a third dedicated to a fax. Guests also may have their own incoming telephone number, enabling them to be dialled direct. A comprehensive secretarial service is available, as is a Poste Restante service.

22 Jermyn Street, 22 Jermyn St, London SW1, 071-734 2353.

## Best Hotel With Less Than 15 Rooms
The Fenja

With its pretty brick facade, black wrought-iron railings and balconies, and surrounding trees and shrubbery, this meticulously restored small hotel resembles the grand private residence that it once was. Fourteen guestrooms range from a charming single to spacious junior suites, each with its own bathroom or shower room, and each named after a famous English writer or painter who lived nearby. The J. M. W. Turner is done in earth tones and features a fireplace and four-poster bed; the J. S. Sargent has magnificent bay windows and frequently doubles as a meeting room; the Jane Austen has a fireplace, writing table, charming breakfast nook with a leafy view, and a bathroom that is pretty in pink. The public areas are splendid, with original pictures and marble busts throughout, including a fine collection of paintings and prints by 18th- and 19th-century English masters. Light meals may be ordered from the room-service menu, accompanied by wines from a thoughtfully assembled list. Rooms have a drinks' tray; drinks also are served in the drawing room with its tufted leather chairs and cheery fireplace. Each room is equipped with dial-direct telephones, and fax facilities are available for business use. This beautiful Cadogan Gardens location is just a few minutes' walk from Harrods and the Victoria & Albert Museum; Peter Jones in Sloane Square is only 100 yards from the door.

The Fenja, 69 Cadogan Gardens, London SW3, 071-589 7333.

## Best Hotel With More Than 900 Rooms
Forum Hotel London

Hotels in London are not typically as gargantuan as the sprawling big-city hotels found in the United States—which means that this large hotel is uncommon. At 27 floors (containing some 908 rooms and suites), the Forum towers above its South Kensington surroundings. Inside, guests will find one of the largest lobbies in any London hotel, appointed in gleaming marble. The rooms are comfortable and standardised, each offering mini-bars, tea- and coffee-making facilities, and

TV with in-house feature films. A large selection of meal choices is available in the hotel's multiple restaurants and bars; of special interest is the popular Sunday jazz brunch in the Kensington Garden Café. The Forum recently underwent a £15 million refurbishment; it is listed in the *Guinness Book of World Records* as "the Tallest Hotel in the U.K."

Forum Hotel London, 97-109 Cromwell Rd, London SW7, 071-370 5757.

## Best Hotel In A Victorian Townhouse
Wilbraham Hotel

Located just off Sloane Street, this small, personally run hotel was created by joining together three good-looking Victorian townhouses. It is full of restored dark panelling and furnished with antiques. The majority of the hotel's 50 rooms have private bathrooms; all have televisions and telephones. Rooms are charmingly decorated with such touches as matching spreads, drapery, and lampshades. The engagingly old-fashioned Bar and Buttery is the spot for aperitifs and pre-theatre cocktails and for simple luncheons and dinners. Located in a fashionable residential area in the heart of Victorian Belgravia, this hotel is within walking distance of Buckingham Palace, Harrods and the other shops of Knightsbridge, and Victoria. This comfortable small hotel provides a quintessential English aura of quiet grace while offering modern conveniences and a central location at affordable prices. Most definitely a spot for good value in good comfort.

Wilbraham Hotel, Wilbraham Pl, Sloane St, London SW1, 071-730 8296.

## Best Bet To Run Into An American
London Kensington Hilton

For American travellers who want to feel at home at a hotel in a good location with—hard to believe, but true!—street parking, this newly-refurbished, 660-room Hilton may be the spot. You'll find American airline flight crews hurrying across the lobby and tourists from Texas, Minnesota, and a variety of points in between enjoying a cocktail and listening to a piano player or yielding to traditional English afternoon tea in the 24-hour Crescent Lounge. There's a wine bar, a carvery-style restaurant, and authentic Japanese cuisine at the adjoining Hiroko restaurant. Comfortable rooms have the kinds of amenities Americans expect—air-conditioning, movies, hair dryers, minbars, and

complimentary tea, coffee, and daily newspaper—
plus an executive level with its private lounge, theatre-ticket desk, and lobby shops. It's an easy
walk to Holland Park tube station along a pleasant
tree-lined street filled with gourmet food shops and
restaurants. Usually, it is easy to find a parking
meter within a block or two of the hotel.

London Kensington Hilton, 179-199 Holland Park
Ave, London W11, 071-603 3355.

## Best American Hotel With Japanese Room Service

London Regents Park Hilton

If you enjoy room service, but think that the food
generally is unimaginative, here's an antidote to
the club sandwich and beef burger—a Japanese
room-service menu. Selections include tempura,
beef teriyaki, and "kaki fry" (deep-fried Japanese
oysters). For sit-down Japanese, you can visit the
hotel's Kashi Noki restaurant. Japanese are among
the international business travellers attracted to
this 377-room hotel which, as part of a major
refurbishment, installed state-of-the-art business
facilities, including a Spectra 2000 training suite
with sophisticated audio-visual equipment and a
built-in "learning wall." In a pleasant location overlooking Lords Cricket Ground (see separate listing), the hotel offers Minsky's New York Deli, a coffee shop lounge with live music each evening, and
an executive floor with club room. There is free
valet parking.

London Regents Park Hilton, Lodge Rd, London
NW8, 071-722 7722.

## Best Hotel To Recite A Nonsense Verse

Edward Lear Hotel

There once was a writer from Highgate/Whose lim-
ericks and artwork were first-rate/In this house he
did dwell/It's now a hotel/Where guests can stay
and luxuriate! With apologies to limerick fanciers,
this nonsensical bit of doggerel does describe the
origins of this comfortable, family-run hotel.
Housed in a connected pair of circa 1780 brick
houses, it was named after Edward Lear, the
famous writer and artist (and limerick composer)
whose one-time home is the westernmost of the
two houses. Its public areas and 30 guestrooms
are full of fresh flowers and bright, cheery adornments. Throughout the hotel, the walls are decorated with illustrated interpretations of its namesake's light verse. Rooms offer tea- and
coffee-making facilities, TV and radio, and direct-

dial telephones. Rates at this homey hostelry start at £37.50 for singles, £49.50 for doubles; these reasonable prices include a full English breakfast and all taxes.

Edward Lear Hotel, 28-30 Seymour St, London W1, 071-402 5401.

## Best Hotel For Business
### London Hilton on Park Lane

Hilton's flagship, 501-room high-rise devotes an entire floor to business, with a battery of fax machines, photocopiers, state-of-the-art audio visual equipment, and expert secretarial support. Eight meeting rooms include the Serpentine Room overlooking Hyde Park and a luxurious boardroom where some of London's top deals are made. A major refurbishment created presidential suites in Oriental and American styles, and launched the Windows of the World, a 28th-floor restaurant patterned on the well-known restaurant in New York's World Trade Center. The restaurant features a live band and a "grazing" menu of light dishes served in the bar until 1 a.m. Also open until that hour is the new Café Brasserie Patisserie Glacier, a continental café with an adjoining shop and patisserie (which purports to be the only place in London where fresh chocolates and pastries may be purchased at a retail counter from 7 a.m. until 1 a.m. the following morning). Rooms feature Georgian-style occasional furniture, deep-pile carpet, chintz hangings, and traditional sporting pictures.

London Hilton on Park Lane, 22 Park Ln, London W1, 071-493 8000.

## Best Hotel Like A Country Home That's Close To Harrods
### The Beaufort

The wonders of Harrods are little more than 100 yards from this wonderful little hotel tucked away from the bustle of Knightsbridge on a quiet, tree-shaded square. The idea, successfully executed, was to create the feeling of a country home—at which you let yourself in with your own key. There is no lobby, no restaurant, no 24-hour coffee shop—and no tipping (a house policy!). Another policy is to include as many services and amenities as possible with the price of a room (which ranges from £150 to £250). At The Beaufort, these encompass breakfast and other light meals served in guestrooms, which are kept supplied with decanters of brandy, Swiss chocolates, fruit, shortbread, and lots of fresh flowers. Also included are drinks from a well-stocked bar in the drawing room, membership at a health club, a VCR and video library, and a portable tape player and tape library (ideal for jogging, for which the hotel will provide a map). All of the 28 rooms are air-conditioned and decorated in pastel colours with rich carpeting and pretty floral curtains. Start the day with freshly-squeezed orange juice, fine tea or freshly ground coffee, and warm, home-baked croissants and rolls served with homemade jams, marmalade, and real lemony lemon curd—all served on fine Wedgwood china.

The Beaufort, 33 Beaufort Gardens, London SW3, 071-584 5252.

## Best Hotel In Little Venice
Colonnade Hotel

This pleasant little hotel is found snug among the residences of the neighbourhood of Little Venice (so-called due to the area's 19th-century canals—the Regent's Canal meets the Grand Union Canal a few blocks south of this hotel). Run for three generations by the same family, it is small—50 rooms—but with high professional standards: It offers plenty of central heating throughout and operates its own soft-water-treatment facility. The rooms are large, some with balconies, Jacuzzis, four-poster beds, and/or air conditioning; all have private baths and/or showers, TV, radio, phone, and hair dryers. The room rates include a full English breakfast. The Colonnade also has a restaurant, a very popular cocktail/piano bar (which often attracts considerable crowds), and a pleasant garden out back.

Colonnade Hotel, 2 Warrington Cr, London W9, 071-286 1052.

## Best Swedish-Owned Hotel
Mornington Hotel

Stepping into this hotel (housed in a Victorian-era building on a quiet residential street, across from Hyde Park and near shopping and sightseeing) is somewhat like travelling to a gracious Swedish inn. The staff and the decor are Scandinavian, and the service is attentive and efficient. The Mornington has 68 rooms, all with private baths, TV, radio, and direct-dial phones; its rates include a Swedish-style buffet breakfast (English breakfasts are available at a surcharge). Of course (considering its heritage), this hotel offers a popular sauna; it also includes a bar for cocktails, snacks, and tea, and a pleasant library for relaxing or quiet conversation. The Mornington's high level of friendly service makes it a good value for the price (and certainly cheaper than a trip to Stockholm!).

Mornington Hotel, 12 Lancaster Gate, London W2, 071-262 7361.

## Best Luxury Flats

"Hyde Park Apartments"

Looking to stay in London for a week of more, but don't want to incur exorbitant hotel costs? Or, perhaps you're trying to save money by splitting lodging costs among a group or even by doing some of your own cooking. If any of these propositions sounds familiar, you can find an economical way to stay (and eat) in London through the "Hyde Park Apartments" program, offered by British Airways Preferred Vacations. These London flats—available in configurations from studio through three-bedroom, two-bath apartments—are fully equipped with appliances and utensils (including TV, radio, telephone, and full kitchen equipment), and also offer five-days-a-week maid service and a full supply of clean bed linen and towels. These secure, privately owned, centrally located apartments can make great "home bases" for families, groups, couples, and even free-spirited singles wishing to explore London at their own pace and on their own budget. (The inclusion of kitchens could potentially save travellers hundreds of pounds on dining alone on a long stay!) The apartments are available for stays of seven days or longer, and include door-to-door transportation from Heathrow or Gatwick Airport.

"Hyde Park Apartments," British Airways Preferred Vacations, 800/AIRWAYS.

## Best Family Bed-And-Breakfast Hotel

Linden House Hotel

This is the sort of small, family-owned and -run hotel that you find on block-after-block at seaside resorts such as Brighton and Bournemouth—the kind of friendly, affordable family hotel that were legion in London long before small hotels became ultra-chic, trendy, and yuppie-fied. The Linden House, in fact, has been in the same family for 22 years. Rooms are plain and simple, clean and comfortable, all with colour televisions and facilities for making tea and coffee. Two-thirds of the hotel's 30 rooms have private bathrooms. Located in Bayswater alongside Hyde Park, the hotel is within walking distance of Oxford Street, Kensington High Street, and Knightsbridge. Included in the price of a room (which begins at £30 for a single, with a 10 percent discount for stays of seven nights and longer) is a full English breakfast. It would be tough to find other lodgings this friendly *and* reasonably priced.

Linden House Hotel, 6 Sussex Pl, London W2, 071-723 9853.

## Best Bet For Staying With *Somebody's* Favourite Aunt...Especially If You're A Vegetarian

Aunties Home Stays

For foreign visitors and out-of-towners who would like to *really* get to know a London family, this organization can arrange home stays in the London suburbs (and in cities, towns, and villages throughout Britain). Stay with a professional couple in North London, artist hosts in East London, or teachers with young children in South London. It's a great way to make new friends as you learn about local lore and legends and get insider's tips on out-of-the way attractions, nature walks and parks, and historic sites, and on locally popular neighborhood eateries. These accommodations are inexpensive (£13-£17 per night for bed and breakfast) and meet British Tourist Authority guidelines for comfort and cleanliness. This is a particularly good option for choosy eaters, since this organization specializes in homes that offer wholefood breakfasts and welcome vegetarians.

Aunties (Great Britain) Ltd, 56 Coleshill Ter, Llanelli, Dyfed SA15 3DA, 0554 770077.

## Best Bet For B&Bs

B&B Booking Agencies

Visitors to Britain's seaside resorts and other prime tourist areas, such as the Lake District and Cotswolds, encounter little difficulty in finding bed-and-breakfast accommodations. They simply wander streets lined with B&B establishments, looking for "vacancy" signs in windows and ringing doorbells. In London, it is more difficult to rely upon such serendipity and is therefore advisable to book ahead through one of numerous agencies that represent B&Bs. Obtain a list from the British Tourist Authority. For example, London Homestead Services (081-949 4455) represents 500 rooms, most within 20 minutes' journey of Piccadilly, while London Home-to-Home (081-567 2998) specialises in placing travellers in selected homes conveniently close to Underground stations. There are many such organisations, through which you might find lodgings with a family owning a small mews house with a pretty garden in south London, in an atmospheric Edwardian townhouse along the Thames near Kew Gardens, at a country-house-style hotel near Hyde Park, or in a guest house near Hampton Court with rooms decorated on a historic theme. Typically, B&Bs charge an average of between £12 and £25 per person; agencies add a service charge. Breakfast usually will include juice, cereal, bacon, eggs, and perhaps sausages and grilled tomatoes, followed by toast, marmalade, and tea or coffee.

British Tourist Authority, Victoria Station Forecourt, London SW1, 071-730 3488.

## Hotel With The Best Formal Gardens

Cliveden Hotel

To relax in the style of Edwardian-era aristocracy, head for this hotel, outside of the town of Taplow, just north of Windsor. The Cliveden is housed in what was the 17th-century mansion of the Duke of Buckingham, which, later, was also the home of the noble Astor family (which included the acerbic Lady Nancy, the first female member of Parliament, who is remembered for her verbal sparring matches with Winston Churchill). In the mid-1980s, this gorgeous and elegant home was converted into a unique hotel, offering 25 rooms and deluxe suites furnished in antiques and lavishly decorated—a meeting of Edwardian style (recalling the heyday of the Astors) and modern comfort and convenience. Adding to the exquisite beauty of this uncommon accommodation are 376 acres of immaculately tended formal gardens stretching along the Thames. These extensive acres of trees, flowerbeds, shrubs, and other greenery are preserved and cared for by the National Trust. The Cliveden also offers a restaurant and bar, tennis and squash courts, a fitness centre, and a heated outdoor pool. In short, the very model of modern aristocratic accommodation!

Cliveden Hotel, Taplow, Buckinghamshire SL6 OJF, 0628 668561.

# PUBS

## Oldest Pub On Fleet Street

Ye Olde Cock Tavern

These days, "Street of Ghosts" may be more appropriate for Fleet Street, the famous, frenetic "Street of Ink." The great dailies, whose presses once rolled in the streets and courtyards off Fleet Street, now have moved away, mostly to the revitalized Docklands area of East London. But "The Street's" oldest pub remains, the domain of curious visitors and the ghosts of the scribes who once hoisted their tankards of ale and glasses of Madeira on these ancient premises. The omnipresent Mr. Dickens was a habitué, Samuel Pepys mentioned the pub in his diary, and Alfred Tennyson once penned a verse, framed and on display, instructing the "plump head-waiter at the Cock" to "Go fetch a pint of port." Origins of the pub are traced to 1549, with the present building serving its pints as early as 1887. On display is a 17th-century wooden sign of the pub's namesake cockerel. Bar food includes steak-and-kidney pie, cold meats, and cheeses; a Carvery is upstairs.

Ye Olde Cock Tavern, 22 Fleet St, London EC4, 071-353 3454.

## Best Pub Worth A Try

Antelope

Football talk at this smart Belgravia pub is more

likely to be concerned with scrums, tries, and drop kicks than it is with strikers and penalty kicks, inasmuch as it is a popular haunt of a sometimes-boisterous group of rugby enthusiasts. The result is a lively, convivial atmosphere in an 18th-century tavern that is relaxed and old fashioned with settles and zinc-covered tables. Dining options include a servery on the main floor and a comfortable dining room upstairs. Selections include steaks, grilled salmon, roast beef, curried dishes, Dover sole, steak-and-kidney pie, jugged hare, and roast beef, plus salads and filled rolls. Brews include Benskins, Tetleys, and Adnams.

Antelope, 22 Eaton Ter, London SW1, 071-730 7781.

## Best Pub Mentioned In A Nursery Rhyme

Eagle

Most of us remember from childhood the "'Round and 'round the mulberry bush...'" verse of "Pop Goes The Weasel," but what you may not know is that deeper into the song, another verse says, "Up and down the City Road/In and out of the Eagle..." The Eagle in question is a lively, historic pub, just off the City Road (on Shepherdess Walk). This once was a Victorian music hall, and its walls offer pictures of old performers; the Royal Grecian Theatre was once next door—the pub displays a scale model showing what the theatre looked like. The pub offers a variety of hot and cold dishes, and has a dining area featuring roasts, barbecue, and the like. Beers on tap include Charrington IPA, Fullers ESB, Bass, and Tennent's Extra. Trivia note: The aforementioned "Eagle" verse of "Pop Goes The Weasel" is thought to refer to pawning ("popping" in the vernacular) goods at pawn shops that once were along the City Road...and then spending the received money in this pub!

Eagle, 2 Shepherdess Walk, London N1, 071-253 4715.

## Best Pub Immortalised In A Music-Hall Classic

Bull and Bush

Most Britons who are familiar with music hall, that most elementary form of entertainment that once was the mainstay of the masses, are familiar with the names, if not the words, of many of its songs. Foremost among these is *Down At the Old Bull and Bush*, popularised by 19th-century music-hall performer Florrie Forde. This is the pub of the song and the bush in question is said to have been planted by William Hogarth, the distinguished painter-engraver-satirist, when this was his country home. This 17th-century tavern is yet another of the Hampstead ale houses said to have been visited by Charles Dickens. Inside is a display of pictures of Florrie Forde and other music-hall stars; outside is a pleasant beer garden. On the periphery of Hampstead Heath, the Bull and Bush is close to two other famous inns—Jack Straw's Castle and the Spaniards (see separate listings). Taylor Walker bitter and Burton bitter are on tap.

Bull and Bush, North End Way, London NW3, 071-455 3685.

## Best Riverside Pub
### Dove

Situated on the edge of the Thames in Hammersmith, and affording patrons excellent views of the river from its terrace (open-air in summer, enclosed in winter), this 300-year-old riverside pub is an ideal spot for an assignation. Reputedly, Charles II and paramour Nell Gwynne once met here over a drink. Inside, three small rooms have original features such as bare floorboards, low beams, and the traditional pub decor of dark panelling and wooden benches. Adding to the decor are many vintage Thames photos and prints. It is said that the celebrated author James Thomson, who penned "Rule Britannia," was a frequent visitor. Other famous patrons include painter J. M. W. Turner and A. P. Herbert, who used a fictionalised version of the Dove in *Water Gypsies*. Today the pub attracts a mix of people, who come not only for the view, but for the reliable food that includes shepherd's pie, cheeses, salads, pâtés, and roast beef. Beer is provided by the local Fuller brewery. This is an excellent example of an authentic English pub, and well worth a visit.

Dove, 19 Upper Mall, Hammersmith, London W6, 071-748 5405

## Best Rivertown Pub
### White Cross

The delightful riverside town of Richmond, Surrey, has an impressive royal past and more than its share of commendable pubs (see separate listing), including many overlooking the Thames. This busy tavern is ideally situated for river watching, sitting just off Cholmondeley (pronounced "Chumley") Walk that stretches along the south bank. Bay windows offer views of the river and of the Richmond bridge, while a quayside terrace connects with the walkway, where low walls provide impromptu alternate seating. This companionable Victorian pub has a pair of cheery fireplaces and big tables in front of and seating around its large picture windows. Traditional bar food includes ploughman's, salads, sausages, and a few hot specialities. Fanciers of roast beef and other joints head for the carvery. Youngs is the brew of choice.

White Cross, Cholmondeley Walk, Richmond, Surrey, 081-940 0909.

# Best Rivertown Pub Crawl

Pubs In Richmond, Surrey

Despite its relative proximity and accessibility to central London, the pleasant riverside town of Richmond, a favourite of Tudor monarchs and site of a royal palace, is almost rural. It also has a clutch of attractive pubs that make it a good destination for lunch and an afternoon of exploration and casual quaffing. Richmond's ancient, tree-lined Green once provided a field for royal jousting. Today, cricketers clad in immaculate whites play there. *The Cricketers* has charming bay windows overlooking the broad Green and along with its neighbour, the *Princes Head*, which dates back to the mid-18th century, has tables on the pavement. Behind the pubs are narrow lanes brimming with galleries and antique shops. The *White Swan* (Old Palace Lane) offers an appealing luncheon buffet and an enclosed garden with picnic tables, and the *Orange Tree* (45 Kew Road) has live theatre (see separate listing). On Richmond Hill, known for its spectacular views of the Thames Valley—which attracted the brushes of Constable and Turner—is the *Roebuck*. Its second-floor restaurant offers a view over high, wooded bluffs of the river twisting along its timeless course, glinting in the sun like spilled quicksilver.

Richmond Tourist Info, Old Town Hall, Whittaker Ave, Surrey TW9 1TP. 071-940 9125.

# Best Pub For A Riverside Lunch

White Swan

International rugby matches, which have been played in Twickenham since just after the turn of the century, are one reason to visit this Thames' suburb. Another is a leisurely riverside lunch at this 17th-century pub. Menu selections typically might include daily homemade soup, pork chops, and traditional dishes such as Lancashire hot pot and steak-and-kidney pie. Snack foods run the gamut of pâtés, ploughman's, and salads. Watneys, Combes, and Webster's Yorkshire are available on tap. In winter there are plain wooden tables pulled up to a cheery log fire. In summer you can enjoy alfresco dining and river views from a terrace and garden. Nearby is the Eel Pie Island Charles Dickens wrote about in *Nicholas Nickleby*, and Marble Hill House, an elegant Palladian mansion built for the mistress of George II. Adjoining this fine Georgian mansion are splendid gardens and Monpelier Row, a terrace dating to 1720.

White Swan, Riverside, Twickenham, Middlesex, 081-892 2166.

## Best Riverview From A Pub

The Angel

For a nonpareil view of the Tower Bridge, find a spot on the riverside balcony of this Rotherite pub, *rebuilt* in the mid-18th century and restored in the 1960s. The balcony, resting on piles sunk into the river, also offers a view downstream to the Pool of London. According to an entry in Samuel Pepys' diary, he purchased cherries for his wife from the quay here, while Captain Cook is said to have quaffed some tots of rum at this inn that once was run by the monks of a nearby priory. The nautical decor includes a ship's wheel, wrought-iron lamps, prints of early life along the river, and captain's chairs. Courage Best bitter and John Smith's Yorkshire bitter are among the brews of choice. There is standard pub food at the bar and a restaurant that specialises in fish dishes.

The Angel, 101 Bermondsey Wall E, London SE16, 071-237 3608.

## Top Towpath Tankards

City Barge

Chiswick, a delightful 18th-century suburb fronting the River Thames, is full of historic houses, including the 1729 Chiswick House, a fine example of a Palladian revival villa. The City Barge, a venerable riverside pub rebuilt after severe damage during the World War II blitz, is located alongside the ancient towpath, neighbouring a number of these historic houses, including those once occupied by Dylan Thomas and Nancy Mitford. The pub has a 15th-century charter and is on the site where a Lord Mayor of London from that period moored his barge—hence, the pub's name. The pub has two barrooms and a terrace that is a delightful spot to relax with a drink on a pleasant summer evening. On hand are Courage beers and

an above-average selection of pub food. It is a size-
able walk to the pub from Hammersmith, the
nearest Underground station, but the charming
pub repays the effort—especially if you combine
your visit with a look in at a neighbouring tavern,
the 350-year-old Bull's Head (15 Strand-on-the-
Green).

City Barge, 27 Strand-on-the-Green, London W4,
081-994 2148.

## Best Pub For Watching The Boat Race

Ship

Here's a pub where you can be absolutely certain
of just the right subject about which to strike up a
conversation. Head here on boat-race day and
simply look to see which colour rosette or scarf a
person is wearing (light blue for Cambridge, dark
blue for Oxford) to determine which university
rowing team that person is rooting for. The universities' rowing crews have been battling each other
since 1829—and since 1845 over the four-mile
stretch of the Thames between Putney and Mortlake. This Mortlake pub has been around consid-
erably longer—since the 16th century—and its terrace provides an excellent vantage point for
watching the crews sprint for the finish line. Decorated with paddles and sculls, photographs and
mementoes from past races, and various nautical
bric-a-brac, this spacious pub offers plenty of conversation starters, as well as Watney's beer (not
surprisingly, since the brewery is next door). The
annual Oxbridge boat race is held late March or
early April (see separate listing).

Ship, Ship Lane, London SW14, 081-876 1439.

## Best Pub For Watching The Bard

George Inn

The only galleried coaching inn remaining in London is a holdover from the time when patrons used
open wooden galleries to watch entertainment provided by itinerant players in the courtyard below.
The tradition continues with occasional performances in the inn's cobbled courtyard of Shakespeare and Chaucer and demonstrations of Morris
dancing and medieval combat. Rebuilt after the
great Southwark fire, the present building dates to
1676 and once was an important coaching stop,
mentioned by Charles Dickens in *Little Dorrit*. Preserved by the National Trust, the pub has dark
beams, bare wood floors, panelled walls, lead windows, some seating in old-fashioned settles, and
cheery open fires in winter. A "Parliamentary

Clock" dates from a short-lived law that imposed a harsh tax on personal timepieces; an ancient beer engine, once used for dispensing ale, is another curiosity. Good bar food consists of sausages, quiche, ploughman's, and homemade meat pies, with more formal dining—roast beef, grilled fish, and roast chicken—upstairs in a half-panelled restaurant. Fullers, Boddington, and Wethered's bitter are available on tap. There also is a wine bar.

George Inn, 77 Borough High St, London SE1, 071-407 2056.


# Best Pub For Watching Street Performers

Punch & Judy (Upper Gallery)

Punch & Judy shows once were popular street entertainment in this neighbourhood. The tradition continues—in the name of this busy pub, and with the itinerant street performers who entertain the Covent Garden crowds virtually non-stop. Fronting the piazza of the much-yuppie-fied former flower, fruit, and vegetable market, this pub offers patrons of its small upstairs bar an unobstructed balcony view of the spectacles below (which normally include a seemingly endless parade of mimes, acrobats, jugglers, singers, fire eaters, sword swallowers, and other assorted street performers). The atmosphere is lively—but often a little too crowded—typically attracting a young crowd. The pub serves hot and cold food, usually including quiche, ploughman's, filled jacket potatoes, sweet-and-sour pork, and cheesecake, and offers on tap a number of beers such as Courage Best and Directors. Prices tend to be a little high, but, given the location, this probably is to be expected.

Punch & Judy, 40 The Market, London WC2, 071-836 1750.


# Best Pastoral Pub Near The City

Sun Inn

Despite its pastoral setting across from Barnes Common, this country-like pub is only a bus ride away from the hurly-burly hustle of the West End. Reconstructed in the mid-18th century, it faces a pond ringed by picturesque weeping willows and complete with ducks, bulrushes, and small boys netting tiddlers. In warm weather, it's pleasant to sit out front surrounded by a display of pretty flowers in planters and chug a pint of Tetley or Taylor Walker bitter and enjoy one of the pub's well-made sandwiches. Inside, the ambience is in keeping with the age of this venerable tavern, with low ceilings, bare wooden floors, period furniture, a cozy Victorian fireplace decorated with antique bric-a-brac, and framed prints of early London scenes. Its location in chic suburban Barnes makes this pub a popular yuppie hangout. At the rear is a bowling green where Sir Francis Drake and Queen Elizabeth I are said to have played bowls together.

Sun Inn, 7 Church Rd, London SW13, 081-876 5893.

## Best Pub Theatre

Orange Tree

The beautiful river town of Richmond is well endowed with splendid pubs (see separate listing), including this sprawling Victorian pub that is known both for its food and its theatre. Upstairs are performances by the Orange Tree Fringe Theatre Group, one of the best of its kind in London that carries on a theatrical tradition at this pub that dates back to the 1920s. Its experimental productions include plays by unknown authors and appearances by local actors. During the summer, there are a limited number of shows for children and some lunchtime productions. The restaurant in the cellar, with exposed red-brick walls, tiled floors, and old panelling, produces some ambitious dishes, such as duck l'orange, osso buco, paella, braised rabbit, game pie, and various curried and casserole dishes. The pub, handily located across from the Richmond Underground station, carries Young's beers.

Orange Tree, 45 Key Rd, Richmond, Surrey, 081-940 3633.

## Best Pub For Theatregoers

Salisbury

In the heart of London's theatre district, this opulent Victorian pub is a popular haunt both for those who go to plays and those who appear in them (or aspire to). Its gilded 1890s decor features moulded ceilings, copper-topped tables, lush red velvet, and bronze light fixtures Among the more appealing aspects of its art nouveau interior are handsome engraved glass panels and mirrors. Potables featured are draft Guinness, Taylor Walker bitter and Ind Coope Burton ale. An excellent cold buffet includes a good salad selection and a variety of homemade pies. In addition to a number of nearby theatres is a cluster of antiquarian bookshops.

Salisbury, 90 St. Martins Ln, London WC2, 071-836 5863.

# Best Pub For Opera Goers
Nag's Head

This cozy, Edwardian-style pub, conveniently located near the Royal Opera House, was the fancy of Cockney fruit-and-vegetable peddlers during the 18th century (because of its proximity to the Covent Garden market). Today, it attracts a mostly young crowd and is frequented by theatregoers; it is busiest either just before or after scheduled performances at Covent Garden. Its interior features opera and ballet posters and other theatrical memorabilia, comfortable seating, and a long bar. Beers include McMullen's Country Bitter, Guinness, Steingold, and Hartsman. The pub offers a selection of basic bar food and traditional Sunday lunches.

Nag's Head, 10 James St, London WC2, 071-836 4678.

# Best Pub For When The Fat Lady Sings
Opera

There's no phantom at this Opera but, according to legend, there *is* a ghost—of a man murdered and buried beneath the cellar nearly 100 years ago. The pub is handy to the revelry of Covent Garden and the eponymous Royal Opera House is nearby. Inside, the operatic theme is furthered by a display of handbills, photographs, and other mementoes. The Victorian pub also is near the Theatre Royal, Drury Lane and to several other theatres and is popular both with theatre-goers and actors. Salads, sausages, prawns, and home-made pies are among the selection of pre- and post-theatre food in which the pub specialises. The brew of choice here is Taylor Walker.

Opera, 23 Catherine St, London WC2, 071-836 7321.

# Handiest Wine Bar For Concert-Goers And Sausage Lovers
Archduke

Given the dearth of traditional pubs close to the multiple concert halls of the South Bank Arts Centre, this congenial wine bar nicely fits the bill for pre- or post-performance food and drink. Artfully built into one of the arches of Hungerford railway bridge, which dates back to the 19th century, it features bare brick walls, red-painted open duct work and is decorated with lots of greenery and framed cartoons of musicians. Wine selections include well-regarded burgundies and bordeaux and imports from California, Australia, and New

Zealand. The Archduke is noted for its variety of excellent sausages, and also serves salads, quiche, and pies. Nightly entertainment features live jazz and blues, with performers such as the Martin Blackwell-Ian Ballantine piano and vibes duo and the Brian Leake piano and bass duo.

Archduke, Concert Hall Approach, London SE1, 071-928 9370.

## Most Inviting Pub Forecourt

Red Lion

During summer, the toney crowd that frequents this stylish pub spills out onto a pretty forecourt decorated with rustic furniture, barrel planters, and coach lamps. Located in a quiet Mayfair back-water, the pub dates from 1723 when it catered to construction workers building neighbouring Berkeley Square. Today, it draws office workers from that same square, as well as a mix of actors, musicians, and models. Inside, the old tavern has a country feeling, with bare wooden floorboards, dark wall panelling, ancient settles, decorative shelves of dishes, and framed prints of early London street scenes. On tap is Websters Yorkshire bitter and Ruddles Best and Country. Good bar food includes ploughman's, steaks, thick-cut sandwiches, and a good cheeseboard, plus sausages, homemade pies, quiche, and lasagne.

Red Lion, 1 Waverton St, London W1, 071-499 1307.

## Best Outdoor Terrace

Windsor Castle

Given the vagaries of English weather, opportunities for alfresco drinking and dining are scarcer than in many of the continental playgrounds to which Britons flock at holiday time. But, given a bright clear day in early summer, it is hard to beat a pub garden for a pleasant interlude with friends or with someone special. This pub off Kensington High Street has a pleasant terrace with teak garden furniture and pretty flowers spilling from hanging baskets. The flagstoned terrace is sheltered by ivy-covered walls and shaded by leafy plane, lime, and cherry trees. There is separate food and liquor service to the garden. Inside, the pub is old-fashioned and unchanged, with hunting prints on dark panelled walls and practical built-in benches. Food selections run to such traditional fare as beefsteaks, sausages, fish and chips, and steak-and-kidney pie. Charrington and Bass are available on draught.

Windsor Castle, 114 Camden Hill Rd, London W8, 071-727 8491.

## Best Pub To Mingle With Sloane Rangers

Admiral Codrington

This upmarket Chelsea pub unquestionably is a fashionable spot to be seen mingling with the Sloane Ranger crowd. But, notwithstanding its affluent, status-conscious patrons, it is worth visiting because of its charming Victorian ambience and its imaginatively prepared food. Among its charms are a mellow gaslit bar decorated with Victorian prints and antique mirrors. At the rear, an agreeable conservatory has a splash of colourful flowers, a pretty grape arbour, and cast-iron tables and chairs. The kitchen offers a good selection of soups, salads, sandwiches, and hot and cold entrées, including homemade meat pies and traditional desserts such as apple pie and treacle tart. Brews include Worthington Best bitter, Bass, and Charrington IPA, and for whisky connoisseurs there is an enticing selection of single malts.

Admiral Codrington, 17 Mossop St, London SW3, 071-589 4603.

## Best Pub To Meet Yuppies

Front Page

Chelsea brings to mind many images—of sticky, sugary Chelsea currant buns, of frock-coated Chelsea Pensioners sunning on benches, and of the wild and weird Chelsea of its Bohemian era. Today, it is perhaps best known as an elegant residential neighbourhood full of tranquil backwaters which, these days, are inhabited by a large per capita number of yuppies. This good-looking pub fits well into its quiet, genteel surroundings. It features panelled walls, heavy wooden tables, seating on pews and benches, and a cheerful open fire. Food is exceptionally good, with daily specials such as ratatouille, salmon fish cakes, and grilled sole posted on huge blackboards. Daily soup specials are consistently good, as is the house pâté. Available on draught are Ruddles Country and Websters Yorkshire.

Front Page, 35 Old Church St, London SW3, 071-352 2908.

## Best Pub To Avoid Yuppies

Barley Mow

This also can be a good pub to avoid late sleepers, since it opens around 5 a.m. (Mon-Sat), catering to those who cater to London's greengrocers. London's central wholesale fruit, vegetable, and flower market, which in 1974 moved to this South Bank site near Vauxhaul Bridge from its historic Covent Garden location, is all business—and so is this pub, which actually is within the market. It serves full English breakfasts, substantial enough to satisfy a porter manhandling sacks of potatoes, as well as ample lunches. Courage is the brew of choice—but don't expect an evening drink, since this pub closes mid-afternoon when the market shuts down. The produce market, sheltered by a vast steel roof, is strictly wholesale, moving about 4,000 tons of fruit and vegetables daily. It is not as colourful as the old market but is interesting to see as a major food hub—particularly if a visit is combined with a solid breakfast or lunch at this busy pub.

Barley Mow, East Bridge, New Covent Garden Market, London SW8, 081-720 5555.

## Best Brew Named After A Postal District
Orange Brewery

What's in a name? Nell Gwynne, the popular "pretty witty Nell" who was mistress of King Charles II, was said to have sold oranges near this pub and hence its name. One of the growing number of pubs that brew beer on the premises, the Orange Brewery names its basic beer SW1 and calls a stronger brew SW2. It also offers Pimlico Light and Pimlico Porter. Decorated with lots of vintage photographs and miscellaneous Victoriana, this Pimlico pub has dark panelling, bare wooden floorboards, and some gas lighting. Another welcome speciality is a variety of homemade pies, including such fillings as chicken and leek and lamb and apricot, served in the appropriately named Pie and Ale Shop. Other food choices include ploughman's, sandwiches, quiche, chili, beef bourguignon, and Sunday roasts.

Orange Brewery, 37 Pimlico Rd, London SW1, 071-730 5378.

## Punningest Pubs For Real Ale
Ferret & Firkin in the Balloon up the Creek

David Bruce, who founded (and later sold) the "Firkin" chain of brew-pubs is known both for his idiosyncrasies (such as playing games with names and having fun with puns), and for his dedicated efforts to revive the time-honoured craft of brewing beer on the premises. Often, the signature name of a Bruce Brewery pub is teamed with a creature or spectral being, the name of which spills over (so to speak) to the beer. Thus, you have the Flounder and Firkin dispensing Whale ale, the Frog and

Firkin with Bullfrog beer, and the Phantom and
Firkin with Spook bitter—you get the idea! The
Ferret (with both Stoat and Ferret ale) is representa-
tive of the chain, with bare wooden floors, traditional seating, and a long bar with lots of room to
congregate in front. Sometime Chelsea resident,
actor Michael Caine, is said to frequent this particular Firkin. Along with the house brews (including
the notoriously potent Dogbolter), there is real
cider (also packing a kick), and such standard bar
food as ploughman's, sausages, pies, and substantial filled rolls. Live entertainment includes sing-
along piano music and a guitarist. Note: A firkin is
a small cask equal to 1/4 barrel.

Ferret & Firkin in the Balloon up the Creek, 114 Lots
Rd, London SW10, 071-352 4645.

## Best Yank Bars With Longest Names

Henry J. Bean's But His Friends All Call Him
Hank Bar and Grill

The flagship of this chain of American-style bars is
a historic Chelsea site that has been a pub since
1596. Formerly the Six Bells, it was the haunt of
artists and writers, including Whistler, Turner,
Walpole, Wren, and Hemingway. A garden, reputedly used by Charles II for lawn bowling, has a
fountain and children's play area. The American-
ised decor includes advertising signs and movie-
star photographs (including the famous pin-up of
Betty Grable inscribed, "To Hank...I love your
hamburgers...How do you like my buns?"). Potables include wine, spirits, and beer, including the
house brand Chicago Old Gold, brewed at a family
brewery in Bedford. Food runs to burgers, chili,
hot dogs, potato skins, nachos, chicken, and other
basket foods. Music is from a collection of 5,000
American recordings from the 1950s and early
1960s. There's a Bean's in Kensington (54 Abing-
don Road) and, if you think this is a long name for
a pub, consider a sister bar in Fulham (490 Fulham Road), Henry J. Bean's But His Friends,
Some of Whom Live Down This Way, All Call Him
Hank Bar and Grill, that caught the eye of *The
Guinness Book of Records*.

Henry J. Bean's But His Friends All Call Him Hank Bar
and Grill, 195-197 King's Rd, London SW3, 071-352
9255.

## Best Pub For Whom The Bell Story Is Told

Founders Arms

This is one tavern that does not claim connections

with momentous historic events and famous personages. As a pub, that is! If you consider it as the
site of a former iron foundry, now that is an entirely
different matter. The pub, recently built, occupies
the site of the foundry that cast the bells for St.
Paul's Cathedral and other churches. The
Founders Arms looks across the Thames from the
south bank and offers a fine unobstructed view of
the City and St. Paul's Cathedral. You can look out
onto the Thames through big picture windows and
from a large riverside terrace that is a pleasant
spot for a drink and a snack when the weather is
fine. Youngs Special and bitter are available on tap
in a stylish barroom that features gleaming
mahogany and green velvet banquettes. The pub
serves traditional food in the bar and has an
adjoining restaurant with such offerings as steaks
and chops, meat pies, pan-fried trout, plaice, and
other fried and grilled fish. City types head across
Blackfriars bridge for weekday luncheons at this
agreeable riverside watering hole.

Founders Arms, Bankside, London SE1, 071-928 1899.

## Jazziest Pub
Bull's Head

"I scream, you scream, everybody loves ice cream."
So go the lyrics of the old jazz classic, and it could
not be more appropriate than when belted out
with feeling by the vocal lead of one of the prominent jazz groups that perform at this large Victorian pub. Its scrumptious home-made ice cream is a
real treat and its jazz, traditional and otherwise,
can be as good as you'll find in a pub—and perhaps anywhere else in London. Internationally
renowned jazz artists—the likes of Johnny
Dankworth—perform here every evening and at
lunchtime on Sundays, interspersed with more
esoteric performers such as Sax Appeal and Mark
Nightingale's Bone Structure. Excellent food
includes such traditional choices as pies, steaks,
chops, grilled plaice and other fish selections, plus
sandwiches, pasta, excellent roasts served at a
carvery, and homemade fruit pies. On tap is
Youngs Special and bitter. This Barnes pub is
pleasantly situated overlooking the River Thames
near the flood wall.

Bull's Head, 373 Lonsdale Rd, London SW13, 081-876
5241.

## Best Pub To "Hang" Out In
Prospect of Whitby

In contrast to the pleasant greenery of London's

westerly riverside neighbourhoods, the Thames embankments in east London house the docks and wharves that once were the grim haunts of thieves and smugglers. Today, many of these areas are being modernised with the construction of sleek condos and shopping complexes. Such a transformation is underway in Wapping, a former dockside area where you'll find the famed Prospect of Whitby. This historic tavern, circa 1520, with a terrace overlooking a murky, moody stretch of the river, has hosted such patrons as diarist Samuel Pepys, artists Whistler and Turner, Charles Dickens, and "Hanging" Judge Jeffreys, who dealt summarily with river pirates right on the premises. You'll find lots of tourists here in search of gruesome tales, as well as lively live entertainment and stout pub food and drink.

Prospect of Whitby, 57 Wapping Wall, London E1, 071-481 1095.

## Best Pub To Get Lit

Viaduct Tavern

Holborn Viaduct, from which this pub takes its name, was an engineering marvel of its day. A series of arches, 1,400 feet long, it was designed to overpass "Hole Bourne," the valley of the River Fleet. It was, in effect, London's first fly-over! The viaduct was completed in 1869, the same year that this namesake tavern was built. The pub's ornate Victorian decor features a tin ceiling and mirrors decorated with gold leaf. Another piece of history related to this tavern is that it was the first pub in the country illuminated by electric light. The current was supplied by the Edison Electric Company, established at 57 Holborn Viaduct in 1882 as the first power station in London. This friendly, historic public house offers Friary Meux beers and ales.

Viaduct Tavern, 126 Newgate St, London EC1, 071-606 8476.

## Best Bet For Most Brews

The Sun

This small, busy pub is like the proverbial tip of the iceberg. Hidden beneath it, stretching out under the street, is a vast network of temperature-controlled vaulted cellars that make it possible to store a prodigious quantity of beer. And therein lies its major attraction! The Sun offers what is said to be the greatest variety of real ales offered by any pub in London, with about 20 varieties on draught at any given time, and up to 50 different kinds rotated over the course of a week or so. If you have an interest in the brewer's art (beyond consumption) it is possible to get a tour of the cellars if you make prior arrangements. Because beer's the major drawing card, most regulars don't mind that the ambience is somewhat sterile and the bar food (available at lunchtime and in the evening) is not especially creative—but tasty all the same.

The Sun, 63 Lamb's Conduit St, London WC1, 071-405 8278.

## Best Pub To Do Your Bidding
Red Lion

This engaging pub in a narrow alley off Pall Mall is close enough to St. James's Palace to be the "local" for the Royals. More realistically, however, you're more likely to find auctioneers and bidders from Christie's slaking their thirsts and grabbing a fast bite here. The famous auction house is located less than a "sold to the gentleman with the carnation" holler away on King Street. Ruddles County and Websters Yorkshire beers are on tap and food selections include quiche, pies, well-made sandwiches, sausages, salads, and savoury snacks such as Scotch eggs. Tucked away as it is, this is a pleasant local pub which provides a haven of calm after a hectic morning or afternoon of watching the pomp and ceremony in and around St. James's.

Red Lion, 23 Crown Passage, London SW1, 071-930 8067.

## Most Civil Pub From The Civil War
Bull's Head

Dating back to the 17th century, this riverside pub is located on a site that is said to have been used as a headquarters by Oliver Cromwell and his Roundhead army during the Civil War. Today, the atmosphere is decidedly civil, with window seats overlooking a peaceful stretch of the Thames and pints of Ruddles Best and County and Websters Yorkshire bitter. Painted white with contrasting black shutters, this pretty pub has a terrace and secluded beer garden. Pub food is standard fare, including sausages, shepherd's pie, ploughman's, and lasagne. The Bull's Head is located along pretty Strand-on-the-Green, an ancient towpath flanked by historic houses and the site of another pleasant riverside pub, the City Barge (see separate listing), named for a jetty where a 15th-century Lord Mayor of London once tied his barge. Both of these Chiswick pubs are well located for a visit during a trip to Kew Gardens (see separate listing).

Bull's Head, 15 Strand-on-the-Green, London W4, 081-994 1204.

## Best Pub For Royalist Plots
Holly Bush

Dig into an old pub—and this one dates back to the late 18th century—and someone will come up with a bit of history involving some famous novelist, poet, painter, highwayman, or insurrectionist who once hung out there. In this case, the claim is that a plot to overthrow Oliver Cromwell was hatched in this Hampstead village pub. The front bar has moody gas lighting, old prints, advertising signs, and miscellaneous Victoriana. A cozy back bar has an embossed ceiling and painted brick walls decorated with framed prints. Partitioned alcoves create private spots for quiet conversation. A variety of beer on draught includes Ind Cooper Burton, Youngs, and Benskins. Traditional bar food runs to Cornish pasties and ploughman's plus Lancashire hot pot and homemade savoury pies. Check the schedule for evenings of live jazz.

Holly Bush, Holly Mount, London NW3, 071-435 2892.

## Best Pub For Royal Rendezvous
The Clifton

In a quiet, leafy residential neighbourhood of St. John's Wood, this cozy pub is a good choice for an assignation, covert or otherwise. It certainly has precedent—royal precedent, in fact, since it was here that Edward VII, then Prince of Wales, arranged his clandestine meetings with beautiful actress Lillie Langtry. The pubs exudes Edwardiana (with some Victorian flourishes), with bare wooden floors, lofty ceilings, a handsome oak bar, cast-iron tables, art deco trappings, and displays of china and photographs of the aforesaid famous trysting couple. Built in 1837, this pub has a country-like ambience, with three fireplaces, a tree-shaded alfresco area out front with marble-top tables, and an agreeable conservatory in the rear. Taylor Walker and Tetleys are among the favoured brews; bar food includes daily hot special such as beef-and-ale stew with dumplings and a good selection of well-made sandwiches.

The Clifton, 96 Clifton Hill, London NW8, 071-624 5233.

## Greatest Pub For Frederick
King's Head and Eight Bells

This historic Chelsea pub overlooks the river in a

neighbourhood with strong literary connections. Scots Essayist Thomas Carlyle lived at 24 Cheyne Row and you may visit his house, furnished with original pieces, and inspect the attic where he wrote (and rewrote after a partially complete manuscript was accidentally burned) his remarkable historical work, *The French Revolution*, and his tome on Frederick the Great. His house, where he entertained Dickens, Tennyson, and Thackeray, is worth a visit, as is this local pub, where Dylan Thomas is said to have hoisted a pint or three. The name is taken from the custom of a nearby church to sound eight bells to signal the approach on the Thames of the royal barge. Food specialities here are seafood—plaice, prawns, swordfish, mussels—plus excellent grilled sausage and Flower's and Wethered's on tap. This charming 400-year-old pub is decorated with historic prints of Chelsea.

King's Head and Eight Bells, 50 Cheyne Walk, London SW3, 071-352 1820.

## Best Pub With Game Pie
Ye Olde Cheshire Cheese

Literary associations abound in London pubs, and Charles Dickens seems to have been at least as well-travelled in his homeland as was George Washington in his. The peripatetic Mr. Dickens is said to have been a habitué of this popular Fleet Street pub, as were Thackeray, Yeats, and lexicographer Dr. Samuel Johnson. In fact, the latter's house is adjacent to the pub and is open for tours. The pub has dark-panelled dining rooms with beamed ceilings, Georgian-style bottle windows, scarred wooden pews, and sawdust-sprinkled floors. In fine weather, patrons spill into a tiny courtyard. As for venerability, this pub was *rebuilt* in 1667, having succumbed to the Great Fire. For a hearty luncheon, try the famous steak, kidney, mushroom, and game pie or pudding or traditional roast beef and Yorkshire pudding. For dessert there are fluffy, light pancakes sprinkled with lemon juice.

Ye Olde Cheshire Cheese, Wine Office Ct, 245 Fleet St, London EC4, 071-353 6170.

## Best Pub For Pub Food
White Horse

After a while, pub food has a certain sameness about it, particularly if it is not especially well done. Here it is extremely well prepared, with no limp lasagne or predictable ploughman's. Although both of these dishes are served, the former features an imaginative combination of carrots and feta cheese and the latter offers a selection of three cheeses. Other choices include creative omelettes, Italian meatballs, house pâté, Scotch eggs, excellent pies such as steak and kidney and tomato pie, good cold cuts, big breakfasts on weekends, and a traditional Sunday joint of beef, lamb, or pork. In fact, this 19th-century Fulham tavern across from Parsons Green is where you will find pub food at its best! The brew is good, too, with Highgate Mild, Adnams bitter, Charrington IPA, and Bass, plus a good wine list and a selection of malt whiskies. Wine tastings and beer tastings are held. The good-looking pub has hanging greenery, ceiling fans, and comfortable seating on couches and banquettes. In warm weather, you can retreat to a shady terrace.

White Horse, 1 Parsons Green, London SW6, 071-736 2115.

## Best Pub For Non-Traditional Pub Food

### Slug & Lettuce

Despite the weird (and unappetising) name, this pub in Victoria offers a pleasant lunchtime alternative to the standard pub fare of bland ploughman's and lasagne. In fact, those who claim that pub food is universally predictable obviously haven't been to this chain of pubs. They tend to be more like spirited bistros than corner pubs. Menus change daily, and include such dishes as Guinness casserole, rack of lamb, salmon cakes, chicken breast with avocado filling, and spicy sausage, as well as made-on-the-premises pies and puddings, and tempting desserts such as bananas with rum and apple tart. In summer, the pub offers alfresco dining. Other locations of the popular chain include Westbourne Grove and Islington. Beers such as Guinness, Holsten, and Carlsberg are offered on tap. Prices are reasonable for the superb quality, but tables often are at a premium.

Slug & Lettuce, 11 Warwick Way, London SW1, 071-834 3313.

## Best Bet For Cheese, Bread, And Ale

### Lamb & Flag

For the best of English cheese served in an historic pub, look no further than this small pub hidden down a short side street from the hordes of Covent Gardens tourists. Its history stretches back nearly 300 years (including its incarnation as the "Bucket of Blood," so-called for the gory bare-fisted prize-fights staged in an upstairs room). Charles Dickens was a patron, and poet John Dryden, also a regular, was beaten-up by hired thugs after making a less-than-favourable comment about Charles II's mistress, Louise. Inside the tiny pub, yellowing walls are embellished with old signs, scraps of manuscripts, and several dark paintings. The pub offers darts in a small front area, and high backed seats in the back room. Space is at a premium and patrons tend to spill out into the courtyard with their plates and pints. Cheeses represented include Blue Shropshire, Red Leicester, Cheddar, and Sage Derby, served with pickle garnish and crusty bread (try some pâté or ham with your cheese; both are excellent). There's also a fine selection of hot dishes including chili con carne, shepherd's pie, and speciality curry dishes. Beer served on draught includes Courage, Guinness, Kronenbourg, Hofmeister, and Smith's Bitter.

Lamb & Flag, 33 Rose St, London WC2, 071-836 4108.

## Saltiest Spot For Munching On Whitebait

Trafalgar Tavern

Moored side-by-side along the river at Greenwich are two famous sailing ships (see separate listings). The *Cutty Sark*, built in the 1860s, is a magnificent clipper ship that once raced between Britain and the China seas. She dwarfs her dockside neighbour, the diminutive *Gypsy Moth IV*, in which Sir Francis Chichester single-handedly circumnavigated the globe in 1966. Also riverside, with handsome bay windows overlooking the Thames, is the restored Trafalgar Tavern, built in the 1830s. It has a suitable nautical theme (including pictures of Lord Nelson and a bar decked out to resemble a forecastle). The pub offers seafood dinners, including whitebait, the tiny, crisp fish that is a local speciality—perfect as a snack or a starter. Roast beef and steak-and-kidney pie are popular dining choices.

Trafalgar Tavern, Park Row, Greenwich SE10, 081-858 2437.

## Best Bar To Shuck An Oyster

Green's Champagne & Oyster Bar

This is the spot to head for during those "r" months for fresh oysters and, at just about any time, to soak up the ambience along with a glass or two of bubbly. Not far from the royal attractions of St. James's and the tourist hub of Piccadilly

Circus, this smart wine bar has a clubby feel with dignified mahogany panelling and a marble-topped bar. But it isn't stuffy; rather, it usually is busy and mostly is fun. There's a varied wine list that includes close to three dozen champagnes and a menu that emphasises seafood. In addition to succulent oysters, choose from lobster, crab, prawns, and Scottish smoked salmon. For traditionalists there is smokey kedgeree, and for Britons who remember the austerity days following World War II there are those old standbys, fish cakes—except that Green's elevates them to greater culinary heights with a crisp finish and the addition of a complementary parsley sauce.

Green's Champagne & Oyster Bar, 36 Duke St, London SW1, 071-930 4566.

## Happiest Highwayman's Haunt
The Spaniards

A London favourite for outdoor recreation—walking, riding, kite-flying—is the natural expanse of Hampstead Heath, with its sprawling sand hills, wooded valley, and borders of thick holly and blackberry bushes (see separate listing). Along its boundaries are some historic and fashionable pubs, including The Spaniards. It dates from the 16th century and was a haunt of notorious highwayman, Dick Turpin. He is said to have watched the highway from the window of what now is a charming upstairs bar, poised to take off after any likely coach passing through the tollgate below. The pub also is another former Dickens' hangout and was used as a setting in *Pickwick Papers*. It's a cozy spot, with low-beamed ceilings, intimate alcoves, and a pretty garden with a terrace, lawn, and rose garden.

The Spaniards, Spaniards Row, London NW3, 071-455 3276.

## Best Pub That Made Its Name In Water
The Flask

These days, patrons of this delightful Hampstead pub go for the Tetley's bitter and Burton's rather than the flasks that once were sold to enable people to draw spa water from the Hampstead springs. This is another pub that claims associations with highwayman Dick Turpin, who roamed this area and is said to have concealed himself in the cellars here. Painter and engraver William Hogarth, known for his social satires, is said to have brought along his sketch pad when supping at The Flask. Originally built in 1663 and rebuilt a centu-

ry later, the pub has low-beamed ceilings and an
agreeable patio with rustic furniture and occasional folk entertainment. A dining room features a
daily roast.

The Flask, 77 Highgate West Hill, London N6, 071-340
3969.

## Best Pub To Follow The Van
### The Lamb

Somehow, this classic, 18th-century pub in
Bloomsbury evokes the old Cockney music-hall
songs, "My old man says follow the van" and "Any
old Iron?" In part, it is because of its Victorian
ambience, that includes sets of the few-remaining
cut-glass-and-mahogany swiveling snob-screen
panels and tables with cast-iron frames and tops
edged with brass rails. But it also is because of the
pub's gallery of sepia prints of Victorian and
Edwardian theatrical performers, including many
who starred on the boards of music halls. And perhaps also because of an 18th-century polygon, a
sort of vintage juke box, that plays large metal
discs. The tavern's name and curious address
derives from William Lamb, an affluent City merchant who installed an underground conduit in
1577. This is yet another pub where Dickens is
said to have visited, credibly enough since his
house was nearby. Latterday attractions include
Young's beers and bar food that features lasagne,
ploughman's, pies, sandwiches, and Cornish
pasties.

The Lamb, 94 Lamb's Conduit St, London WC1, 071-
405 0713.

## Best Pub Near A Railway Station
### Railway Tavern

Before the nationalisation (and homogenisation) of
Britain's rail system and the creation of the
colourless British Rail, the names of the private
railway companies beckoned like a gazetteer—
Great Western; London, Midland, and Scottish;
London North Eastern. A holdover from those days
is the sprawling Gothic brick-and-cast-iron building that houses Liverpool Street Station. Built in
1875 on the site of a burial pit used during the
Plague, it currently is being modernised along with
adjacent Broad Street Station. Across from Liverpool Street Station is this pub that glorifies the
early days of Britain's railways. A display includes
insignia of the once-powerful railway companies,
model trains, and a fascinating assortment of photographs, prints, and early advertisements. This is

a Whitbread house that also carries Flowers,
Wethered's, and Boddington's beers.

Railway Tavern, 15 Liverpool St, London EC2, 071-
283 3598.

## Best Pub *Not* Near A Railway Station

Crockers

Fanciful to a fault, extravagant in the extreme, and
ornately picturesque—the architecture of this pub
is so excessive as to befit its earlier nickname of
Crocker's Folly. The folly, in this case, was not the
building, but the location. Frank Crocker built this
Maida Vale pub believing that it would thrive on
business drawn from soon-to-be-built Marylebone
Station. This turned out to be a major miscalcula-
tion, because the station rose much further from
his pub than he had anticipated. In true "folly"
fashion, the Victorian pub sports marble pillars,
bronze reliefs, an intricate moulded ceiling, pil-
lared fireplace, and a grand marble bar. Real ales
available include Boddingtons, Greene King Abbot,
Samson, Youngs, and Wards Weizenbier, an
unusual wheat beer. Bar food includes steaks,
pies, lasagne, Scotch eggs, and sandwiches. Nearby
is the Regent's Canal footpath.

Crockers, 24 Aberdeen Pl, London NW8, 071-286
6608.

## Best Pub Underneath Waterloo Station

Hole In The Wall

Located virtually beneath the noise and confusion
of Waterloo train station, this pub is a popular
watering hole with daily commuters. The attraction is the large selection of beers and ales, such
as Adnams, Youngs Special, Burke's Best, Braks-
pears SB, Godsons Black Horse, and Ruddles
County, available on tap, as well as food served in
large portions, including such basics as filled rolls,
chili con carne, quiche, steak-and-kidney and
chicken-and-ham pie, ploughman's, and burgers.
The dark ceiling above the pub's main bar is actually a brick railway arch supporting the station's
tracks above. Occasionally, a train shakes up the
pub—but such incidental interruptions usually
are felt rather than heard, due to the boisterous
after-work crowd and the blasting jukebox.

Hole In The Wall, 5 Mepham St, London SE1, 071-928
6196.

## Jolliest Pub From Dickens

Grapes

Always in search of grist for his literary mill,

Charles Dickens is said to have used this Lime-house pub as a model for the "Six Jolly Fellowship Porters" in *Our Mutual Friend.* Dating from the 16th century, this quiet pub is set amidst a gentrified area of former dockland. It offers pretty views of the river from an enclosed terrace and also from a well-regarded upstairs dining room. Seafood is the speciality, including basic fish and chips, fish pie, seafood risotto, oysters, Dover sole, plaice, turbot, halibut, and prawn curry. Popular brews include Taylor-Walker bitter and Friary Meux bitter.

Grapes, 76 Narrow St, London E14, 071-987 4396.

## Dickens' Favourite Wine Bar

The Olde Wine Shades

Chalk up another one for the peripatetic Mr. Dickens! He is claimed to have supped a glass or two at this City tavern off Cannon Street. With all the wine bars and alehouses the author is said to have visited, it is a wonder he found the time (or sobriety) to become such a prolific writer. In any event, this bar has the credentials. Built in 1665, it claims to be London's oldest wine house, having been ravaged, but not totally destroyed, by the Great Fire. The present facade is early Victorian. Inside, are thick, dark beams and antique tables. Framed prints and early political cartons add to the ambience. Find yourself a cozy alcove, slip into a plain, high-backed settle, and enjoy some fine wine and above-average bar food, including quiche, pies, sliced ham and roast beef, pâtés, cheeses, beef salad, and jacket potatoes. This is a traditional bar where they insist on jackets and ties for men and appropriate dress for women (jeans definitely are frowned upon).

The Olde Wine Shades, 6 Martin Ln, London EC4, 071-626 6876.

## Best Pub That Dickens *Didn't* Sup At

Dickens Inn

Here's a pub that *looks* like and *sounds* like it might have been visited by Charles Dickens—but wasn't! The Dickens Inn is a contemporary pub, transformed in the 1970s from a derelict brewer's warehouse and moved to its present site to accommodate the gentrification of the old St. Katharine's Dock. Incorporating 17th-century timbers, the handsome pub offers a traditional galleried facade and low-ceilinged barrooms with heavy beams, exposed bricks, and bare floor boards. Enhancing this traditional ambience are scrubbed tables, old wooden settles, a brass-covered bar, and sawdust on the floors. The three-level pub has a terrace with views of the yacht marina and Tower Bridge, and flower-bedecked dining-room balconies offering views across the water. Available brews include Courage Best, Directors, and the pub's own Dickens Special. Food, served on all three levels, includes seafood specialities and solid English fare such as shepherd's pie and sausages and mash. For traditional fish and chips try the Great Expectations Eating Parlour.

Dickens Inn, St. Katharine's Way, London E1, 071-488 1226.

## Best Pub For A Peek At Pepys

Samuel Pepys

Samuel Pepys' London is well-documented through the one-and-a-quarter million words in his famous diaries, including details of the many pubs he frequented. This is *not* one of those original pubs, but it is an interesting recreation and an agreeable riverside restaurant and bar. Created from a warehouse on a Thames' wharf, it has a cellar bar with a flagstone floor, a passably good restaurant, and a well-mounted collection of artifacts, letters, and other memorabilia relating to the famous diarist that also chronicles his days as secretary to the Admiralty. This admittedly is a theme bar/restaurant, but the river views and pretty good food make it a worthwhile visit. Meals run to robust traditional fare, such as roasts, beef Wellington, various pies and puddings, and oxtail soup. Charrington brews and various imports are available. (Those interested in Pepys will find his monument at nearby St. Olave's church; in late May or early June the Lord Mayor traditionally places a wreath there as part of a commemorative service that includes 17th-century music.)

Samuel Pepys, Brooks Wharf, 48 Upper Thames St, London EC4, 071-248 3048.

## Best Spot To Say, "Great Scott!"

Sherlock Holmes

In warm weather, you'll find a few tables shaded by white-and-yellow umbrellas and flanked by hanging baskets of flowers outside a pub in a pleasant tree-shaded backwater. This once was the Northumberland Arms, a hotel frequented by Conan Doyle and mentioned in the *Hound of the Baskervilles*. Decor includes theatrical posters and playbills, movie and TV stills, photographs of the author, and showcases filled with such Holmes' memorabilia as a magnifying glass, pipe, violin, forensic-science paraphernalia, and the green, luminous head of the legendary hound. Upstairs, adjoining the dining room, is a detailed creation of the detective's study at 221b Baker Street. Downstairs, savoury pies, sausages, cheese, and other decent pub food is available.

Sherlock Holmes, 10 Northumberland St, London WC2, 071-930 2644.

## Pub Mark Twain Would've Liked
Anchor

While the river it overlooks is the Thames and not Twain's beloved Mississippi, we think the American author would've felt at home among the history and draughts of this historical water's-edge pub (the present building of which dates back to around 1750, and was meticulously restored in the 1960s). The pub does have literary credentials. Dr. Johnson was a habitué, and rumour has it that in 1666 diarist Samuel Pepys watched from the pub's original building as London's wooden city was ravished by flame. Today's patrons enjoy watching the busy river traffic on the Thames and the fine view of St. Paul's across the river. In summer, there is seating on an outdoor terrace. Within walking distance of the pub are the original sites of the Globe Theatre and Clink Prison. The current building, a combination of old and new structures, contains many small rooms and a larger, separate restaurant, all of which retain their historical character. Adding to the ambience, is a decor that includes detailed Georgian panelling, old-fashioned high-backed seats, and comfortable leather chairs. A varied bar menu includes hot and cold dishes, such as cottage pie, steak-and-kidney pie, casseroles, lasagne, curries, ploughman's, cheeses, and assorted pâtés. This is extremely popular; plan to arrive early for lunch.

Anchor, 1 Bankside, Southwark, London SE1, 071-407 1577.

## Best Pub For This Sceptred Isle
Ye Olde Mitre Tavern

On a pleasant weekday afternoon, after the City lunch crowd have gone back to their computers and commodities, you can linger over a pint in the narrow courtyard squeezed between this pub and neighbouring St. Ethelreda's church and contemplate its considerable history. This tavern originally was built in 1546 as quarters for the servants of the Bishop of Ely. This powerful clergy had his

London residence in Ely Place, where Henry VIII once embarked on a five-day feasting orgy and which was the locale in Shakespeare's *Richard II* of the much-quoted "this sceptred isle" speech. Nearby the pub are the diamond merchants of famous Hatton Garden. The pub itself, rebuilt in the 18th century, has dark oak panelling, beams with hanging jugs, and antique settles. On display is a preserved segment of a cherry tree around which it is claimed Queen Elizabeth I danced a maypole. Bar food runs to sandwiches, Scotch eggs, pork pies, and some good cheeses. Friary Meux bitter and Ind Coope Burton ale are popular potables.

Ye Old Mitre Tavern, 1 Ely Ct, Ely Pl, London EC1, 071-405 4751.

## Best Pub Where There's Usually A Doctor In The House

### Hand & Shears

Sometimes it is hard to know if those gents in the long white coats are doctors or porters! This pub, close to the Smithfield Meat Market, also is the "local" for staff from St. Bartholomew's Hospital. In fact, because of its proximity to St. Barts, the unspoiled Victorian pub was used to film some of the extracurricular exploits of Dr. Simon Sparrow and friends in the vintage movie, *Doctor in the House.* The pub's name dates back to a 12th-century tavern on this site that was the haunt of tailors from the Cloth Fair. Later, upstairs rooms were used to pass sentence on criminals from Newgate Prison, some of whom were permitted to quaff their last ales here before walking the steps of the gallows. Courage beers are on tap.

Hand & Shears, 1 Middle St, London EC1, 071-600 0257.

## Best Pub For Homesick Canucks

### Maple Leaf

Should someone at this pub end a simple declarative sentence with a question and pronounce "out" as "oat"—as in "I'm going oat and aboat, eh?"—you'll know that you've just met a Canadian. And that wouldn't be surprising, because this comfortable and popular pub is full of Canadian-themed memorabilia (photos, posters, signs, etc.), attracts expatriate Canadians, and may just be the best place in London to stir up a conversation about North American ice hockey. The Maple Leaf serves an interesting mix of English and Canadian dishes in hearty portions. Pub-food entries include a Canadian-style chicken casserole, smoked beef sandwich on rye bread, lean ham sandwiches served on granary-bread, lasagne, and a selection of minced beef-stuffed pasties. Wash your meal down with Ruddle's County, Elridge Pope Royal Oak, Webster's Yorkshire Bitter, Guinness, or Combes Bitter—or, better yet, try a Molson, direct from Canada! There are plenty of seats and friendly service.

Maple Leaf, 41 Maiden Ln, London WC2, 071-836 4108.

## Best Pub To Make A Pilgrimage To
Mayflower

Historians and Americans have a special interest in this 17th-century dockland pub, formerly the "Spreadeagle & Crown," and refurbished in the 1960s following wartime damage. The reason is an historic delivery that is believed to have been made here. The master of *The Mayflower* was said to have received his orders to sail to America while sipping a pint at this bar in 1611. The pub changed its name to honour that historical event. Heavy black ceiling beams, lattice windows, and high-backed wing seats help create a 17th-century ambience. Decorations include models and drawings of the famous Pilgrim ship. A wooden pier looks onto the Thames, from where tall ships once sailed. The pub serves such hot and cold dishes as meat rolls, ploughman's, pâté, steaks, casseroles, salads, and cheeses, as well as a variety of beers including Bass ale, Guinness, Carling Black Label, Tennent's lager, and Charrington IPA. At night, there is full-service restaurant upstairs.

Mayflower, 117 Rotherhithe St, London SE16, 071-237 4088.

## Best Pub For Workers Of The World To Unite At
Museum Tavern

This Victorian-style pub is the perfect retreat after a long day touring the British Museum, directly across the street (see separate listing). The pub has the reputation as a writers' hangout, and also attracts students and faculty from nearby London University, plus museumgoers who drop by to see what all the fuss is about. It is said that Karl Marx worked on his *Das Kapital* writings here over a pint and a meal. (However, history has failed to record how the father of Communism counseled the workers who served him!) Decor features oak panelling and ornate cut glass, accented by plush velvet and an interesting mix of 19th-century memorabilia. The pub is a popular lunch spot (in summer, tables are placed outside) offering hot and cold dishes such as smoked mackerel, beef in beer, ploughman's, shepherd's pie, turkey and ham pies, and a selection of salads and English cheeses. On Sunday, the pub offers a full roast lunch menu.

Museum Tavern, 49 Great Russell St, London WC1, 071-242 8987.

## Most Cheerful Fireside
Star Tavern

With not one, but two, open fires crackling cheerfully in its hearths, this pretty pub is a snug spot for an after-work drink on a damp winter's evening. Its location in a Georgian mews in Belgravia makes it a popular watering hole with staffs of the nearby embassies and it also attracts the occasional entertainment celebrity, along with a crowd of thirsty office workers. Its other charms include comfortable upholstered settles and a general Victorian ambience with dark green walls, ornate mouldings, crammed bookshelves, and lots of mahogany reflecting the glow of globe lamps. This is a Fuller, Smith, and Turner house with Fullers Chiswick and London Pride among the beers of choice. A food counter offers such dishes as vegetable quiche, salads, steaks, and ham plates.

Star Tavern, 6 Belgrave Mews W, London SW1, 071-235 3019.

## Best Pub To Talk To Your Local MP
St. Stephen's Tavern

You would hope that the Member of Parliament for your home constituency would be warming one of the benches in the House of Commons and attentively listening to, and perhaps taking part in, the debate. But MPs need sustenance, too, and this congenial pub across from the Houses of Parliament has become the local of many of these duly elected representatives. So if you do run into your MP here, it could be that he is busy lobbying on behalf of his constituents—or simply enjoying a sandwich and a Webster's Yorkshire bitter or a Ben Truman. Along with members, the pub attracts political scribes in search of fresh copy, and the occasional novelist or two (could that been Jeffrey Archer leaning on the bar?). If you know there is a critical vote imminent in the House, and your man is still quaffing, have no fear. The pub has installed a "division bell" to summon MPs back to the House in time to register their ayes or noes. The pub has a traditional look with mahogany and etched glass. Both bar food and more substantial restaurant fare is available.

St. Stephen's Tavern, 10 Bridge St, London SW1, 071-930 3230.

## Favourite Wine Bar With MPs

Methuselah's Wine Bar

About the only thing long in the tooth here are some of the vintage wines—although there also are plenty of eminently drinkable younger selections. Of course, when this popular wine bar was named by New Zealander Don Hewitson, who also runs the Cork and Bottle and Shampers (see separate listings), he probably had in mind not Noah's 969-year-old ancestor, but the extra-large wine bottle containing a little more than six litres that also is known as a Methuselah. The wine bar-restaurant is a favourite with local office workers and with Members of Parliament who stroll over from the nearby House of Commons. There are a good selection of Australian wines, a wide range of reasonably-priced vintage champagnes, and good values on end-of-line specials, which are posted on a chalkboard. In addition to a ground-floor bar, there are two wine bars in the basement—both serving food—and a more formal restaurant known as the Burgundy Room. Hot and cold snacks and more substantial offerings include the likes of terrines, seafood salad, and Scotch sirloin steaks.

Methuselah's Wine Bar, 29 Victoria, London SW1, 071-222 3550.

## Best Pub After You Pass The Bar

Seven Stars

Were you to walk into this tiny pub and say, "Good afternoon, m'lud," you'd probably get a few takers. Close to the Law Courts, the offices and chambers of Lincoln's Inn, and the city greenery of Lincoln's Inn Fields, this early-17th-century pub is a haunt of barristers, solicitors, and a judge or two. Dickens is said to have visited this pub and, since he once worked as a solicitor's clerk, this claim may have some merit. In any event, the pub acknowledges the writer with a collection of caricatures of Dickensian characters. With its small, cluttered ambience, wooden floor, and cartoons of members of the legal profession, this is a pleasant, but busy, weekday lunchtime spot to enjoy a pint of Director's bitter and decent bar food.

Seven Stars, 53 Carey St, London WC2, 071-242

8521.

# Best Bar After You've Tried Your Case
## Magpie and Stump

This "local" for the Old Bailey is the spot to celebrate, commiserate, and generally discuss the
wheels of justice, depending upon how the day
went in court. The pub is right across from the Old
Bailey—more properly the Central Criminal
Court—and derives much of its patronage from the
business of London's famous seat of justice. It
does not, however, serve the gristly purpose that it
once did. When the infamous Newgate Prison also
was located at this site, those interested in watching public hangings would hire upstairs rooms
offering a view of the public executions held outside the prison gates that were a major spectator
event from the late 18th century until the mid-
19th century. The pub, partially rebuilt in the
early 1930s, offers Charrington beers and good
lunches. An upstairs bar is known as Court No.10,
sort of like the 19th hole in golf, inasmuch as the
Old Bailey once had only nine courtrooms.

Magpie and Stump, 18 Old Bailey, London EC4,
071-248 3819.

# Best Bar With The Longest Bar
## Cittie of York

Not far from Lincoln's Inn and the law courts, this
is another pub that attracts thirsty members of
the bar and the bench. There has been a pub on
this site since 1430, although for most of the 18th
century it was known as the Gray's Inn Coffee
House. The present building dates from Victorian
times and was reconstructed from some of the
original material. Notable features of this large pub
include trussed wooden beams, a phalanx of
1,000-gallon wine vats, and what is claimed to be
the longest pub bar in London—perhaps in
Britain. Preferred seating is in intimate cubicles
embellished with decorative carving. A curiosity is
a three-sided working fireplace. A food counter
offers ploughman's, filled rolls, burgers, and daily
specials such as casseroles, curry, goulash, chili,
and lasagne. Old Brewery bitter drawn from a
wooden barrel is a popular potable.

Cittie of York, 22-23 High Holborn, London WC1,
071-242 7670.

# Best Pub Where Your Sedan Chair Awaits
## Shepherd's Tavern

Shepherd Market seems always to have had this
Jekyll and Hyde personality. Beginning in the late

17th century, it was the site of a boisterous fair held each year in May—which eventually was supplanted by the growing gentrification of the area and the building of elegant townhouses. In more recent history, the area gained notoriety as the domain of high-priced call girls. Today, this area of Mayfair (after the original fair) is a charming village of antique shops, cafés, restaurants, and pubs— the latter including this engaging 18th-century alehouse. It, too, is imbued with more recent history, as a noted hangout of RAF types during World War II. The handsome main bar has wood panelling and comfortable upholstered chairs. Antique furnishings include a sedan chair reputed to have been the property of the Duke of Cumberland, son of George II. Ruddles, Watneys, and Webster beers are served. An upstairs restaurant does a good job with traditional English fare.

Shepherd's Tavern, 50 Hertford St, London W1, 071-499 3017.

## Best Pub To *Not* Order Punch
Tom Cribb

Unless you're sipping shandy or neat lemonade, you'd expect a pub's potables to pack a jolt. They do, and at one time, so did this pub's proprietor! This pub is named for Tom Cribb, a famous barefist prize-fighter who was the top English boxer in the early 1800s. He owned this pub after retiring from the ring in 1811 (at the then-ripe old age of 30) when it was called the Union Tavern. Back then, there were regular cockfights, boxing matches, and other sporting contests in the pub's basement. Today, the pub attracts a mix of professionals, locals, and, especially, boxing fans, who pore over the vintage boxing photos on the pub's walls. You'll find Charrington on tap here.

Tom Cribb, 36 Panton St, London SW1, 071-839 6536.

## Most Potent Potables For Medicinal Purposes
The Old Dr. Butler's Head

More captains of commerce than men of science frequent this ancient City inn, despite the scientific connotation of its name. William Butler was a noted 17th-century chemist who, during the reign of James I, ministered to the monarch's sciatica with a tankard of ale. For whatever reason, this eminently palatable treatment is said to have coincided with remission of the king's ailment. An honorary degree of Doctor was conferred on Butler who served "medicinal ale" from a tavern on this site that succumbed to the Great Fire and was rebuilt in 1667. The renovated inn is atmospheric with wood panelling, dark heavy beams, gas lights, and sawdust on the floor. Many regulars will claim that the Marston Pedigree and Tolly Cobbold Original beers dispensed here are indeed medicinal—or, at least, restorative. An upstairs restaurant offers traditional English cooking.

The Old Dr. Butler's Head, 5 Mason's Ave, Coleman St, London EC2, 071-606 3504.

## Best Former Architect's Office
Ye Olde Watling

During busy weekday lunch hours, this pub on London's oldest street draws its clientèle from the surrounding City offices and exchanges. It is close to St. Paul's Cathedral and, back in the middle of the 17th century, Sir Christopher Wren built the dark-beamed, heavy-timbered pub as headquarters for the architectural and construction team he assembled to work on the great cathedral. With its handsome arched doorways and leaded windows, and seating at trestle tables, this mellow City pub provides a perfect setting for such sturdy traditional edibles as steak-and-kidney pie and roast beef and Yorkshire pudding and such contemporary pub fare as lasagne, ploughman's, and chili con carne. Bass and Charrington's IPA are the brews of choice.

Ye Olde Watling, 29 Watling St, London EC4, 071-248 6252.

## Hauntingest Pub For The Best Bloody Marys
Grenadier

Slip into a quiet, cobbled mews, tucked away from the frenetic pace of Hyde Park Corner, and you'll encounter a Sunday tradition—the Bloody Mary, made from a guarded recipe and sold in prodigious numbers. This 1812 pub has plenty of other traditions, most of them associated with The Duke of Wellington, whose Grenadier Guardsmen were said to have used it as a sort of unofficial officers' mess. There's a sentry box outside, a stone in the adjoining alley with lineage as the Iron Duke's mounting block, and by way of interior decor a portrait of the Duke and masses of military pictures and memorabilia such as swords and uniforms—and beef Wellington and pork Grenadier with pride of place on the menu of the pub's intimate candlelit restaurant. There's also said to be a military ghost, of a guardsman who allegedly was flogged to death for cheating at cards. Among the pub's more upstanding former patrons was King George IV.

Grenadier, 18 Wilton Row, London SW1, 071-235 3074.


## Highest Pub Above Sea Level
Jack Straw's Castle

Dick Turpin and the other notorious highwaymen who once roamed Hampstead Heath in search of booty are associated with this pub, as are novelist William Makepeace Thackeray and all-time-champion pub crawler, Charles Dickens (with whom Thackeray quarrelled). Its origins, however, are much earlier. It was named for one of leaders of Kentishman Wat Tyler's peasant revolt of 1381 against harsh taxation. The present pub, however, was rebuilt in the 1960s to the specifications of an old coaching inn, including distinguishing weatherboarding. It replaces a predecessor lost to World War II bombing. Among its charms are its pleasant gardens and its lofty perch atop the heath. At 443 feet above sea level, it is London's highest pub. The bar has a terrace overlooking the heath and the spacious upstairs restaurant, a Toby Carving Room, offers a panoramic view of the sweeping parkland and the distant hills of Kent. Phone ahead to reserve a window seat and enjoy the view, a roast beef dinner, and some Charrington's ale.

Jack Straw's Castle, North End Way, London NW3, 071-435 8374.


## Best Wine Bar For Shoppers
Le Metro

After prowling the food halls of Harrods and poring over the designer labels and high fashions of chic Harvey Nichols, this stylish Knightsbridge wine bar is the destination for a glass of wine and an assortment of choice pâtés as you regather your energies and ponder your budget for the next onslaught of until-you-drop shopping. The selection is superb, with fine burgundies, bordeaux, and Alsace wines, and a good representation of champagnes featured on a lengthy (and pricey) wine list. If you're up for a wine-tasting session, the wine bar keeps its opened bottles in a Cruviér, enabling you to order quality wines by the glass. This open, roomy wine bar, in a basement attached to the Capital Hotel, has access to a splendid kitchen that produces the likes of filet of lamb, roast duck, smoked mackerel pâté, and steamed mussels.

Le Metro, 28 Basil St, London SW3, 071-589 6286.

## Best Wine Bar Down Under
Cork & Bottle

In this context, "Down Under" refers to the location of this popular wine bar (in a basement below Leicester Square), to its owner (New Zealander Don Hewitson), and to its product (a large selection of Australian and New Zealand wines). Of course, an ever-evolving inventory of wines includes French, Spanish, German, and Californian varieties—among others. Usually, there are more than 20 wines available by the glass and, for the bubbly crowd, about 30 champagnes. If you don't mind the crowds (but *do* try to avoid the traditional lunch hour), the knowledgeably assembled wine list is a good reason to give this wine bar a try. Another is the food. It includes the expected pâtés, salads, cold meats, and English and French cheeses (there is a good selection of each), but also provides some exceptional hot dishes, such as roast chicken, casseroles, sausages, and an exceptional ham-and-cheese pie which is far and away the most popular choice of regulars. Syllabub and chocolate roulade are recommended desserts.

Cork & Bottle, 44-46 Cranbourn St, London WC2, 071-734 7807.

## Best Wine Bar Up Top
Shampers

Tucked away on a narrow alley on the fringe of Soho, this is another wine bar owned by New Zealander Don Hewitson, who also runs the Cork and Bottle (see separate listing). It is extremely popular with button-down types from the nearby cluster of advertising and public-relations agencies, and is especially busy at lunchtimes. As with its sibling, the choice of wines is mind-boggling, with nearly 200 selections from around the world, including 20 or more wines by the glass and a similar number of champagnes—not unexpectedly, given the bar's name. Good buys on wine are marked on a blackboard. A downstairs brasserie features sensational salads, pâtés, and hot dishes such as sautéed lamb's kidney in madeira sauce, grilled rabbit with mustard sauce, lamb cutlets, and Oriental chicken. There is an excellent cheese board. French posters and a background of recorded jazz help provide the desired setting for conversation and sipping.

Shampers, 4 Kingly St, London W1, 071-437 1692.

## Best Art Nouveau Pub

Black Friar

This corner pub, located in the City, probably is *the* best example of art nouveau decor in London. Designed in 1905, in a collaborative effort by respected sculptor Henry Poole and architect H. Fuller Clark, this extravagantly decorated establishment is a literal feast for the eyes. It features: a low vaulted ceiling crowned with an intricate mosaic inlay; pink marble walls with a matching recessed marble-pillared fireplace; opulent stained-glass; an interesting selection of shimmering mirrors; a long curving bar that includes three copper bas reliefs; and various reliefs of playful friars and droll mottos such "Finery Is Foolery!" and "Don't advertise, tell a gossip." A large carpeted backroom with a barrel curved ceiling and exposed beams provides plenty of comfortable seating, much of it ingeniously built into nooks and crannies. Decor aside, a major reason to visit this pub (and the reason it's packed at lunchtime and early evening by hordes of City types) is the large selection of ales (such as Adnams, Bass, Charles Wells Eagle, and Morrells) plus the further inducement of well-prepared pub food, including shepherd's pie, beef-and-ale pie, and lasagne.

Black Friar, 174 Queen Victoria St, London EC4, 071-236 5650.

## Best Pub To Escape From Petticoat Lane

Dirty Dick's

It anchors the Bishopsgate end of the Petticoat Lane (Middlesex Street) Sunday-morning street market (see separate listing), and when you tire of the pushing and shoving, bustling and bargaining of the market's milling crowds, this is the perfect, convenient retreat. On warm summer mornings, in particular, you'll appreciate its cool, dark air-conditioned interior as a spot for potables and good pub food. The ground floor room has a beamed ceiling decorated with casks and wrought-iron chandeliers, planked floors, and a winding staircase serving a loft. Stone-floored vaults are dedicated to preserving the pub's legend of 18th-century mountebank, Nat Bentley, who, after the death of his fiancée, vowed never to wash himself nor clean his premises. Mummified cats and fake cobwebs complete the illusion.

Dirty Dick's, 202 Bishopsgate, London EC2, 071-283 5888.

# Best Pub Where They Still Charge In Pounds And Shillings

King's Head

This pleasant pub near the shopping of Camden Passage has steadfastly refused to be dragged into the decimalisation of English currency—even though the switch occured nearly 20 years ago, back in the early 1970s. It still charges in the old-style amounts of pounds, shillings, and pence, leading to a bit of mental arithmetic for locals—and very often blank-faced confusion for tourists! But, rest assured, the archaic pricing is purely stubborn nostalgia, not an attempt to baffle patrons. For fun, try to figure out your bill by keeping in mind that at the time of conversion there were 12 pence to every shilling and 20 shillings to a pound—thus 240 pence to a pound instead of the decimalised 100. (If your brain locks up at this math—not inconceivable after a few pints!—the bar help will assist in the economic translation.) Beyond its unique pricing scheme, the King's Head is famous as a theatre pub, offering performances on a small stage in the back at lunchtime and in the evening (with dinner beforehand) on many days. There also is live music, featuring jazz, folk, and rock performers, after many of the theatre performances. The pub is decorated with vintage and contemporary theatre posters and handbills.

King's Head, 115 Upper St, London N1, 071-226 1916.

# Best Pub Architecture

Princess Louise

This Victorian pub, voted Pub of the Year by the *Evening Standard* in 1986, is an architectural delight. Inside are stone columns, etched-glass mirrors, an ornate moulded plaster ceiling in red and gold, luxurious green banquettes, glazed floral tiles, stained glass, and plain wood floors contrasted by lots of mahogany and brass. The attractive exterior has marble pillars and a handsome bay window. But it is the food and drink as well as the ambience that draws a steady stream of patrons. A good selection of real ales includes such brands as Vaux Samson, Wards Best, and Boddingtons. Bar food is available downstairs; upstairs is a restaurant with well-prepared standard selections such as Lancashire hot pot, steak-and-kidney pie, chili, and lasagne.

Princess Louise, 208 High Holborn, London WC1, 071-405 8816.

## Best Pub To Play Skittles Or Pall Mall

Freemason Arms

This is the place to head if you're "game" for a little bit of traditional pub fun to go along with your pints. Located near Hampstead Heath, the Freemason Arms offers both a 90-plus-year-old indoor skittle alley (which has been extensively refurbished recently) and an outdoor lawn for pall mall (also called "pell mell")—a game of lawn billiards similar to croquet that once was very popular. (Both the Mall and Pall Mall owe their names to this game, which was once played on the wide grassy areas of St. James's Park near those thoroughfares.) This is a popular pub with London celebrities, such as actors and TV personalities. It offers a large garden (claimed to be the largest pub garden in London) and courtyard, making it a perfect spot for a relaxed outdoor drink, even if you're not going to bowl a few balls. There is a selection of basic bar food (ploughman's, lasagne, pies), and Charrington IPA and Bass on tap.

Freemason Arms, 32 Downshire Hill, Hampstead, London NW3, 071-437 2799.


## Best Pub With A Continental Flair

Alma

Some pubs are made-to-order for convivial quaffing, others are excellent destinations for a good meal. This toney Battersea pub offers a good measure of both, while putting a definite emphasis on good food imaginatively prepared. With tables supported by ornate cast-iron, covered with red-and-white checkered tablecloths, and paired with bentwood chairs, this pub gives out the flavour of a Continental bistro—despite its Victorian ambience of polished mahogany, bevelled glass, and ornate friezework. Youngs bitter, Special, and London Lager and Beamish stout are among the popular brews. Featured food might include onion soup, house pâté, taramasalata, beefsteak, grilled lemon sole, lamb chops with mustard sauce, and Lyon sausages. The pub's namesake Battle of Alma (waged victoriously in 1854 by British and French forces against the Russians during the Crimean War) is pictured in mosaics.

Alma, 499 Old York Rd, London SW18, 081-870 2537.


## Best Pub That Isn't A Coffee House

Old Coffee House

In the 18th century, London coffee houses were centres of commerce as well as social gathering places, where City traders, gentlemen of leisure, and men of arts and letters congregated to do business, socialise, and exchange gossip. Over the years, things haven't changed much, except that now these establishments serve the brewer's finest instead of the "devil's brew" (as coffee once was called), and they're called pubs and not coffee houses. Except this pub—which calls itself a coffee house. In this case, the potable of choice is Watney's, with Ruddles Best and County and Websters Yorkshire available on tap. There's a carvery with joints of beef, lamb, and pork, plus a variety of hot dishes such as steak-and-kidney pie, hot pot, and chili. Once voted the Soho Pub of the Year, it features a narrow panelled bar and a museum-like collection of prints, old photographs, vintage posters and theatrical handbills, stuffed wildlife, and old musical instruments.

Old Coffee House, 49 Beak St, London W1, 071-437 2197.

# MUSIC, ENTERTAINMENT & NON-PUB NIGHTLIFE

## Best Place To See A Rock or Pop "Event"

Wembley Stadium

With roaring crowds and massive banks of amplifiers pumping out a continuous wall of sound, this famous stadium is literally aquiver with noise during the many mammoth rock concerts booked in every year. Twice voted "Top International Facility" by *Performance* magazine, the 80,000-seat venue in northwest London has played host to a pantheon of popular music stars, including the Rolling Stones, Bob Dylan, Bruce Springsteen, Madonna, and Michael Jackson. Wembley also was seen by millions of television viewers around the world in the summer of 1985, when it served as the British nerve centre for the momentous Live Aid benefit that raised millions of dollars to fight hunger in Africa. During Live Aid, singer Phil Collins became probably the only pop star in history to play a gig on both sides of the Atlantic in one day when he flew to America after his Wembley set to play drums for a reunited Led Zeppelin. Wembley also hosts a variety of sporting events; behind-the-scenes tours of the massive facility are available (see separate listings).

Wembley Stadium, Empire Way, Middlesex HA9 ODW, 081-900 1234.

## Best Place For Rock Concerts Not Quite Big Enough For Wembley, But Too Big For The Clubs

The Hammersmith Odeon

This pop music fan's dream of a theatre in the heart of Hammersmith is known for treating concertgoers to intimate sets in civilised surroundings. While queuing up to see Bob Dylan, Johnny Mathis, or even Motorhead (all acts recently booked into the Odeon), check out the immense art deco chandelier reflected in a mirrored wall of the lobby, and take time to admire the border of intricate, leaf-pattern moulding. An even more stunning visual—and aural—experience awaits inside the cozy 3,485-seat theatre. You'll be so close to artists more often seen performing in huge stadia that you'll be able to see such details as actual fingers plucking at actual guitar strings. You get the feeling that if Sting turned the spotlight around for a second, he would be able to see the smile (or grimace!) on your face as you respond to the great acoustics.

Hammersmith Odeon Theatre, Queen Caroline St, London W6, 071-748 4081/2.

## Best Concert Auditorium Mentioned In A Beatles Song

Royal Albert Hall

This regal Kensington venue was a prominent image in the British consciousness long before the chart-smashing success of "Sgt. Peppers Lonely Hearts Club Band," the Beatles album on which it's mentioned (in "A Day In The Life"). Prince Albert, consort of Queen Victoria, conceptualised the great hall in 1853 as part of a larger cultural centre. When it finally opened in 1871, the theatre had been fitted with 2,500 seats and an immense pipe organ that remains to this day one of the largest and finest in the world. Little did the Prince imagine that one day the Royal Albert would become known as an elegant jack-of-all-entertainments, hosting events ranging from glittering galas and classical concerts to heated tennis matches, bloody prize fights, and rock 'n' roll spectacles. It seems fitting that such a gem among theatres should be so equally enjoyed by audiences of every stripe. After all, its rounded shape and heavily ornamented exterior (complete with a lavish extended and arched entranceway), looks something like an exotic, welcoming place of worship in the rich glow of the afternoon sun. Certainly, worshipping fans by the thousands make a pilgrimage to the Royal Albert when it becomes the Blues-

Rock equivalent of Mecca during the annual series of performances held there by guitar great Eric Clapton.

Royal Albert Hall, Kensington Gore, London SW7, 071-589 3203.

## Best Annual Concert Series

The Promenade concerts ("The Proms"), Royal Albert Hall

Properly called the BBC Henry Wood Promenade Concerts, but popularly referred to simply as "The Proms," this summertime series of classical concerts was founded by Wood in 1912, and have been held at the Royal Albert Hall (see separate listing) since 1941. Regarded as one of the top music festivals in the world, it attracts orchestras, choirs, ensembles, and solo performers from around the world. Individual concerts in the mid-July to mid-September series are held at various London venues, with major performances—including the extremely popular Last Night—presented at the Royal Albert Hall. The seats on the main floor of the hall are cleared for the Proms performances, meaning that non-seat-holders stand or mingle during the concerts—thus the name "Promenade," harking back to the casual classical-music garden parties that were popular during the Edwardian era. Tickets are available the day of each concert at the door—except on the Last Night, tickets for which are sold by means of a lottery and are booked well in advance. Besides the lucky ticket-holders, the Proms are heard by approximately 150 million people around the world (thanks to the wide-reaching endeavours of the BBC).

"The Proms," Royal Albert Hall, Kensington Gore, London SW7, 071-927 4296.

## Best Open Air Concerts

Kenwood Lakeside Concerts, Kenwood House, Hampstead Heath

For a nice night out, perhaps a picnic, and some music under the stars, head to Hampstead Heath on Saturday nights from June to August for these concerts at Kenwood Lake, near historic Kenwood House. The concerts are presented on the shore of the lake, in an area surrounded by a heavy halo of leafy trees—a very attractive site. The fare tends to "popular" classical, with the occasional jazz or brass-ensemble performances. The sightlines are acceptable, but the sound can best be described as "typical outdoor acoustics"—which is to say they are questionable, at best. But a pleasant night, with a picnic on the lawn, is the objective here, not pristine sound. (Fireworks are also offered after the performances.) For early-arrivers, a tour of Kenwood House is a nice way to pass the time. This lived-in old mansion (remodelled in 1764 by famed architect Robert Adam) offers the late Lord Iveagh's fine collection of art (including Rembrandt, Gainsborough, Reynolds) and a handsome garden with a great view of the city to the south. Tickets for the Lakeside concerts are available in advance at the Duke of York's Theatre in St. Martin's Lane, or at the site on the evening of the performance.

Kenwood Lakeside Concerts, Kenwood House, Hampstead Heath, London NW3, 081-348 1286. Sat evenings Jun-Aug. Near Hampstead and Highgate Underground stations.

## Best Symphonic/Orchestral Music Hall

Royal Festival Hall

Built for the 1951 Festival of Britain (and the only notable building remaining from that national celebration), this concert hall is considered one of the finest post-war buildings in London. The Royal Festival Hall is located in the South Bank Centre (which also has two smaller halls) and is the home base of the Royal Philharmonic. (As a bit of trivia, the Philharmonic always performs with a bust of Beethoven on stage; Beethoven wrote his beautiful *Ninth Symphony*—the composer's last great work— for this then-new orchestra in the early 19th century.) The hall mostly hosts large orchestral and choral performances, but also presents the occasional jazz and pop concert. In general, the schedules of all of the South Bank Centre halls are big on "theme" series—e.g. Beethoven, "Russian/Soviet Composers," Mozart—meaning many of the performances offered are of "safe," long-established music. (Not that this is necessarily a bad thing— just the facts of the matter.) No less an authority than the great Italian conductor Toscanini proclaimed that the Royal Festival Hall has some of the finest acoustics in the world.

Royal Festival Hall, South Bank Centre, Belvedere Rd, London SE1, 071-921 0682.

## Best Home Of The London Symphony Orchestra...And Much More

Barbican Centre

With an annual offering of 2,000 events playing to two million visitors, this "City's gift to the nation" truly is Europe's largest arts centre. Many visitors don't make it past the London Symphony Orchestra's performances in 2,000-seat Barbican Hall or the world-famous productions of the Royal Shakespeare Company in the 1,150-seat Barbican Theatre. But the play's not the only thing in this colossal complex that has risen above the ruins of the ancient City of London, just half a mile from St. Paul's Cathedral. A barbican is the ancient term for a fortified watchtower in the walls of a city or castle, and, as a protector and purveyor of the arts, Barbican Centre lives up to its name. Within this modern concrete-and-glass structure (flanked by two residential towers) are two art galleries, three cinemas, two theatres, a conservatory, a public library, and a conference hall. Should you still not find something that appeals among this cornucopia of culture, you can pop next door for a recital or play at the Guildhall School of Music and Drama, or across the way to the wide-ranging exhibits of the Museum of London (see separate listing).

Barbican Centre, Silk St, London EC2, 071-638 8891.

## Best Spot To See The World's Leading Opera Performances (*If* You Can Get—Or Afford—Tickets)

Royal Opera House

Amidst a decor awash in crimson and gold, this is where the world's top touring opera companies appear, as well as where opera superstars such as Placido or Luciano perform (with astronomical ticket prices attached) when they're in town. Built in 1858 (on the site of theatres dating back to the Restoration), this is one of the most respected theatres in the world for opera and ballet. Performances are very popular among the cognoscenti; the tickets are usually hard to get and are very expensive. For a shot at getting a last-minute bargain, keep in mind that a few dozen seats in "the gods" (i.e., nosebleedingly high in the theatre) are available the day of the performance—but only one ticket is allowed per person (so you have to convince your date to join you in the often-long queue for these seats). Unlike some of the more staid top houses in other cities, the Royal Opera House presents both classics *and* modern / experimental works. (And, also unlike other venues, subtitles are shown above the stage during foreign-language works.) The Royal Opera House is also home to the Royal Ballet (see separate listing).

Royal Opera House, Covent Garden, London WC2, 071-240 1066.

## Best Spot For Opera Performed In English (Which You *Can* Get Tickets To)
London Coliseum

Look for the illuminated globe defining the night sky near Trafalgar Square; that's the capital's largest theatre and the home of the innovative English National Opera. With its blend of classic and current works (all performed in English), the company draws more than 400,000 fans a year to its 200-odd performances—representing almost 45 percent of the national opera-going audience. Surprisingly, however, tickets are easy to come by, and they're cheaper than those at the Royal Opera House. In the summer, either The Royal Ballet or the London Festival Ballet sets up camp.

London Coliseum, St. Martin's Ln, London WC2, 071-836 3161.


## Best High-Tech Cinema
UCI Whiteleys 8 Cinema

From the latest comic-strip hero adaptation to a Stallone or Schwarzenegger muscle flick to the social-epic-sweep of the obvious Oscar contenders...The best—and most popular—from among today's Hollywood movies are offered at this "octoplex." This sizable cinema attracts large crowds for movies on its eight screens, but it also offers plenty of ticket and concession facilities to keep the crush (or the wait) from getting unbearable. For entertainment before the show, check out the huge wall of video screens (showing music videos and coming attractions) in the cinema's dazzling lobby. And, when you finally get settled in to watch the latest Roman-numeralled sequel in your favourite film series, you'll likely appreciate the comfortable seating and Dolby sound offered in all eight theatres. This United Cinemas International cinema is located in the gleaming Whiteleys shopping center (see separate listing); advance tickets can be reserved by credit card.

UCI Whiteleys 8 Cinema, Whiteleys of Bayswater, Queensway, London W2, 071-792 3324.


## Europe's Biggest Street Party
Notting Hill Carnival

It started in 1964 as a small street party and it has grown into Europe's largest street festival, attracting up to half a million people. You'll hear reggae, calypso, soul, soca, and some less familiar sounds of Africa played from stages and even from the backs of lorries. And you'll taste curried goat, callaloo, breadfruit, green bananas, saltfish and ackee, and spicy Jamaican patties. Rows of stalls are filled with African and Caribbean books, tapes, records, folk art, crafts, and colourful clothing. A highlight of the carnival is the colourful, flamboyant costumes and exotic floats that are presented in the main parade—as well as in boisterous, impromptu processions. Although the carnival has become a multi-national Carib-Afro affair, it owes its origins and much of its current impetus to London's Trinidadians. As in Trinidad's own big annual carnival, steel bands abound. Although earlier carnivals were disrupted by outbreaks of violence, things have been relatively calm in recent years— even during the carnival's big 25th-birthday bash in 1990. This chaotic street party is, however, fair game for pickpockets and purse snatchers. Leave valuables at home!

Notting Hill Carnival, Ladbroke Grove and Notting Hill, London W11. Aug Bank Hol Sun & Mon.

## *The* Jazz Capital Of Europe
Ronnie Scott's

While jazz may be among the few artforms with American roots, that doesn't mean that Londoners don't appreciate and recognise terrific jazz music. When it comes to presenting the very best in jazz by artists from around the world, this crowded, classy club in the heart of Soho bows to *no* one— not even to such jazz capitals as New Orleans, New York, or Hamburg. Ronnie Scott's club consists of three levels: the large, ground-level Main Room, where you can enjoy hot jazz and a hot meal (mostly Italian cuisine); the Downstairs Bar, with live entertainment in an intimate atmosphere, often including prominent jazz musicians on their nights' off; and the Upstairs Room, offering dancing to live or recorded music. Ronnie himself often acts as MC, and is known for the terrible jokes and convoluted puns he uses to introduce acts and good-naturedly heckle audiences. The club attracts a mix of patrons, none of whom seem very interested in getting to bed before 4 a.m. or so. Get plenty of sleep before your visit, and join them in soaking up the music and atmosphere all night long.

Ronnie Scott's, 47 Frith St, London W1, 071-439 0747. Mon-Sat 8:30 pm-3 am. Membership or cover charge £8-£12.

## Best Jazz Club With An Address You Won't Forget
The 100 Club

From cacophony to calm: Where punk groups

such as the Sex Pistols and Siouxsie and the Ban-
shees once played, now smooth modern and "trad"
(traditional) jazz is offered. This basement club—
the name of which is its street address—has been
popular for years for its varied programmes of
music. It is a smoky and crowded place—"atmospheric" in the euphemistic vernacular—and is
generally shabbier than Ronnie Scott's (see separate listing)...But it's also cheaper than Scott's and
is thought to offer jazz as good (or, at worst, just a
step below) that offered at London's more famous
jazz club. The 100 Club also presents the occasional folk, rock, or new-wave act, and serves
drinks and a limited menu of Oriental food.

The 100 Club, 100 Oxford St, London W1, 071-636
0933. Mon-Sat 7:45 pm-1 am, Sun 7:45-11:30 pm.

## Best Club Located In A 19th-Century Wine Cellar

The Rheingold Club

Below street-level, just around the corner from the
Bond Street Underground station, is this delightful
nightspot. The Rheingold Club (open since 1959)
offers a variety of entertainment and nightlife,
incorporating into a single club a restaurant, a
pair of bars, and a dance floor. Live dance music is
presented every night; the club also presents occasional cabaret-style performances by singers and
comedians. This was considered a "singles club"
before there was such a term. Today, it remains a
good place for couples or even single men and
women to meet—without the pressures or predato-
ry atmosphere that often pervades other singles
spots. The Rheingold Club also offers solid dining
choices from a simple German- and continental-
influenced menu, and a good, varied selection of
German draft beers and French wines.

The Rheingold Club, Sedley Pl at Oxford St, London
W1, 071-629 5343. Mon & Tue 7:30 pm-1:30 am,
Wed & Thu 7:30 pm-2 am, Fri & Sat 7:30 pm-2:30
am.

## Best Club To See Up-And-Coming Rock Groups

Rock Garden

Attracting a mix of tourists, locals, and young
music fans, this brand-name-ish (i.e., sanitised)
rock venue may be better known for who has
played here than for who will. Such current and
recent top bands as U2, Dire Straits, Talking
Heads, and the Police played at the Rock Garden
on their way up. Today, the performers found here

are usually hungry newcomers (as those superstar bands once were), meaning you may have a shot at seeing one of tomorrow's stars in a fairly intimate setting...Either that, or you'll just see an OK band that you'll never hear of again. Such are the vagaries of rock 'n' roll—and of the Rock Garden. The club consists of two levels: Upstairs is a some-what-pricey restaurant for burgers, and ribs, etc. (sort of a minor-league Hard Rock Café—see separate listing); downstairs, in a former vegetable warehouse, is where the action is, with up to three bands performing seven nights a week (this is one of the few venues to offer music on Sunday nights). The Rock Garden also offers outdoor din-ing in summer...and has been known to host the *occasional* (emphasis placed on that word so as not to disappoint) top-name guests for an impromptu song or two.

Rock Garden Restaurant & Rock Music Venue, 6-7 The Piazza, Covent Garden Market, London WC2, 071-240 3961. Mon-Sat 7:30 pm-3 am, Sun 7:30 pm-midnight.

## Best Club To See Well-Known Rock Musicians On Their Nights Off

The Marquee

Nobody wants to see musicians on an off night... but on their *night off*, well, that's a different propo-sition altogether. This classic rock club has moved a few blocks away from its crowded old site on Wardour Street—but its reputation as London's top small rock club has followed the physical move. The Marquee's new digs are bigger (the site once housed a cinema), but the place still is atmo-spherically grungy. Most of the big rock acts of the '60s (the Stones, the Kinks, the Who) played at the original Marquee. Occasionally, members of bands such as those—or some of today's top British rock stars—can be seen in here when they're in town or between gigs at other venues. Whether they're checking out the competition or just grooving to the sounds, their presence (or even the possibility thereof) makes this a popular and fun club for rock fans. And, of course, when you get famous musicians together on their nights off, can super-star jam sessions be far behind?

The Marquee, 105 Charing Cross Rd, London WC2, 017-437 6603. Daily 7-11 pm.

## Best Club That's—Literally!—The Talk Of London

The Talk of London

With the once-renowned Talk of the Town

cabaret/nightclub converted into the chic Hippodrome disco (see separate listing), this recent
nightclub has come along to carry on the flavour of
its famed predecessor. Located just off Drury
Lane—in the midst of London's theatre district—
this is the largest venue for cabaret-style dining
and entertainment in the West End. Nightly entertainment packages include a four-course dinner
from an international menu, dancing to live music,
popular cabaret performers, and a chorus of span-
gle-and-feather-bedecked dancers. A unique, in-
the-round seating scheme (on varying levels)
ensures perfect sightlines to the stage for all
patrons. A package price of £26-£28 (plus drinks)
covers an 8 p.m.-to-midnight evening of entertainment; special group packages and prices are also
available.

The Talk of London, Parker St, London WC2, 071-408
1001. Daily 8 pm-midnight.

## Best Disco You Can Get Into

The Hippodrome

Disco impresario Peter Stringfellow has transformed the old Talk Of the Town theatre into a
mammoth dance club, attracting London's smart-
ly-dressed trend-setters. Quite possibly London's
ultimate high-tech dance club (and perhaps its
most popular non-member club), the Hippodrome
is decked out in chrome and plush carpeting, features six bars, giant-screen video monitors, and a
dance floor with all the trappings—such as lighted
floor, spotlights, strobe lights, mirrored balls, and
rotating speakers. The disco also has a battery of
special effects, including fog machines and laser
lights. Music is a mix of the latest dance hits and
an occasionally requested oldie. Unlike its members-only sister club, Stringfellow's (see separate
listing), the Hippodrome is open to the public.
However, this general door policy doesn't deter
celebrities from making an occasional appearance
here. The club also hosts occasional performances
by international entertainers on its elevated stage.

The Hippodrome, Cranbourn St (Charing Cross Rd &
Leicester Sq), London WC2, 071-437 9933. Mon-Sat
9 pm-3 am. £6-£12.

## Best Disco You *Might* Be Able To Get Into

Stringfellow's

Owner Peter Stringfellow's hopping hot spot theo-
retically is a members-only club. In reality,
patient, sharply-dressed non-members can be

granted admission after a brief ritual that includes enduring the slights of a scrutinizing doorman and waiting outside the door in a long queue. Why go through all this just to enter a disco? If you have to ask, you probably don't really want to go here! Nonetheless, inveterate nightclubbers and trend-chasers seem to enjoy being dazzled by the club's over-the-top glitz (lots of flashing lights, a glass dance-floor, a booming sound system), rumoured to have cost in excess of £1 million. You may spot stars...or you may merely spot other vaguely disaffected star-gazers. Both the cover-charge and the drinks are expensive; also offers a limited nouvelle cuisine menu (and it, too, isn't cheap!). Stringfellow also owns the similar—if not as exclusive—Hippodrome disco (see separate listing).

Stringfellow's, 16 Upper St. Martin's Ln, London WC2, 071-240 5534. Mon-Sat 8 pm-3:30 am. Admission £8-£15.

## Best Gay Disco

Heaven

Fans of the glitzy, high-energy gay dance scene will feel like they've died and gone to you-know-where when they enter this jumping joint. The largest and most popular gay dance club in London (and perhaps in all of Europe), Heaven is a split-level club, offering lots of room for dancing downstairs and a more casual bar—perfect for drinks and conversation—upstairs. A labyrinth of dark hallways, bars, stairways, and open spaces connect the high-tech dance areas (where the theory seems to be that bigger is better among the three Ls of clubland: Lights, Lasers, and Loud). Heaven also offers scheduled "mixed" nights—although the crowd here on any given night is likely to include more than a sprinkling of "straights." Other notable gay clubs are Paradise, the Hippodrome on Monday nights, and, for south-of-the-river action, the Fridge on Tuesday nights.

Heaven, Villiers St, London WC2, 071-839 3852. Mon-Sat 10:30 pm-3:30 am.

## Best Disco Named After An Inert Gas

Xenon

This massive complex, containing three separate bars (one a piano bar; see separate listing) and two restaurants featuring Italian and Japanese cuisine respectively, is a trendy, fun place to visit at least (and perhaps only!) once. Inevitably, you'll find some sort of entertainment—perhaps a mime, jugglers, magician, or a choreographed dance by the club's own dance troupe. The dance floor is equipped with the usual high-tech electronic gadgetry such as laser lights, mirror balls, and the like, backed by a decent sound-system and a DJ spinning loud dance tracks. This upscale club attracts native Londoners and visitors (particularly from the continent) alike, indistinguishable, except for language and accents, in their smartest, dressed-to-kill party garb.

Xenon, 196 Piccadilly, London W1, 071-743 9344. Nightly 10 pm-3 am.

## Best Disco That Lives Up To The Name Of Its Creator

Camden Palace

The early 1980s was a strange period in London's nightlife and music scenes. And perhaps chief among this strangeness was the appropriately pseudonymed Steve Strange, a key impresario among that period's "Blitz" and "New Romantic" movements (which combined mostly moody—but danceable—music with over-the-top fashions, such as circa-1975 Elton John or circa-*anytime* Liberace outfits). Strange created this club, and it used to be full of strange (or Strange) people...It has calmed down a bit, but is still a colourful and entertaining place. Housed in a former theatre, Camden Palace boasts a huge dance floor, bombarded by loud music and flashy lighting. Big-beat dance music is offered most nights; there also are regularly scheduled nights of soul, pop, and alternative rock music, as well as more esoteric types of dance music (such as acid funk, hip-hop, and house). Also presents occasional live performances.

Camden Palace, 1 Camden Rd, London NW1, 071-387 0428. Mon-Thu, Sat 9 pm-2:30 am; Fri 8 pm-2:30 am.

## Best Recreated Victorian Music Hall

Cockney Cabaret and Music Hall

"I say, I say, I say...my wife just went on holiday to the West Indies." "Jamaica?" "No, she went of her own accord!" That hoary joke gives you a good idea of what kind of entertainment you're in for at this theme cabaret, which purports to be a recreation of a Victorian music hall. The evening's package starts off with a cocktail reception around a rickety upright piano for honky-tonk sing-alongs. (Try a large "Mother's Ruin"—Cockney vernacular for gin.) This is followed by a four-course, meat-and-potatoes East Enders repast (complete with unlimited wine and beer), cabaret performers emoting tunes of the era in costume, and dancing to a period band. The night's inclusive packages run from £25-£27 per person (depending upon the night); group rates are also available. Overall, this can be a bit hokey. But it can also be an entertaining evening if you're in the proper mood to be carried back to a time when performers in loud checked suits and cloth caps sung about "boiled beef and cabbage" and comedians adopted comic names, such as Nosmo King (purloined from a "no smoking" sign).

Cockney Cabaret and Music Hall, 161 Tottenham Court Rd, London W1, 071-408 1001. Daily 8 pm-midnight.

## Best Spot Where Music Hall Lives (And Where The World's Top Entertainers Perform)

The London Palladium

Whether you call it music hall or, as Americans do, vaudeville, this popular, often-corny form of stage entertainment lives on (if in somewhat modified form) at this legendary theatre. Built in 1910, the Palladium long has been known as the venue where performers considered that they had "made it" when they played here. In years gone by, it hosted Frank Sinatra, Sammy Davis, Jr., Danny Kaye, Max Bygraves, Julie Andrews, and other top American and British stars; recently it has offered a variety of entertainments, from light theatre (such as Gilbert and Sullivan revivals and touring musicals) to interesting rock concerts (Lou Reed, Elvis Costello) to the aforementioned vaudeville-type shows. This large old theatre is also known as the site of the annual Royal Command Performance.

The London Palladium, 8 Argyll St, London W1, 071-437 7373.

## Best Selections From *The Pirates of Penzance*, *The Mikado*, and *H.M.S. Pinafore* With Your Roast Beef

Mansion House at Grim's Dyke

If you desire to dine with a Pirate King, three little Japanese school maids, and the Yeomen of the Guard, then an evening at this attraction is for you. This Middlesex site is the one-time home of William S. Gilbert (who wrote the words) and is where he and Arthur Sullivan (who composed the music) collaborated on some of their famous operettas. On most Sunday evenings, an entertaining combination music-dinner package is offered here, featuring the music of Gilbert and Sullivan (as performed by the English Heritage Singers) and a full Edwardian-style dinner; packages cost around £30 per person. The costumed performers sing during and after dinner, and patrons can request their favourites from the Gilbert and Sullivan catalogue. (Put the singers to the test—see if one of them knows all of the words to the famous rapid recitative of "I Am the Very Model of a Modern Major-General" from *The Pirates of Penzance!*)

Mansion House at Grim's Dyke, Old Redding, Harrow Weald, Middlesex, 081-954 4227. Sun evenings (inquire for schedule).

## Best Place For A Medieval Banquet
Beefeater Club By The Tower Of London

Your presence is requested by His Royal Highness, King Henry VIII. He may not have been much of a committed husband (going through six wives, and separating two of them from their heads!), but apparently he knew how to throw a royal party. This dinner/entertainment club, located in an historic building in the shadow of the Tower of London, relives the boisterous days of the court of the hedonist Henry. For an all-inclusive price, patrons can enjoy a five-course medieval banquet (featuring pâté, soup, chicken, beef, vegetables, and thick, fresh-baked apple pie), unlimited tankards of ale and mead, and merriment by court jesters, saucy wenches, valiant knights, balladeers, and other royal entertainers. All of this, hosted by Henry VIII—in a better mood than usually depicted by history (although women may want to avoid catching the wandering eye of the oft-lustful and -vengeful king!). The package price for the four hours of dinner (and high jinks) is around £28 per person (price varies for different nights or for groups).

Beefeater Club By The Tower Of London, Ivory House, St. Katherine's Dock, London E1, 071-408 1001. Daily 8 pm-midnight.

## Best Nightspot To Yell "Opaa!"
The Elysée

At this lively nightspot, the popular and friendly proprietors, the Karegeorgis brothers—George, Michael, and Ulysses—take turns playing *Zorba*. They preside over dancing and general merry-making (to sprightly bouzouki music) at this combination Greek cabaret and restaurant. There's belly dancing, of course, but also lively sing-alongs, and—watch out!—George's don't-quit-your-day-job wine glass-balancing act. This veritable embodiment of "breads and circuses" fills the two indoor levels of the club, with the third being the Roof Garden (purportedly the largest in London), which offers delightful outdoor dining. The menu choices are typical Greek-restaurant fare (dolmades, souvlaki, moussaka, spit-roasted lamb, etc.), offered with friendly aplomb. But the focus is often on the plates that end up on the floor rather than on the tables! Want to join in on the vigorous plate-smashing? Go ahead, but you'll be charged for the pleasure (around £6 per dozen plates—not a bad bargain if you've been shopping housewares lately!).

The Elysée, 13 Percy St, London W1, 071-636 4804. Mon-Sat 7:30 pm-3 am.

## Best Turkish Restaurant That Once Hosted A PM
Gallipoli

This is a curiously named restaurant—curious not because of geography or culture (Gallipoli is a peninsula in eastern Turkey and this is a Turkish restaurant), but because of connotation. As followers of history or viewers of the film *Gallipoli* (which starred a young Mel Gibson) will recall, Gallipoli is best known as a World War I battle in which the Turks overwhelmingly defeated Commonwealth forces. Despite this ironic naming, this is a popular restaurant, as the prominently displayed photos of Margaret Thatcher and Aristotle Onassis dining there (separately, of course) will attest. The Turkish food offered here is similar to the familiar fare found at Cypriot/Greek restaurants, including kebabs, dolmades, and grilled beef and lamb. Included in the somewhat-pricey cost of dining is rousing entertainment by cabaret performers and belly dancers, as well as live music and dancing six nights a week. Gallipoli is open until 3 a.m., making it one of the latest-closing kitchens in London.

Gallipoli, 7-8 Bishopsgate Churchyard, London EC2, 071-588 1922. Mon-Fri 11:30 am-3 pm, 6 pm-3 am; Sat 6 pm-3 am.

## Best Place To Laugh It Off
The Comedy Store

The so-called "New Comedy" movement—fueled by late-night comedy shows and cable TV in the U.S.—has reached London in a big way, and this established club leads the way. Considered the principal comedy club in Britain, it attracts top stand-up talent from the U.K. and the U.S. Tickets are available at the door only, which can mean long queues, especially when a top act is playing (typically on Friday and Saturday nights, when The Comedy Store is already very popular). The Comedy Store Players, an improv revue troupe (à la Chicago's famous Second City group) performs on Wednesdays; there also is music on Thursdays.

The Comedy Store, 28A Leicester Sq, London WC2, 071-828 7827. Wed-Sun, hours vary.

## Best Nightlife Area
Leicester Square

As you narrow your nightlife focus in London, the progression is likely to go from the West End to Soho to the neighbourhood around Leicester Square. This lively (if a bit seedy at times) area draws tourists and local nightclubbers, all attracted by the variety of activities to be found in Charing Cross Road, Shaftesbury Avenue, St. Martin's Lane, and the square itself. Highlights include a clutch of restaurants and pubs, four large cinemas, and, especially, some of London's top dance and music venues. Within a few blocks of the historic square, you can listen to music at two of London's top jazz clubs (Ronnie Scott's and the 100 Club), see famous rock musicians on their nights off at the Marquee's new location, and dance the night away at the Hippodrome, Stringfellow's, the Limelight, or the Empire Ballroom. Also here is the Leicester Square Half-Price Ticket Booth, offering same-day bargains on theatre tickets (see separate listing). In general, things stay open late in this area—later than the Underground runs, so it's best to plan the time of departure for your return trip and keep an eye on your watch—or expect to walk or catch a cab.

Leicester Square, London WC2; sites near Leicester Square, Piccadilly Circus, and Tottenham Court Road Underground stations.

## Best Weekly Information On The London Entertainment Scene
*Time Out*

From fringe theatre to rock concerts, movie listings to sporting events, this weekly magazine covers the eclectic London scene (or, more accurately, *scenes*) with style, clarity, wit, and, perhaps most importantly, readability. Each issue offers separate sections covering arts, film, music, literature, theatre, sport, TV, radio, children's activities, dance, the gay and lesbian scenes, and even views on and reactions to the previous week's news. The hip, upbeat writing in *Time Out* includes feature articles, interviews with the famous and the near-famous, and plenty of current and ongoing listings of events in and around London. In general, this is a great guide for the London visitor or resident who wants to experience what the city offers in the way of entertainment beyond the latest West End theatre blockbuster (*Cats*, *Les Misérables*, *Phantom of the Opera*, etc.). *Time Out* also produces a yearly magazine-style *London For Visitors* guide (which condenses listings into capsule commentaries on the leading cultural and nightlife highlights in London) and a book, *The Time Out London Guide*, which offers more of the same, plus some lively and breezy summarised history (as it relates to sights and sites about town), and additional sections on accommodations, dining, and pubs.

*Time Out,* Time Out Magazine Ltd, Tower House, Southampton St, London WC2, 071-836 4411. Published weekly on Wednesdays. £1.20.

# MUSEUMS, THEATRES, & OTHER CULTURAL SITES

## Best Art That's a Head-*Turner*

The Tate Gallery

Located on a site that once was a jail, along the northern bank of the Thames, this popular museum houses the country's best collection of modern art (and more). It was founded by sugar magnate Sir Henry Tate in the 1890s, with a dual gift of money and his respected collection of British art. Complementing the collection of the National Gallery, the Tate exhibits the British national collection from the 16th century on, as well as a large selection of international modern art. Among the well-represented British masters are Reynolds, Hogarth, Gainsborough, and Turner (more about him below); modern painters collected include Cézanne, Monet, Picasso, Matisse, Dali, Chagall, Rothko, Warhol, and Hockney. One of the gallery's highlights is the multi-million-pound Clore Gallery, added in 1987, which houses a huge collection of J. M. W. Turner works—almost 300 paintings and 20,000 drawings—which the artist bequeathed to the National Gallery. At least 200 of these works are on display at any one time. The museum also has an excellent café, the Tate Gallery Restaurant (see separate listing), perfect for lunch and wine (from a list noted for its quality *and* affordability), after a morning of gallery exploring. General admission to the gallery is free, but there often is a charge for special exhibitions.

The Tate Gallery, Millbank, London SW1, 071-821 1313. Mon-Sat 10 am-5:50 pm, Sun 2-5:50 pm. Free.

## Best Place To Scout Out The Next Turner, Reynolds, or Hogarth

The Royal Academy's Summer Exhibition

For more than two centuries, this annual exhibition of new art has included many of Britain's best contemporary drawings, engravings, sculpture, and architecture. More than 150,000 people now come to the academy every year to browse and buy the latest works of the best up-and-comers, which are displayed right alongside the newest items from such luminaries as Peter Blake, David Hockney, Phillip King, and Norman Foster. Representing the true cream of England's newest art, the fifteen hundred or so works on exhibit are chosen by Royal Academy artists from about 15,000 submissions. It's also worthwhile to tour the beautifully appointed halls (decorated by Benjamin West and Angelica Kaufmann) any time of year for everchanging regular exhibitions.

The Royal Academy of Arts, Burlington House, Piccadilly, London W1, 071-734 9052. Daily 10 am-6 pm. Admission fees range from £1.50 to £4.50, depending on the exhibition.

## Best Place To Come Face-To-Face With England's Greats

National Portrait Gallery

This collection will help you put faces to the names of nearly every Briton ever mentioned in a history book, from artists to architects, seamen to scientists, executives to explorers, and Royals to roustabouts. Since its 1856 acquisition of a portrait of William Shakespeare (painted by an unknown artist around 1610), the gallery has amassed more than 10,000 portraits covering every facet of British history. Each painting was completed while its subject was alive, making this one of the most accurate collections of pre-photographic portraiture anywhere. Starting at the top floor in the acclaimed Tudors display, each room covers a distinct era or theme, including periods of exploration, the struggle for America, and Great Britain at war. Even a brief survey of the museum reveals delightful surprises. The collection of Royals, for instance, includes a series showing Henry VIII growing more fearsome with age, as well as a 1980 likeness of a casually dressed Diana, painted before she became Princess of Wales. And this is one of the few places to find a visual record of the Brontë Sisters, in a portrait painted by their brother Branwell. Other notables on display include Charles Dickens, a long-bearded Charles Darwin, Gilbert and Sullivan, and John Maynard Keynes. Americans might suffer a slight case of culture shock when they read the biographies next to portraits of a few favourite sons. For example, John Paul Jones, commonly known in the States as the father of the American navy, is described here as a "seaman, adventurer, smuggler, and slave trader."

The National Portrait Gallery, St. Martin's Pl, London WC2, 071-306 0055. Mon-Fri 10 am-5 pm, Sat 10 am-6 pm, Sun 2-6 pm. Free admission.

## Best Place To Find Works By Da Vinci, Van Gogh, Renoir, Michelangelo, Et Al.

The National Gallery

Spanning eight centuries, the more than 2,200 paintings displayed in the classical-style gallery on the north side of Trafalgar Square comprise one of the world's most-revered collections of Western art. This is the spot to view a wide range of all-time greats: Jan Van Eyck's "The Arnolfini Marriage;" da Vinci's "The Virgin and Child with Saint Anne and Saint John the Baptist;" Titian's "Bacchus and Ariadne;" "The Straw Hat" by Rubens; "The Water-Lily Pond" by Monet; van Gogh's "The Chair and Pipe," and many others. To put this remarkable collection—which includes paintings dating back to 1260—into context, the Gallery often asks contemporary artists to thematically group their choice of works for display in the continuing "Artist's Eye" exhibit series.

The National Gallery, Trafalgar Sq, London WC2, 071-839 3321. Mon-Sat 10 am-6 pm, Sun 2 pm-6 pm. Free admission.

## Best Place To Mingle Among Ming Vases

Percival David Foundation of Chinese Art

Fine teas are not the only Chinese imports enjoyed by the British. Thanks to the keen eye and deep pockets of the late Sir Percival David, the best collection of Chinese ceramics outside of China resides in a building nestled between Tavistock and Gordon squares on the University of London campus. Especially strong in polychrome items from the 15th through the 18th centuries, many of the collection's 1,700 pieces were purchased from the emperor's Imperial Collection in Bejing. Visitors who closely inspect the stunningly beautiful objects—such as the milk-white vase laced with flowered branches on which two intricately painted green-and-white birds hold forth in animated conversation—might find Sir Percival's passion for them quite infectious. Covering mainly the Song, Yuan, Ming, and Qing dynasties, many pieces in the collection bear names and dates inscribed at the time of their manufacture, as well as poems and notes brushed on in later periods at the instruction of Chinese emperors. (The strokes of the emperor Qianlong himself appear on several objects.) Don't miss the Ming vases, the blue-and-white wares of Jingdezhen, and the remarkable group of refined 18th-century polychrome pieces traditionally known as *Gu yue xuan.*

Percival David Foundation of Chinese Art, 53 Gordon Sq, London WC1, 071-387 3909. Mon-Fri 10:30 am-5 pm. Free.

## Best Place To Learn That "Philately" is Not A Relative Of Clem Attlee

The National Postal Museum

Ardent philatelists, casual collectors, and just about anyone interested in the historic, colourful world of postage stamps will find something to write home about in this first-class museum next to the London Post Office. Thousands of Victorian-era stamps, donated to the nation by a private collector in 1965, join the Post Office's near-complete collection of worldwide stamp issues since 1878 and its exhibits of artwork, essays, and British stamp registration sheets to form one of the world's most comprehensive philatelic museums. Historic general issues are displayed alongside rare items such as the Coronation stamp of Edward VIII, which was held from issue when the king abdicated. The non-stamp collections are impressive as well, such as a cylindrical 1856 Scottish letter box, painted bright red and black and topped with a gold-and-red crown. Ornate stamp boxes of ormolu, silver, brass, and wood—mostly of the Victorian period—are displayed. Other artefacts include antique cancelling, vending, and meter franking machines. Remember your visit with a one-of-a-kind souvenir: a collector's card with a special museum postmark.

The National Postal Museum, King Edward Bldg, King Edward St, London EC1, 071-239 5420. Mon-Thu 9:30 am-4:30 pm, Fri 9:30 am-4 pm. Free.

## Best Museum To Analyze

The Freud Museum

After escaping to London from Nazi-occupied Austria in 1938, the father of psychoanalysis spent the last year of his life working in surroundings painstakingly arranged to resemble his Vienna residence of 47 years. The famous analysis couch, with its richly patterned cover and plump, velour-covered pillows, is perfectly placed, right next to the green tub chair where Freud would sit, just out of sight, and listen to the free associations of his patients. Also transferred to the two-story Hampstead house were his large collection of Egyptian, Roman, and Oriental antiques, portraits of Freud by Ferdinand Schmutzer and Salvador Dalí, and, resting on the shelf behind his desk, favourite works by Goethe, Shakespeare, Flaubert, Dostoievsky, and Anatole France. Should you doubt the authenticity of the arrangement, a video presentation, focusing on photos of Freud taken in his Vienna study a few weeks before he was forced to flee, invites direct comparison to his old digs. Close scrutiny of the eminent psychiatrist's possessions certainly will give visitors insights into his mysterious character, but as Freud himself might caution, it's best to remember that sometimes a couch is only a couch.

Freud Museum, 20 Maresfield Gardens, London NW3, 071-435 2002. Wed-Sun Noon-5 pm. Adults £2, children £1, children under 12 free.

## The *Only* Place to Find A Shakespeare First Folio, The Rosetta Stone, Two Copies Of The Magna Carta, The Elgin Marbles, And One Copy Of Every Book Published In The UK

The British Museum and Library

You needn't galavant to the ends of the earth like Indiana Jones to discover the greatest artefacts of human history: It's far easier to leave your bull-whip at home and instead navigate the halls of the British Museum, perhaps the world's richest repository of antiquities. Each of the more than 100 exhibition rooms contains numerous awe-inspiring items from early civilisations, such as the Assyrian lionhut reliefs, Egyptian mummies, Lewis chessmen, and the Lindow Man. Permanent exhibits catch the broad and exciting cultural sweep of societies such as Italy before the Roman Empire, Hellenistic Greece, Ancient Iran, and Pre-historic Britain. Among the museum's most famous objects are the Elgin Marbles (sculptures that once graced the outside of the Parthenon), the Rosetta Stone (the tablet that led to the translation of Egyptian hieroglyphics), and a large assortment of other Greek, Roman, and Middle Eastern antiq-

uities. All of the temporary exhibits, which have
included Swords of the Samurai, Archaeology and
the Bible, and Ancient Egyptian Sculpture, are
accompanied by lectures and films. And as if those
collections didn't cram enough history under one
monumental roof, the British Library displays
many of its greatest treasures here as well, such
as two copies of the Magna Carta, a Gutenberg
bible, the first printed editions of Shakespeare's
plays, and many original manuscripts by such
noted authors as Jane Austen, Jonathon Swift,
and Samuel Pepys.

The British Museum and Library, Great Russell St,
London WC1, 071-636 1555. Mon-Sat 10 am-5 pm,
Sun 2:30 pm-6 pm. Free.

## Best Place To See (But Not Touch!) Uranium
Geological Museum

You don't have to dig very deep here to mine some
valuable and fascinating information! Established
in 1837 and moved to its present site in 1935, this
museum looks at things on and under the surface
of the earth and (especially) Britain.   Among the
museum's highlights are: An extensive collection of
gemstones—diamonds, emeralds, rubies, etc.—
both in raw and cut states (this also includes a
model of the massive Koh-i-Noor diamond, which
weighs in at more than 100 carats and is part of
the Crown Jewels); "The Story of the Earth," an
audio-visual presentation tracing the history of the
planet; models and maps showing the geography,
geology, and topology of England, Scotland, and
Wales; and a model and display explaining off-
shore oil and gas retrieval. While many of these
exhibits encourage patron-participation, a definite
hands-off item is the encased display of raw
radioactive uranium! The museum offers special
events and (especially on Saturday) family activities, such as movies, tours of exhibits, and lectures.

Geological Museum, Exhibition Rd, London SW7,
071-938 8765.  Mon-Sat 10 am-6 pm, Sun 1-6 pm.
Adults £1, children 50p.

## Best Place To See A Sopwith Camel And A Spitfire
Imperial War Museum

As you pass by the huge twin guns dominating the
entrance of this museum, get ready to let your
imagination soar as, via dramatic re-creations, you
scramble for shelter as shrill sirens signal a raid

during the London Blitz and fly with the RAF on a daring World War II raid over France. Then tour the poignant exhibits chronicling the history of battlefields from World War I to the Falkland Islands and beyond. War often has cast its long shadow over the British landscape, and these displays help visitors better understand its impact. Reminders of the island nation's tenacity and perseverance in the face of incredible odds include a Battle of Britain Spitfire, a tiny wooden sailboat, *Tamzine*, one of the hundreds of small craft used to pull off the miraculous evacuation of Dunkirk, and "Ole Bill," a rickety double-decker bus once used to ferry troops to the Western Front. (Also here is the famous "Peace in our time" agreement that Prime Minister Neville Chamberlain brought back from his historic meeting with Hitler; unfortunately the Prime Minister's optimism was misguided.) Touch monitor screens to learn about the Battle of the Atlantic, devastating attacks by German V1 and V2 rockets, and other harrowing events of war. Or get down and dirty in a re-created WW I trench, complete with the sounds, sights, and smells encountered by front-line soldiers. The impressive film and photo collection showcases images as grim as a group of Australian troops passing through an eerily devastated French forest in 1917 and as gregarious as a smiling T.E. Lawrence, his resplendant white robes set against the sands of Arabia.

Imperial War Museum, Lambeth Rd, London SE1, 071-416 5000. Daily 10 am-6 pm. Adults £3, children 5-16 £1.25.

## Only Place In London Where You Can Still Catch A Tram Or Trolley
London Transport Museum

"In the Blitz, they never closed/Though they blew up half the roads/Oh, it hurts me just to see 'em/Going dead in a museum," sang British rock performer Robyn Hitchcock in a nostalgically beautiful song called "Trams of Old London." Hitchcock or any other Londoner (or visitor, for that matter) who is feeling a bit sentimental for the old ways and old days of London transportation can head for this very alive museum housed in the former Covent Garden flower market building. You'll find double-decker buses, Tube cars, trams (streetcars that ran on rails), trolleys (buses powered by overhead wires), and even a replica of London's first horse-drawn bus (circa 1830). Many of these are definitely hands-on—patrons can climb behind the wheel of a variety of vintage and modern buses and trains. Also here are exhibits examining the sociological impacts of affordable transportation for the masses; displays of vintage maps, photos, and tickets; and a shop offering a great collection of postcards, posters, maps, and books (see separate listing).  To get the full effect, take the Underground to the museum; it is near the Covent Garden, Charing Cross, and Leicester Square stations.

London Transport Museum, 39 Wellington St, London WC2, 071-379 6344. Daily 10 am-6 pm. Adults £2.60; children 5-16, students, & OAPs £1.20; under 5 free.

## Good Place To Learn About London *Before* You Explore It

Museum of London

Nestled within the square mile of the City of London (the historic financial district), is this fascinating free-admission museum celebrating and explaining London's history.  Within this modern facility are exhibits looking back to the time when London was the Roman-built encampment of Londinium, including remains of the six-foot wall erected around the colony in the 3rd century A.D., still standing in its original location (the museum was built around it). You'll also find chronological displays depicting London's colourful past, including artefacts from Roman and Saxon ancestry, period costumes, pictures, tools, coinage, and weaponry. Two somewhat morbid must-sees are the excellent exhibits reliving the horrific plague of 1665 and Great Fire of 1666 which destroyed much of London (paving the way for Christopher Wren to rebuild much of the city, including a staggering array of beautiful churches). Be sure to visit the Museum Shop, offering—among other souvenirs—an extensive selection of books on London's history, many published by the Museum. A museum restaurant offers hot and cold snacks and an outdoor dining area.

Museum of London, London Wall, London EC2, 071-600 3699. Tue-Sat 10 am-6 pm, Sun 2-6 pm. Free.

## Best Place To Learn About Tribal Cultures

Museum of Mankind

This is a quiet, mostly undiscovered spot that is one of London's museum treasures. It consists of the British Museum's (see separate listing) ethnography department—meaning it is devoted to the study of the way people live.  Accordingly, it contains an immense collection of art and artefacts from cultures around the world, most notably those in Africa, the Americas, and the South Sea islands (many of the items from the last of these areas date to the 18th-century exploratory voyages of Captain Cook). The museum has more than 300,000 objects in its collection, only a small portion of which are exhibited at any given time. Typical examples of artefacts on display include wood carvings, bronzes, gold jewelry and decorative items, tools and utensils, religious icons, and clothing. There also is a collection of rare Aztec objects, including masks, weapons, and adornments. The museum offers films, lectures, and an extensive research library.

Museum of Mankind, 6 Burlington Gardens, London W1, 071-437 2224.  Mon-Sat 10 am-5 pm, Sun 2:30-6 pm. Free.

# Best Spot To Spend A Morning At The Movies

Museum of the Moving Image

Treat yourself to a "reel" romp through the history of the moving image in the company of actor-guides—dressed as magic lantern operators and movie directors—who will take you all the way from the earliest pre-cinema experiments, such as the Javanese Shadow Puppets of 2000 B.C., to a modern television studio. At this state-of-the-art media museum in the South Bank arts centre, you'll have a chance to stare into the camera's unblinking eye as a newsreader, draw some Daffy Duck and Goofy frames in an animating studio, and emote your heart out in an old-fashioned Hollywood screen test. Pop-culture artefacts, such as Marilyn Monroe's shimmy dress from *Some Like It Hot* and Charlie Chaplin's signature "Little Tramp" hat and cane, will get you in the mood for the 20 compilation films that examine the history of motion pictures. Subjects include British film pioneers, German Expressionists, newsreels, animation, television advertising, 3-D movies, science fiction, and a presentation called "Precious Images," a six-minute montage, assembled by the Directors' Guild of America, of 500 extracts from Hollywood films. Next door to the museum, the British Film Institute's National Film Theatre shows more than 2,000 movies a year, from early silents to new mainstream releases (daily memberships are 40p and admission is £3.95 for adults; £2.75 children 5-16.)

Museum of the Moving Image, South Bank Centre, Waterloo, London SE1, 071-401 2636. Tue-Sun 10 am-8 pm. Adults £3.95, children 5-16 £2.75.

## Best Spot To Find The Bones of Bonaparte's Horse

National Army Museum

You can't miss this museum—it's the only building in London with a 51-ton tank in front! The National Army Museum celebrates the noble history of the British Army, from Henry VII's Yeomen of the Guard in 1485 to the controversial Falklands War against Argentina in 1982. On display here are weapons, decorations and medals, paintings, photographs, and a comprehensive collection of military uniforms (numbering more than 20,000 pieces). Among the more interesting (or perhaps simply more *bizarre*) items in the museum's collection are a recreated World War I trench, containing original materials from the battlefield at Ypres; the hand-written order that commanded the Light Brigade to its doomed charge in Balaclava (in the Crimea) in 1854, as immortalized in Tennyson's famous poem; and the skeleton of Marengo, Napoleon's horse. In general, this is a good place to bone up (no pun intended!) on the highlights of British history.  (The museum adjoins the Royal Hospital, home to that group of retired soldiers popularly known as the Chelsea Pensioners.)

National Army Museum, Royal Hospital Rd, London SW3, 071-730 0717. Mon-Sat 10 am-5:30 pm, Sun 2-5:30 pm. Free.

## Best Museum Where Britannia Still Rules The Waves

National Maritime Museum

Britain's proud maritime heritage, both in peace and at war, is colourfully brought to life in a series of exhibits at this museum by the Thames in the heart of historic Greenwich. The proud sea-faring era of Sir Francis Drake and Sir Walter Raleigh is well-represented in the "Discovery and Seapower" display, but a more-melancholy note is struck in "Exploring the Arctic," which includes relics of Sir John Franklin's ill-fated expedition to find the North West Passage. The most impressive full-size vessels on hand are the beautifully gilded barges once used to transport royalty on the river and the paddle tug *Reliant*, which dominates the hall dedicated to merchant shipping and pleasure-craft. Other highlights include an unrivalled collection of original 17th-century Admiralty Board models of great naval ships and a wooden-shipbuilding gallery that takes a look at Britain's earliest shipyards and the tools of the traditional marine craftsman.

National Maritime Museum, Greenwich, London

SE10, 081-858 4422. Mon-Sat 10 am-6pm, Sun noon-6 pm. Adults £1.50, children 75p.

## Best Place To See A "Whale" Of A Collection
Natural History Museum

It's got twin horns and gruesome choppers, and it just might be your distant cousin. Yes, the 35-million-year-old Arsenotherium, found in Egypt near the Ancient tomb of Queen Arsinoe, is quite possibly the stumpy root of the mammalian family tree. You can see old Arsen, along with hundreds of exhibits covering the earth's entire natural history, in this cathedral-like South Kensington museum. Anything but a dull repository of dusty bones, this is *the* place to stand beneath a full-size model of a Blue Whale, stare into the fearsome jaw of Tyrannosaurus rex, and explore the world of Creepy Crawlies (including scorpions, tarantulas, and other fearsome creatures). Excellent examples of the art of taxidermy await in the Rowland Ward pavilion, where you'll be transported to a waterhole in Kenya, a grassland in Angola, and a central African rain forest, where you can see examples of the secretive okapi and bongo, rare jungle animals. Even fossils come to life in the fascinating "Britain before Man" exhibit, an investigation of the northwestern edge of the Eurasian continental mass.

Natural History Museum, Cromwell Rd, London SW7, 071-692 7654. Mon-Sat 10 am-6 pm, Sun 11 am-6 pm. Adults £3, children 5-17 £1.50.

## Best "Please Touch" Museum
Science Museum

You won't be ready to lead the London Philharmonic, but you can become a great conductor by visiting the human battery exhibit in this collection of more than 200,000 objects from the world of science, technology, and medicine. This electrifying experiment (where visitors can allow electrical current to safely flow through their bodies) is one of hundreds of hands-on exhibits that trace the rise of industrial society from the first steam locomotive and the beginnings of photography to the latest advances in computers and space flight. Become a part of the action by building a bridge, operating a model grainpit, or riding the Energy Bike. The most popular exhibits include Exploration of Space, Aeronautics, Land Transport, and Chemical Industry; the Wellcome Museum of the History of Medicine—with its numerous full-scale reproductions of important medical events—chronicles the important discoveries and events in the history of medicine. From the muddy 1896 X-ray of a hand (the first in Britain to show part of the human body) to the 1969 Apollo 10 spacecraft (showing wear incurred during its re-entry into the earth's atmosphere after circling the Moon), these collections celebrate past scientific achievements and inspire visitors to imagine the advances of the future.

Science Museum, Exhibition Rd, South Kensington, London SW7, 071-938 8000. Mon-Sat 10 am-6 pm, Sun 11 am-6 pm. Adults £3.50, children 5-15 £1.75.

## Best Misnamed Museum

Victoria & Albert Museum

The collections of this South Kensington fortress of culture concentrate not on its namesake Queen and her consort, but on a variety of lively decorative arts. Conceived during the Great Exhibition of 1851 to promote high standards of excellence among manufacturers and designers, the V & A (as it is casually referred to by Londoners) celebrates the items relating to everyday life—ceramics, jewelry, furniture, metalworks, textiles, glassworks, and clothing—from early Christian times to today. Focusing primarily on the cultures of England, China, India, Japan, and a loose grouping of Islamic nations, the museum also contains one of the finest collections of Italian sculpture outside Italy, in addition to a group of Rodin bronzes. The museum occupies a fine Victorian building, which is virtually an exhibit in its own right. You can admire its remarkable period rooms while touring the national museum of the theatre and the national collections of sculpture, watercolours, portrait miniatures, art photography, wallpaper, and posters also contained in the V & A.

Victoria & Albert Museum, Cromwell Rd and Exhibition Rd, South Kensington, London SW7, 071-938 8363. Mon-Sat 10 am-5:50 pm, Sun 2:30-5:50 pm. Free.

## Best Place To See Marie Antoinette And Sylvester Stallone Under One Roof

Madame Tussaud's

This may be the only place you'll see Prince Charles and Princess Diana together for an extended period: Wax figures of the Prince of Wales and his bride stand in an ornate hall with effigies of the entire Royal Family, including an especially realistic Fergie, Duchess of York. Prestigious despite its medium, Madame Tussaud's has been attracting popular-culture and history buffs with its exact waxwork likenesses of the famous and infamous since 1770. Besides Royals past and present, the museum features a constantly changing cast of recognizable characters from the entertainment world, including new James Bond Timothy Dalton aiming his Walther PPK, Cher in one of her oh-so-revealing Bob Mackie creations, and quintessential movie star and native Londoner Michael Caine at his sartorial best in a classic tux. The museum also presents timeless faces of true greatness, such as an elderly Pablo Picasso, Roundhead leader Oliver Cromwell, William Shakespeare (waxing poetic, of course), Mahatma Gandhi, Archbishop Desmond Tutu, even Abraham Lincoln (who looks as honest as his face is long). A stickler for up-to-date appearances, Tussaud's has re-cast many figures several times. The museum's makeover king is Sir Winston Churchill, whose likeness has been remade 13 times since his 1908 debut. Top that, Phyllis Diller!

Madame Tussaud's, Marylebone Rd, London NW1, 071-935 6861.  Mon-Fri 9 am-5:30 pm, Sat-Sun 9:30 am-5:30 pm (from 10 am in winter). Admission £4.95.

## Best "Gem" Of An Attraction
The London Diamond Centre

Had enough of gazing at beautiful, but unobtainable gems and jewels? The tempting allures of the Crown Jewels at the Tower of London (see separate listing) need not cause you to emulate a certain Colonel Blood of the 17th century, who managed—briefly—to steal the royal baubles (the only such occurrence in British history). Instead, head to this attraction in the western section of Soho to see—and even buy!—a variety of precious gems. The Diamond Centre offers the largest collection of diamonds (plus other fine gemstones) in London, a selection of which are available for sale. Can't find anything in your price range? Not to worry—take a tip from the centre's exhibition detailing the creation, mining, and cutting of diamonds, and bury a lump of coal under tons of rock in your backyard. Give it about a million years (give or take a few thousand), and, presto!—dig up your "instant" diamond.

The London Diamond Centre, 10 Hanover St, London W1, 071-629 5511. Mon-Fri 9:30 am-5:30 pm.

## Super Spot For Superlatives
Guinness World of Records

This is the strangest, the most interesting, the

wildest museum in London! Excuse the hyperbole, but...it's understandable, considering that hyperbole is this museum's stock in trade. The Guinness World of Records consists of six pavilions housing bizarre records and spectacular feats from the Human World, Animal World, Entertainment World, the realm of Structures and Machines, and Our Planet Earth. Here you can gain a wealth of conversation-starting trivia in an odd and playful atmosphere reminiscent of a circus sideshow. After a glimpse of Britain's most-tattooed lady, Rusty Field, and the other manic mannequins on the Human World's fairground carousel, move on to a display that will have you all abuzz—a video of a man wearing a beard of 35,000 live bees! If it's a really big show you desire, step on the scale and see how you stack up against the world's heaviest human, or walk into the jaws of a Blue Whale. All the records are real, of course; the only tall tale you'll see is the literal one of Robert Wadlow, the world's tallest man, who reached a towering 8' 11". Multi-media reenactments of awesome sporting achievements, a chronology of the space race from Sputnik to the space shuttle, a hall of Great British Achievements, and replicas of the earth's heaviest, largest, and tallest landmark structures—all authenticated by the *Guinness Book of World Records* crew—also are represented here, believe it or not.

Guinness World of Records, at the Trocadero, Piccadilly Circus, London W1, 071-439 7331. Daily 10 am-10 pm. Adults £4.50, children 4-15 £2.85.

## Best Sight That's A Blast

HMS Belfast

Moored on the Thames across from the Tower of London, this relic of World War II is the last surviving big-gun ship in Europe. Referred to as "that straight-shooting ship" by the U.S. Navy, the *Belfast* played a decisive role in several naval battles and was one of the first ships to fire on German fortifications during the D-Day invasion of Normandy Beach. Visitors can imagine defending the ship against an air attack from a gun turret on the ship's deck, enter the massive turret of a six-inch gun, sit in the captain's chair on the bridge, and wander through the tangle of pipes and gauges in the engine and boiler rooms. Exhibits focus on D-Day, the development of battleships, mine warfare, gunnery, and other naval subjects. The newest attraction is the Arctic Convoy Experience, a dramatic re-enactment of a "surface action" played out in the Operations Room. As you roam freely about the ship's seven decks, the audio guide soundtrack and authentic smells emanating from the galley and boiler room immerse you in the atmosphere of a battleship on active duty.

HMS Belfast, Morgan's Ln, Tooley St, London SE1, 071-407 6434.  Daily 10 am-5:20 pm. Adults £3.50, children 5-16 £1.75.

## Best "Out Of This World" Spot
The Planetarium

This is the only spot in England where you'll find a cloudless night sky every day. Thanks to the advanced, multi-lens Zeiss projector (which looks like a probe craft from a far-off world), Britain's largest planetarium can in seconds flash across its domed ceiling universe-spanning events which took millions of years to unfold in real time.  During the half-hour "Star Show," you'll see familiar constellations up close, land on other planets, and fly through distant galaxies, all while learning how our ideas about the stars have changed through the centuries. Less educational but equally mind-expanding are the Planetarium's evening laser light shows, set to the music of groups such as Pink Floyd, Genesis, and the Beatles.

The London Planetarium, Marylebone Rd, London NW1, 071-486 1121. Mon-Fri 9 am-5:30 pm, Sat-Sun 9:30 am-5:30 pm (from 10 am in winter). £2.95.

## Largest Collection Of Historic British Cars In One Place
British Heritage Motor Museum

From the first wobbly Wolseleys (in the 1890s) to today's sleek styles, this museum offers the single largest collection of British automobiles gathered anywhere. There are nearly 100 vehicles on display, dating from 1895 to current models, with a heavy concentration on sporty Jaguars and Austins (which arguably represent the collective peak of British car-making). For the most part, the cars are lined up in close ranks, making the museum seem like somewhat of a carpark for time-travelling motorists! Audio-visual presentations offer information about the cars displayed; lectures and tours are available by appointment (otherwise, pre-recorded cassettes can be used to accompany a self-guided tour). The Museum is on the grounds of the garden-filled Syon Park (see separate listing). And, if you're looking for the largest collection of *contemporary* British (and German and Japanese) cars in one place, we suggest you try the M25 on a Friday afternoon before a Bank Holiday Weekend...

British Heritage Motor Museum, Syon Park, Brentford, Middlesex, 081-560 1378. Mar-Oct daily 10 am-
5:30 pm, Nov-Feb daily 10 am-4 pm. Adults £2, children 6-16 & OAPs £1, under 6 free.

## Best Classic Ballet
The Royal Ballet, Royal Opera House

From new offerings such as David Bintley's and
Wilfred Joseph's adaptation of Rostand's *Cyrano
de Bergerac* to classics such as *Swan Lake* and
*Agon*, the ultimate Balanchine/Stravinsky neo-
classical ballet, the Royal Ballet offers up performances of unmatched passion in a breathtaking
setting. The multi-tiered, 2,158-seat theatre is
resplendent with lights in ornate sconces and
crimson curtains embroidered in gold with Her
Majesty's Crest. Bring your opera glasses to see
how masterfully the company uses every inch of
the massive stage. It's often difficult to obtain tickets for the most popular productions, but 65 seats
in the Rear Amphitheatre are sold on the day of
every performance, beginning at 10 a.m. These
tickets are available only to personal callers, with
a limit of one seat per person. After all 65 are sold,
some standing-room tickets usually will be available for £6.50-£7.50. The Royal Opera House also
plays host to some of the world's leading opera
companies and performers (see separate listing).

The Royal Ballet, Royal Opera House, Covent Garden, London, WC2, 071-240 1066. Box office open
Mon-Sat 10 am-8 pm.  Unrestricted view seats for
full-length ballets, £20.50-£45; matinées, £15-£33.

## Best Theatre Complex
Royal National Theatre

Even if you don't have tickets to one of the six
shows in repertoire at the Royal National on any
given evening, stop by the complex while you're in
the South Bank Centre area. You'll find at least
two free exhibits on the history of British theatre,
free music in the foyer, an extensive theatre bookshop, and an enjoyable restaurant with a great
view of the Thames. The complex's three theatres—the Olivier, Lyttleton, and Cottesloe—are
each unique in design and purpose. The fan-
shaped Olivier seats 1,160, but it maintains an
aura of intimacy during large productions with two
banks of sharply raked seats which sweep down to
the stage. The mid-size Lyttelton is remarkably
versatile: Part of its proscenium stage can be lowered to form a pit, and the main acting area can be
angled to suit the needs of particular shows. A
flexible floor plan makes the 400-seat Cottesloe

ideal for experimental works. Tea-and-Tour packages let you tuck into a leisurely tea of sandwiches, scones, jam, and cream before taking a trip backstage to see the inner workings of all three theatres—the scenery docks and workshops, as well as the auditoria and front-of-house areas.

The Royal National Theatre, South Bank, London SE1, 071-928 2252. Box office open Mon-Sat 10 am-8 pm. Show tickets range from £6.50-£16.

## *The* Classic London Theatre
### Drury Lane, Theatre Royal

Known today for its blockbuster musicals, "Old Drury" has been putting up spectacular productions of one kind or another on the same site for more than 325 years, making it the oldest theatre in the world still in continuous use as a playhouse. Now in its fourth building (constructed in 1812 after the third one burned down), this thespian landmark has attracted every monarch of England since Charles II to its Royal Box to see performances by nearly every English actor of note. Since its establishment by Royal Charter in 1660, all manner of unlikely beasts and improbable stage sets have graced the boards of the theatre. Real horses were led onstage in 1870 during *Henry V*, a production of *Carmen* used bulls, and, in 1897 in *The White Heather*, actors in diving suits staged an underwater fight to the death in a large tank. In recent years, dazzling productions of *42nd Street* and *Miss Saigon* have been sell-out successes. But the theatre's record for consecutive performances (2,281) still is held by the 1958-63 production of *My Fair Lady*, starring Rex Harrison and Julie Andrews. For a show to become a hit here, legend suggests that it must first please a 17th-century apparition known only as "The Man in Grey." For many years, it seems, audience members have reported seeing a ghost wearing a tri-cornered hat, powdered wig, ruffled shirt, riding cloak, and dress sword walking through walls in the Upper Circle section on the opening days of soon-to-be-smash productions.

Drury Lane, Theatre Royal, Catherine St, London WC2, 071-836 8108. Performances Mon-Sat 8 pm, matinées Wed and Sat 3 pm.

## Best Restored 19th-Century Theatre
### The Old Vic

The facade and interior of this 170-year-old workhorse have been restored to their 19th-century appearance, when this was a classic, ornate example of Regency-period architecture. But theatregoers will appreciate just as much the modern improvements made during the recent remodelling effort. The proscenium arch has been moved back to improve the Old Vic's sight lines, air conditioning has been installed, more seats and stage boxes have been constructed, and the stage has been trebled in size. Best of all, these major changes have been made without sacrificing the integrity of the original structure. The backstage areas have been almost completely modernised, however, allowing the theatre to offer the most current productions in an historic playhouse setting. The theatre's offerings range from revivals of classic plays to new, experimental works. Before or after a performance, you can toast these efforts in one of the theatre's five bars.

The Old Vic, Waterloo Rd, London SE1, 071-928 7616. Box office open daily 10 am-8 pm. Performances Mon-Fri 7:30 pm, Sat 4 pm and 7:45 pm; Wed matinée 2:30 pm. Unrestricted view seats £9-£17.50. Wed matinée £7.50-£16.

## Best Established Theatre For New And Non-Traditional Works
### Royal Court Theatre

Ever since the English Stage Company's ground breaking 1956 production of John Osborne's *Look Back in Anger*, the Royal Court has been a champion of new writers and the principal home of the theatrical avant garde in Britain. The pioneering program—which launched the careers of well-known playwrights such as Edward Bond, Ann Jellicoe, David Hare, and Howard Brenton—remains committed to helping the future stars of cutting-edge drama cut their teeth with a maximum amount of artistic freedom. This is thought-provoking theatre, where writers from all segments of society address the social, economic, political, and personal problems of the day. Especially exciting is the annual Young Writers' Festival, which showcases the newest, most diverse works by playwrights as young as 10 years old.

Royal Court Theatre, Sloane Sq, London SW1, 071-730 1745. Performances Mon-Sat 8 pm, matinée Sat 4 pm. Tickets £5-£15.

## Best Theatre-Ticket Bargains
### Leicester Square Half-Price Ticket Booth

Or, in other words, how to catch some of the best shows in London theatre without planning ahead or paying full price. Head for the colourful wooden hut on the north side of Leicester Square; open from noon to 2 p.m. (for matinées) and 2:30 to 6:30 p.m. (for evening shows), this booth sells unsold or returned tickets for same-day performances. These tickets are available for cash only (half of their face value, plus a service charge of £1-£1.25), and there is a four-ticket limit per person. A board outside the booth lists what's available each day—and these do not usually include the biggest hits (since these are often sold out and seldom returned)...But, since the available tickets change every day, patience and diligence can be occasionally rewarded with a couple of scarce ducats for the latest Lloyd Webber extravaganza. Don't be intimidated by the sometimes-long queues stretching around the booth—they usually move quickly.

Leicester Square Half-Price Ticket Booth, Leicester Square, London WC2. Mon-Sat noon-6:30 pm.

## Best Transatlantic Theatre Tickets

British Airways

Travellers from the United States can get access to the best seats in the house at more than 38 London theatres, plus performances of the London Philharmonic, the Royal Opera and Ballet at Covent Garden, and other entertainment events. British Airways' passengers may choose from among London's hottest shows, including *Phantom of the Opera*, *Miss Saigon*, and *Les Misérables*, and receive a voucher for the seat and performance of their choice. Then, in London, they simply exchange the voucher for a ticket at one of two Edwards & Edwards West End theatre agencies. Theatre bookings are available up to seven days in advance of departure through travel agents and from British Airways.

British Airways sales offices, 800/AIRWAYS.

# SPORTS (SPECTATOR)

## Best Place To Sleep Through A Cricket Match

Lords Cricket Grounds

With its famous Old Father Time weathervane (the game isn't *that* boring!), Lords is the home and shrine of cricket. A test match (the English equivalent of America's baseball World Series) pitting an England team against a touring Commonwealth eleven, is played there each year, along with a schedule of professional and amateur fixtures. Lords is the home of the Marylebone Cricket Club (MCC), dating from the late 18th century, and of the sport's governing body. The Memorial Gallery chronicles the game and houses the terra cotta urn containing the ashes of an 18th-century wicket—the prized "Ashes" competed for by English and Australian teams. The new "Gestetner Tour of Lords," began in 1990, is a must for cricket fans, but may also interest others, particularly tennis players. Expert guides take visitors on a tour of Lords and its exhibits, and videos screen great moments in the sport—the likes of England's Len Hutton and Australia's Don Bradman smacking mighty boundaries. The rules of lawn tennis were drawn up by the MCC, and the Lords' Tennis Court provides an opportunity to see tennis played as it was in the time of Henry VIII.

Lords Cricket Grounds, St. John's Wood Rd, London NW8, 071-289 1611. Tours daily (except Sunday morning—check for other exceptions) at 10 am, noon, 2 pm, 4 pm. Adults £3.50, children & OAPs £1.50.

## Best Behind-The-Scenes Look At The Cup Final

Wembley Stadium Tours

The immaculate turf of Wembley Stadium often has been referred to as "hallowed ground," but by none so tellingly as Bobby Charlton, star of England's 1966 World Cup championship team. It is ground that also has been stomped upon by massive, 25-stone William "Refrigerator" Perry of the Chicago Bears (who play that other, funny kind of football). But football, despite such big-draw events as cup finals and international matches, accounts for only 15 percent of the activity at Wembley (which has completed a £1-million facelift). Since King George V opened the Empire Exhibition in 1924, Wembley has seen appearances by the Pope, Billy Graham, the Beatles, Michael Jackson, the annual *Holiday On Ice* skaters, Muhammad Ali, racing greyhounds, and performers in the Live Aid Concert and Nelson Mandela 70th Birthday Tribute. The popular "Horse of the Year" show (see separate listing) has created such equestrian stars as Pat Smythe and David Broome. You can capture a lot of this history and excitement with a behind-the-scenes tour of the stadium that includes visits to the Royal Box, dressing rooms, and the famed tunnel where teams emerge to the mighty Wembley roar.

Wembley Stadium, Empire Way, Wembley, Middlesex HA9 0DW, 081-903 4864.

## Best Battle Of The Blues

Oxford And Cambridge Boat Race

Compared to such over-hyped, drawn-out spectacles as the American Super Bowl and the World Cup football matches, this venerable sports rivalry is downright genteel. Genteel, perhaps, but certainly not subdued...Cheering fans line the banks of the Thames, from Putney to Mortlake, rooting for their favourite among the blue-clad teams of eight rowers apiece: Cambridge (light blue) or Oxford (dark blue). First held in 1829—and rowed on this stretch of the river since 1845—the four-mile race is run annually in late March or early April on a Saturday afternoon. The Fulham/Putney Railway Bridge (the busiest of the Thames bridges) is the starting spot for the race upstream—marked officially by the Universities' Stone on the south bank of the river near the bridge. The best—and perhaps most crowded—vantage point for the start of the race are the riverside terraces of Bishop's Park, adjoining the Fulham Palace, which used to be the residence of the Bishop of London. Shortly following the famous race—sometimes held later the same day or the following week—is the Head of the River Race, open to all crews of eight, and usually rowed downstream (the opposite, *easier*, direction than the Oxford-Cambridge race).

Oxford And Cambridge Boat Race, River Thames, from Putney to Mortlake, Sat in late Mar/early Apr (usually nearest Easter).

## Best Regal River Romp

Henley Royal Regatta

This international rowing regatta, held in early July, dates from 1839 and is as much a crucial engagement on the British social calendar as it is an athletic event. Ostensibly, it matches, on a course marked out along a straight stretch of the Thames, international rowing teams who compete in boats of various configurations, ranging from single scullers to crews of up to eight. But the big doings are beside the river, with tailgate picnics conducted from gleaming Rolls Royces and on sleek motor launches tied up on the river. With high society out for its annual river romp and corporate launches stretching travel and entertainment budgets to the limit, it's a time of old-school ties, the old-boy network, multi-hued blazers, straw boaters, fashionable sun dresses, and floppy sun hats. The fare runs to champagne, strawberries, and pâté de foie gras toted in expensive picnic hampers equipped with all of the trappings for elegant alfresco dining. The event also attracts the plebian masses who stretch out along the public towpath with picnic cloths and coolers. Henley-on-Thames, Surrey, is an English country town well worth exploring, with lots of tearooms, Georgian cottages, half-timbered inns, and quaint riverside pubs. Landed gentry like to land at the Red Lion Hotel, a former coaching inn dating from the 16th century. The Bull is the town's oldest pub, dating from the 15th century. Regatta brochures available from:

Henley Royal Regatta, Regatta Headquarters, Henley-on-Thames, Oxon RG9 2LY.

## Most Famous Grass-Court Tennis In The World

All England Lawn Tennis & Croquet Club

From "Big Bill" Tilden to Billie Jean King to Bjorn

Borg to Steffi Graf, this club (which commonly is known simply as Wimbledon) has hosted the very best players in tennis. The tournament is held annually over a fortnight from late June through early July, and, as you might expect, it is very difficult to get tickets—hopeful visitors should plan months ahead and send in for the ticket lottery for the best seats, queue up (overnight waiting is necessary at times) for a limited number of less-desirable same-day seats, or be prepared to pay top price to a scalper (up to £1,000 for a prime Centre Court seat). Even if your visit does not coincide with the hectic championship fortnight, you can visit the club to watch other matches and to visit a museum featuring displays on past champions, changing tennis fashions, and audiovisual presentations of famous matches; there also are exhibits of trophies and other memorabilia. During the tournament, museum admission is limited to ticketholders. (To be included in the annual ticket lottery, you must place your request by January 31 of the year in which you wish tickets—but try by September of the preceding year to get your request in before the crush. Write to: Ballot Office, All England Lawn Tennis & Croquet Club, PO Box 98, Church Road, Wimbledon, London SW19 5AE.)

All England Lawn Tennis & Croquet Club, Church Rd, Wimbledon, London SW19, 081-946 6131. Championship tournament held annually late Jun-early Jul. Museum hours: Tue-Sat 11 am-5 pm, Sun 2-5 pm (closed to non-ticketholders during tournament).

# Best Equestrian Star-Maker

Horse of the Year Show

Britons love show jumping, perhaps because it is one of the few sports in which they continue to excel in world competition. That may account for the popularity of the "Horse of the Year Show" which brings to Wembley Stadium every year in early October six days of jumping and riding in individual and team competition. This show is a star-maker. Every year since 1949 (since 1958 at Wembley), hopeful young men and women, immaculate in their traditional scarlet jackets, vie for the top prizes and international fame and fortune. The public loves Cinderella stories, such as that of Pat Smythe, an unknown rider mounted on her dam Kitty, who pulled the milk float in her home village. Together, young woman and horse overcame the established champions and their prized thoroughbreds; Pat became the heroine of the show and went on to a long and successful career as an international star. The show itself has become a national institution.

Horse of the Year Show, Wembley Stadium, Empire
Way, Middlesex HA9 ODW, 081-900 1234.

## Best Close-in Horse Track
Epsom Race Course

For a combination horse race and social spectacle
second only to a posh outing at Royal Ascot (as
famously depicted in *My Fair Lady*), head to this
track early each June for the annual running of
the Derby (pronounced "DAR-bee") Stakes. This
famous event attracts a widely mixed (and large)
crowd of make-a-quid punters and see-and-be-
seen socialites, and can be a fun outing—especially if your pony comes in on the money! To hone
your wagering skills, journey to Epsom when the
crush isn't as great—the track hosts a year-
around varied schedule of racing, including meetings both during the week and on weekends, as
well as on summer evenings; these schedules vary,
and are not continuous (i.e., they do not run every
day in a row). Epsom also offers nice dining
options throughout the park, ranging from formal
feasting to quick bar bites and beverages. (Kemp-
ton Park and Sandown Park are also convenient to
London; the Epsom phone number can give information for the schedules at all three tracks.)

Epsom Race Course, Epsom, Surrey KT8, 0372
726311. Days and hours vary.

## Best Place For A "Di" At The Races
Royal Ascot

Toffs in toppers, Royals doing their best to look
regal, fashionable society showcasing the season's
latest fashions, plenty of champagne and caviar,
and convoys of Rolls Royces and Bentleys—expect
all of this, and more (including some superb thor-
oughbred horseracing) during Royal Ascot week.
Held annually during mid-June, Royal Ascot is a
four-day meeting of flat racing attended by the
Queen, Princess Diana, and other members of the
Royal family. A daily highlight is the Royal Procession each afternoon. The pretty Ascot Racecourse
(about 30 miles west of London, near Windsor) has
had royal connections since it was opened in 1711
under the aegis of Queen Anne. Spectators will
find that varying admission prices gain them
entrance to such public enclosures as Tattersalls
and the Silver Ring. Diversions include numerous
bars, restaurants, and refreshment tents.
Although the comings and goings (and winnings
and losings) at Royal Ascot grab the international
headlines, Ascot offers an excellent year-around
calendar of race meetings, both flat races and

National Hunt fixtures. In Ascot, the Royal Berkshire, built in 1705 in (appropriately) Queen Anne
style, is *the* place to stay and/or dine in a restaurant with a charming garden view.

Ascot Racecourse, Ascot, Berkshire SL5 7JN, 0990
22211. Royal Ascot held mid-Jun.

## Best Bets For Watching Association Football

To millions of fans in Britain, football is the game
played mostly with the feet that is known to Americans as "soccer." (The word "soccer" is actually a
corruption of "Association Football," the correct
English name for the game.) London is well-
endowed with a dozen professional football teams.
The glamour clubs are the north-London sides of
Arsenal and Tottenham Hotspurs. Football fans
have strong local affiliations—south Londoners
support Crystal Palace and Charlton Athletic (who
share a ground since Charlton lost its famous
venue at The Valley); east Londoners follow the
fortunes of West Ham United and Leyton Orient;
central Londoners often are fans of Chelsea (nicknamed "The Pensioners"), Fulham, and Queens
Park Rangers. Teams play in four ascending divisions. At the end of each season, the top teams in
each lower division are "promoted" to a higher division, while the teams at the bottom of each division's standings are "relegated" to a lower division.
Besides league competition, there are international
matches (all-England sides versus other national
teams), and play in the FA Cup, an annual knock-
out competition with pairings determined by lottery (regardless of division standing), with the two
surviving teams meeting at Wembley in the FA cup
final. The season runs from late August to May
with games every Saturday, usually with a 3 p.m.
kick-off. Traditionally, British fans watch football
standing up, sometimes packed shoulder-to-shoul-
der, on terraces. Reserved grandstand seating is
recommended for visitors—especially in view of the
sometimes-violent hooliganism that has marred
football matches in recent years.

League and cup play at various London stadia; international matches and FA Cup Final at Wembley.

## Best Bet For Watching Rugby Football
Twickenham Rugby Union Football Ground

Twickenham is to rugby union football what Wembley is to association football. It is the home of the
sport's controlling body and the spot to see major
matches, such as "internationals," where all-Eng-

land teams take on the best from France, Argentina, Australia, and other countries. Here is where
you'll also see traditional rivals Oxford and Cambridge battle it out in the Bowring Bowl. For the
uninitiated, this 15-a-side strictly amateur sport
had accidental beginnings. It was in 1823 during a
football match at England's Rugby School that a
schoolboy, disregarding the "feet only" rule,
scooped up the ball in his arms and sprinted
toward goal. Although visiting Americans can see
their own brand of football played in London (see
separate listing), they may be interested in watching this game that was the forerunner of American
football. London has 10 first-class rugby union
clubs—such as the London Welsh, the Harlequins,
the Saracens, and the Wasps, with matches
scheduled on Saturday afternoons from September
through April. Grounds are at various locales
around London, with Twickenham the major
venue for big matches (and also housing a rugby
museum with old uniforms, photographs, a film
about the sport, and behind-the-scenes tours of
the stadium).

Twickenham Rugby Union Football Ground, Whitton
Rd, Twickenham, Middlesex, 081-892 8161.

# Best Bet For Watching American-Style Football

Wembley Stadium

Ever since weekend telecasts of National Football
League games from the United States began in the
mid-1980s, many Londoners have grown fond of
the rough-and-tumble American game. Additionally, to give their British fans a taste of the real
thing, top NFL teams (such as the New York
Giants, Chicago Bears, and Dallas Cowboys) have
been coming to London each summer to participate in an exhibition game, dubbed the American
Bowl, at Wembley. Now—just starting as of this
writing—London has its own American-style football team, the London Monarchs, who compete in
the new, NFL-sponsored World League of American
Football, which plays during the spring months.
(The W.L.A.F. has two other European teams—in
Frankfurt and Barcelona—and seven in the U.S
and Canada.) The Monarchs are owned by Jon
Smith (a noted London sports promoter), are run
by executives and coaches who were formerly with
NFL teams, and play their home games at Wembley; the team's players are a mixture of onetime
NFL players, fresh-from-college prospects, and
even some local amateur footballers. Some deride
the W.L.A.F. as "minor league." While savvy fans
will never mistake Monarchs starting quarterback

John Witkowski for superstar QB Joe Montana, they may just grow to like this interesting experiment in sport importing.

Wembley Stadium, Empire Way, Middlesex HA9 ODW, 081-900 1234. London Monarchs season runs generally from late Mar-late May/early Jun; American Bowl usually held in Jul or Aug.

## Best Place To Be Snookered Into Watching Championship Snooker
Wembley Conference Centre

For legions of fanatical British snooker fans, the sight of red, yellow, green, brown, blue, pink, and black solid-coloured balls on a green felt, six-pocketed table does not look at all unusual. Nor does the fanfare surrounding the annual championship, held at the Wembley Conference Centre each January. For Americans used to the red and white balls of cushion billiards or the "solids and stripes" of pocket billiards (simply referred to as "pool" in the United States), snooker may be foreign, but it can be a simple game to appreciate (if not master!): Players alternate sinking red balls (of which there are 15) and the other six coloured balls; the reds are worth a point each and the coloureds ascend from two to seven points. The game's unusual name refers to a situation in which one player is left without a legally playable shot (due to the position of his cue ball)—he has been "snookered" by his opponent and must pass a turn. This championship is widely televised, and can be a fun spectacle of geometric precision, skill, and cut-throat competition. To get in on some snooker action, contact the sport's official governing body, the Billiards and Snooker Control Council (in Leeds, 0622 440586), for information about snooker venues, clubs, and events; in London, the Centre Point Snooker Club is a good spot to begin or continue your appreciation of this sport.

Wembley Conference Centre, Empire Way, Middlesex HA9 ODW, 081-900 1234. Snooker Championship held each Jan. Centre Point Snooker Club, New Oxford St, London WC1, 071-240 6886. Daily, 24 hours.

## Best Place To Go To The Dogs
Greyhound Racing, Wembley

If the Derby and Royal Ascot are morning coats and top hats, greyhound racing is shiny suit jackets and cloth caps. The sport of dog racing was imported to England from the United States in the mid 1920s, and quickly became a hit with members of the working class who couldn't attend horse races because the tracks were generally too far out of the city and the races were run during working hours. And while a night watching the lean pups chasing a mechanical hare is somewhat of a working-class institution, it is by no means a not-suitable-for-the-family outing. The dog track at Wembley (which is set up in a cordoned-off area along one side of the huge stadium) is clean, attracts a mixture of upmarket as well as more plebian patrons, and features a restaurant and bar. Bets can range from 10p and up—and you never know when any particular dog is going to have its day (or night, in this case). Other nearby dog tracks are at Wimbledon (which recently underwent £2 million in refurbishments), Catford (small and less upmarket than Wembley), Hackney, and Walthamstow.

Wembley Stadium, Empire Way, Middlesex HA9 ODW, 081-908 8833. Mon, Wed, Fri, Sat starting at 7:30 pm. Wimbledon Stadium, Plough Ln, London SW19, 081-946 5361. Tues, Thu-Sat starting at 7:30 pm. Catford Stadium, Ademore Rd, London SE26, 081-690 2261. Mon, Wed, Sat starting at 7:30 pm.

# Best Spot For The Swiftest, Farthest, And Highest Track And Field Achievements
Crystal Palace National Sports Centre

Does the U.K. have another Sebastian Coe or Daley Thompson (Britain's most notable track and field Olympians of the 1980s) ready to burst on the international sporting scene? Head to the track and field events held at this sports centre to scout possible future British Olympics stars—or just to enjoy some hard-competed amateur athletics. These track and field events are sponsored by the Amateur Athletic Association; the championships of the A.A.A., open to any amateur athlete from anywhere in the world, are offered here each June or July. (Special women's and college championships also are held at the Crystal Palace in spring and early summer.) The A.A.A. can provide information about local track and field events, clubs, and facilities. In addition to running ovals and field-event areas, the Crystal Palace National Sports Centre also has an Olympic-sized swimming pool and racquet-sports courts. Built in the late 1950s and early 1960s, the sports centre was named after the famed Crystal Palace (the centrepiece of the 1851 Exhibition), which was moved to this site, in Sydenham, in 1854; it burned down in a spectacular fire in 1936 (its foundations remain; a museum on the site commemorates the once-impressive edifice).

Crystal Palace National Sports Centre, Ledrington Rd, London SE19, 081-778 0131. A.A.A. championships held Jun or Jul. Amateur Athletic Association, Francis House, Francis St, London SW1, 071-828 9326.

# SPORTS (PARTICIPANT)

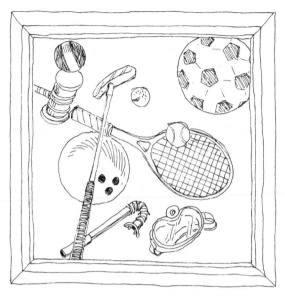

## Most Grueling Guided Tour Of London

The London Marathon

This may not be the ideal way to see the sights of London—by running 26 miles, 385 yards (just under 42 kilometers) through it—but to its devotees, there is no greater challenge. The London Marathon has only been around since 1981, but it has already become one of the largest marathons in the world (along with the massive New York race; the Boston Marathon attracts a prestigious field, but isn't as large). Run each April, the marathon begins at the Tower Bridge, and runs to the Isle of Dogs, Tower Wharf, Victoria Embankment, the Mall, St. James's Park, and finishes up at Westminster Bridge; the race takes a little more than two hours for the leading runners to complete. Due to its convenience to the marathon's starting line, the Tower Thistle Hotel (see separate listing) is the unofficial headquarters for runners and officials; its bar and lounge are good spots to watch televised coverage of the race after its spectacular massed start.

The London Marathon, 081-948 7935. Run each Apr.

# Savviest Cycling Routes In And Around London

The Cyclist's Touring Club

The countryside around London can be ideal for exploration by bicycle, provided you know how to avoid traffic-congested arteries. For help organising a tour of the hundreds of miles of cycling lanes around London, don't spin your wheels poring over disparate maps and brochures. Instead, ask the club that's been helping cyclists gear up for area trips since 1878. More than 40,000 Britons currently wear the CTC's winged-wheel badge, and most are happy to introduce visitors to the joys of coasting along the sun-dappled lanes around London or of pumping hard over the surrounding hills and rolling downs. The CTC offers extensive guided tours, tips on self-guided trips ranging from 15-100 miles (24-160 kilometers), several regular publications, and a complete cycling shop where you can pick up clothes, books, maps, spare parts, and other accessories.

The Cyclist's Touring Club, 69 Meadow, Godalming, Surrey GU7 3HS, 0483 426994.

# Nicest Ice Fit For A Queen

Queens Ice Skating Club

Get with the floe on this indoor club's 14,000 square feet of ice, an immaculately groomed surface that carries the blades of awkward amateurs and world-champion British skaters alike. If you're in need of a pointer or two, a refresher lesson from one of the club's 16 pro instructors will have you quietly gliding to the sounds of Alan Marshall at the electric organ quicker than you can say "Peggy Fleming." Nor need you worry about being bowled over by a speed demon; Queens doesn't allow hockey or speed skates on the ice. If you like to turn your figure eights at a higher tempo, however, show up for fast-paced disco sessions on Saturday and Sunday nights. After hanging up your rental blades, you can head for the Queen's Bar (open seven days a week) to view the panoramic procession on the rink as you enjoy ice of a different kind, sipping a tall drink from the bar's on-high vantage point.

Queens Ice Skating Club, Queens Court, Queensway, London W2, 071-229 0172.

# Best Park For Hacks

Horseback Riding In Hyde Park

Soapbox speakers, boaters, bathers, and courting

couples seek their place in the sun—or in the shade—amid the green expanse of London's largest park. And so do equestrians, who enjoy cantering along Hyde Park's leafy bridle paths, as did gentlefolk in the 17th and 18th centuries who would hope to gain notice of the court by parading in their sartorial splendor along Rotten Row, corrupted from the regal French *Route de Roi* (see separate listing). Horses long have been associated with the park's history. It has contained a royal hunting preserve and a racecourse, and, to this day, members of the elite Household Calvary stable and exercise their mounts in the park; you can see them drill at dawn along Rotten Row. Experienced riders can hire horses from the stables of the nearby Ross Nye riding school. For novice riders, lessons are available (£12 groups, £16 private).

Ross Nye Riding School, 8 Bathurst Mews, London W2, 071-262 3791. Tue-Sat 7 am-4:30 pm, Sun 10 am-4:30 pm.

## Best Course For Hackers

Richmond Park

The calibre of surroundings and play here are not likely to get you ready for a round at Royal St. Andrews, but this course probably is the best bet for public golfing close to London. Richmond is a huge park—the largest Royal Park in England—and it offers a variety of scenic splendors, as well as a lodge that is a perfect spot for alfresco tea (see separate listing). Its two 18-hole courses are very popular with local duffers, but are surprisingly well-groomed for a well-trod public facility. Reservations for tee times are available by phone, and there is equipment available for hire and a fully stocked pro shop. Prices are £5 per round on weekdays, £7.50 per round on weekends; computerized teaching sessions run £25 per, and a driving range lets you practice whacking at balls for £3.50 per hour. There are also decent public courses at Wimbledon Common and Mitcham Common, and several private courses (with temporary memberships available to members of comparable clubs or to guests of certain hotels) just outside of London.

Richmond Park, Roehampton Gate, Priory Ln, Richmond, Surrey, 081-876 3205. Open daily; hours vary by season.

## Best Tennis Courts

Holland Park and Battersea Park

Tennis in and around London isn't all strawberries

and cream and Wimbledon fortnight. Most of the city's parks have some sort of hard-court tennis facilities; the following two examples are among the most notable. Holland Park, in fashionable Kensington, offers six hard courts, and is considered somewhat of a trendy spot for area residents and visitors; court fees are £3 per hour, no reservations are taken. Battersea Park, a huge park along the south bank of the Thames (see separate listing), is another good spot for tennis. It offers 20 hard-surface courts, including nine which are lit at night; reservations are available three days in advance, and court fees run £2 per hour. There are also good hard courts at Hyde Park, Regent's Park, and Lincoln's Inn Fields. For tennis on grass courts (à la Wimbledon), contact the Lawn Tennis Association—at 071-385 2366—for a list of lawn-tennis clubs and courts.

Holland Park, Kensington High St, London W8, 071-602 2226. Open daily, hours vary by season. Battersea Park, Battersea Park Rd, London SW11, 081-871 7542. Open daily, hours vary by season.

# Best Swimming Pools

## Seymour Leisure Centre or Chelsea Sports Centre

If you've a desire to undertake some indoor diving and paddling, the pools at these sports centres are sure to keep you in the swim of things. Mornings and evenings during the week and all day on weekends are the best times to suit up for a dip at Chelsea Sports Centre. Adults and children can take lessons here by the half-hour, but adventurous types might want to enroll for a lesson at Chelsea's Mermaid Diving Centre. A two-hour session includes an hour's dry-land instruction on scuba diving and an hour practising looking for "sunken treasure" in the pool. At the Seymour Leisure Centre, you can put on the goggles for a dip any time of the day, or slap on a green eyeshade for pool of a different sort in the snooker room. Both centres also offer a wide variety of other indoor pursuits, such as squash, badminton, volleyball, net ball, and aerobics. Seymour also offers a popular Kid Morning every Saturday, when the little ones can have a go at games such as bouncing castle, badminton, and football.

Chelsea Sports Centre, Chelsea Manor St, London SW3, 071-352 6985/0366. Open daily (hours & admission fees vary). Seymour Leisure Centre, Seymour Pl, London W1, 071-798 1421. Open daily (hours & admission fees vary).

# Best Bets For Compleat Angling

London Reservoirs

Since Izaak Walton's day, fishing around London has sadly deteriorated, especially in the lakes and ponds. Of course, it is possible to dunk a line as close in as the lake in Battersea Park and the Serpentine in Hyde Park—or head out to the Hollow Ponds at Whipps Cross in East London where anglers cast for tench, perch, and pike, and small boys collect newts in jars and ride their bikes over the sandy hills. But for quality fishing, anglers hie to two major reservoir areas where good ecological management has created productive fishing waters and havens for waterfowl and other birds. You can fish for game fish at Barn Elm Reservoir, stocked with salmon and brown and rainbow trout: this is also a major breeding ground for reed warblers and a preserve where ornithologists go to spot such species as goosanders and great crested grebes. Boats are available for hire. The Walthamstow Reservoirs, in the valley of the River Lee, also are ecologically protected, and are another popular bird-watching area. These waters are stocked with trout as well as coarse fish such as tench, roach, and bream. (To fish in the Thames area you'll need a rod licence available from angling shops or from the Thames Water Authority—Nugent House, Vastern Rd, Reading RG 8HQ, Berkshire, 0734 593921.) A permit and fee are required to fish the reservoirs.

Barn Elm Reservoirs, London SW13, 081-748 3423, near Hammersmith Underground station; Walthamstow Reservoirs, London N17, 081-808 1527, near Tottenham Hale Underground station.

# Best Health Clubs

London offers a wide variety of choices for residents or visitors who want to keep in shape. Among its myriad health clubs, a few stand out: *Flames* is more of a traditional gym than a modern health club, but it is good. It offers a large gym area, considered one of the best in the entire city, and includes pedal bikes, treadmills, and free weights, as well as a full complement of Nautilus machines. You'll work extra hard to work up a sweat here—the gym is pleasantly air conditioned. Day memberships are a bargain at £10, including all facilities. *Lambton Place Health Club* is a bit more posh and more of a complete health club (more expensive, too). It has a large swimming pool, a spa and steam baths, and a full complement of gym equipment and weight machines. Day memberships are priced from £15-£23, depending upon which facilities are desired. *The Sanctuary* is a women-only club where patrons can be pampered (with sauna, spa bath, massage, facials, and make-up consultation) or work up a satisfying sweat (with aerobics and weight machines). A bit pricey at £28.50 per day (or £19.50 for evening only), but the cost includes plenty of activities and services. Many hotels have full or partial health clubs or usage arrangements for guests at nearby clubs; one of the most attractive and complete hotel health clubs is the *Aquilla Health Club* at the Rembrandt Hotel (see separate listing).

Flames, Galena House, Galena Rd, London W6, 081-741 8536. Mon-Fri 7 am-10 pm, Sat 9 am-6 pm, Sun 10 am-4 pm. Lambton Place Health Club, Lambton Pl, London W11, 071-229 2291. Mon-Fri 7 am-11 pm, Sat & Sun 9 am-5 pm. The Sanctuary, 11-12 Floral St, London WC2, 071-240 9635. Mon-Fri 10 am-10 pm, Sat 10 am-6 pm, Sun noon-8 pm.

# Best Jogging Area

Hyde Park

Where boars, bulls, and other wild animals once roamed for the hunting pleasure of Henry VIII, today you'll often find humans dashing along park paths. Hyde Park is not only London's leading spot for outdoor recreation—it is also a prime spot for jogging. Hyde Park is the biggest Royal Park in London, and, along with the contiguous Kensington Gardens to its west, it offers an inviting 600 acres of green parkland, broken only by pleasant rows of shade trees and attractive stretches of water. Paths crisscross wide expanses of rolling lawns, connecting in spokes that lead to the park's corners and edges, and skirt the water of the Serpentine lake (an especially scenic and popular spot for running). The park is generally considered safe, but, for prevention's sake, solo jogging at dusk and after is not suggested. Other sightseeing highlights in Hyde Park include Rotten Row and Speakers' Corner (see separate listings). Regent's Park (to the north of the West End) and Battersea Park (on the south bank of the river, across from Chelsea) also offer some good paths for jogging.

Hyde Park, London W1; near Hyde Park Corner and Marble Arch Underground stations.

# KIDS

## Best Museum For Kids—Of All Ages

Bethnal Green Museum of Childhood

For children, it's a marvellous storehouse of toys and games that provide a perspective of history and a lively introduction to the function of museums. For adults, it's a place to awaken memories of childhood—of Ludo games and bagatelle, Hornby train sets and magic lanterns. With about 4,000 toys, this museum contains the largest collection on public view in the world. There also are more than 1,400 dolls and 46 doll's houses, ranging from a 15-room Victorian mansion to tiny home-made cottages. You'll find a toy butcher shop, circa 1880, and a puppet collection that includes Punch and Judy, Chinese glove puppets, and a rare 18th-century Venetian marionette theatre. There are German miniature market stalls, circa 1920, games galore, exquisite toy soldiers, musical toys, optical toys, model trains and boats, and an entire section of educational toys. Look for a fascinating model of an early, itinerant toy seller. There is a companion collection of childhood clothes and furnishings, and a small gift shop.

Bethnal Green Museum of Childhood, Cambridge Heath Rd, London E2, 081-980 3204. Mon-Thu & Sat 10 am-6 pm, Sun 2:30-6 pm. Free.

# Robert Louis Stevenson's Favourite Museum For Kids

## Pollock's Toy Museum

Paper and cardboard toy theatres, replete with cut-out sets, props, and tiny actors, were as ubiquitous among British children of the Victorian era as Lincoln Logs were among American children of generations past. This museum, named for Ben Pollock, one of England's most-famous toy-theatre craftsmen, preserves the memory of the toy theatre and countless other playthings from long-ago eras and numerous nations. The collection, displayed in two little houses on Scala Street, brims with antique dolls, board games, toy animals, model cars and railways, early children's peep shows, lead miniatures, folk toys from Eastern Europe, and, of course, rainbow-hued examples of Pollock's hand-coloured theatres. Adults and children alike will delight in exploring the small, toy-stuffed rooms connected by narrow, winding staircases before paying a visit to the ground-level museum shop for cardboard toy-theatre replicas. As Robert Louis Stevenson once remarked: "If you love art, folly, or the bright eyes of children, speed to Pollock's."

Pollock's Toy Museum, 1 Scala St, London W1, 071-636 3452. Mon-Sat 10 am-5 pm. Adults £1, children 50p.

# Best Zoo That's *Not* The London Zoo

## Battersea Park Children's Zoo

Unlike London's big zoo in Regent's Park (see separate listing) that usually is considered a destination for a major outing, this compact children's zoo in Battersea Park is made-to-measure for shorter visits on days when you want to crowd in a variety of diversions. And it is perfect for younger children whose attention span may not be up to a full day, or even a half-day, of peering at animals. At this recently remodelled zoo youngsters can enjoy pony rides and get up close to animals at a petting enclosure. The collection includes monkeys, wallabies, sheep, pygmy goats, an aviary, and a reptile house. Battersea Park (see separate listing) is kid-friendly. Other activities include boating, roller skating, tennis, and special events that include a fun fair at Easter culminating in a big parade. There is a deer enclosure and playing fields.

Children's Zoo, Battersea Park, London SW11, 081-871 7540; near Sloan Square Underground station (then bus). Easter-Sep Mon-Fri 1:30-5:30 pm, Sat & Sun 11:30 am-6 pm.

## Best Teddy Bears' Picnic
London Toy and Model Museum

Teddies deserve a day out too, don't you think? Bring your—or your kids'—cuddly bear to this museum on a selected day in July (inquire with the museum for the exact date each year), and join guests from the museum's collection of teddy bears for a lovely garden picnic. Housed in a pair of Victorian houses, this is one of the world's best toy museums, offering more than 3,000 toys and models, some dating from the 1700s. Its eight galleries contain large collections of dolls and dollhouses, toy soldiers, boats and cars, and a huge train layout; passenger-carrying steam trains run in the garden outside on Sundays. (There's also a pond for model boats out back.) When they're not sipping tea in the shade with visitors, the museum's large assemblage of teddy bears reside in the Nursery, where London's own Paddington Bear has pride of place. (If your kids know the Paddington stories, you may want to take them to the nearby Paddington Station that gave the plucky little bear his name.)

London Toy and Model Museum, 21-3 Craven Hill Rd, London W2, 071-262 7905. Tue-Sat 10 am-5:30 pm, Sun 11 am-5 pm. Adults £2.20, children 80p.

## Most Fun Jogga Lesson
Commonwealth Institute

Rhythmic steel bands in Trinidad, vast sheep stations in New Zealand, colourful costumes and customs from South Seas' islands, rugged Mount Kenya, and the lore and legend of the Royal Canadian Mounted Police. This museum, opened in 1962 in a singular building with a green copper roof and the flags of close to 50 Commonwealth nations fluttering colourfully out front, focuses on the far-flung alliance of countries that form the British Commonwealth. It offers cultural events, educational programmes, and special activity sheets for children. Three floors of galleries focus on the peoples, history, wildlife, landscapes, arts and crafts, and economic structure of the Commonwealth countries—like a World's Fair covering those vast and diverse areas of the globe that were coloured pink during the halcyon days of the Empire. For kids, it is like a "jogga" lesson—only much more fun. There's an auditorium for films, a restaurant, and a wonderful museum shop that is bazaar-like with unusual crafts, toys, books, games, etc., from around the globe. This museum is recommended for children ages seven and up; booking suggested for special programmes.

Commonwealth Institute, Kensington High St, London W8, 071-603 4535. Mon-Sat 10 am-5 pm, Sun 2-5 pm. Free.

## Best Attraction That You Wouldn't Want To Get Stuck In After Closing Time
### The London Dungeon

As fact often is stranger than fiction, so reality can be more chillingly frightening than fantasy. This series of macabre, life-size tableaux is based on actual grisly events from Britain's past. As you step through the heavy Dungeon doors into the huge, dark vaults beneath London Bridge Station, the eerie lighting and sound effects will send a jolt through your system. Scary though it may be, you're not nearly as bad off as the poor chap hanging by a noose in the Dungeon's reconstruction of Tyburn Gallows, where you'll learn that hanging was the most common means of execution in the days when 300-plus crimes carried the death penalty in Britain. Not for the faint of heart, this hit parade of the nation's most infamous acts of mayhem and murder includes the burning of Protestant martyrs at Smithfield, a depiction of the "art" of drawing and quartering, a working model of "the rack," and the beheading of one of Henry VIII's wives, Anne Boleyn. Elaborate multi-media exhibits immerse you in the Great Fire of London and events surrounding the use of the Guillotine during the French Revolution. Terrified travellers should heed this warning from the proprietors: "Under no circumstances can we be held responsible for any subsequent nightmares."

The London Dungeon, 28-34 Tooley St, London SE1, 071-403 0606. Daily 10 am-4:30 pm. Adults £5, children 14 and under £3.

## Best Children's Theatre
### The Unicorn Theatre For Children

This unicorn isn't extinct, but it certainly is one-of-a-kind! The Unicorn Theatre is the only professional theatre in the West End especially for young audiences—which explains why families from throughout Greater London travel to the theatre district to watch productions with such peculiar titles as *Frankie's Monster* or *Stig of the Dump.* Peculiar-sounding or not, children definitely think the trip is worthwhile. Founded in 1947 on the principle that children should be introduced to the "adult" atmosphere of theatre through professional productions filled with adolescent whimsy, the Unicorn Theatre company offers well-scripted and

-performed plays at the Arts Theatre on Great Newport Street. There are a few differences between Unicorn performances and those of the prestigious Royal Shakespeare Company, of course. For one, afternoon performances are the rule—to better accommodate early bedtimes—and the audiences, made up mostly of four- to 13-year-olds, tend to be fairly exuberant, rather than quietly respectful. But when it comes down to such basics as production values and pure entertainment, each season's four or five plays at the Unicorn are top-flight flights of fancy.

Unicorn Theater for Children, 6-7 Great Newport St, London WC2, 071-836 3334.

## Best Puppet Show (With Strings Attached)

The Little Angel Marionette Theatre

Children and adults enjoy seeing the world on a string at this theatre especially constructed for the presentation of puppetry in all of its forms. If the puppets, sets, and costumes look like hand-made, one-of-a-kind masterpieces-in-miniature, it's because they are. (Craftsmen turn out every element required for a performance—except the scripts and puppeteers!—in a workshop adjacent to the theatre.) The Little Angel's unique audience policy makes it easier for all concerned to enjoy the finer details of each performance; Saturday morning performances are reserved for three-to-six year olds, while afternoon shows on both Saturday and Sunday are open to adults and children over age six. Adults enjoy a cup of cappucino in the theatre's foyer coffee bar while their offspring bounce along to deliciously diverting tales.

The Little Angel Marionette Theatre, 14 Dagmar Passage, Cross St, London N1, 071-226 1787.

## Best Overall Children's Entertainment Destination

Polka Theatre for Children

This comprehensive junior fine arts centre sends young minds galloping into the land of imagination with an overwhelming array of playful activities. Shows in the Adventure Theatre range from bold offerings such as *The Adventures of Star Dog*, about a space mutt's adventures on Earth, to a series of productions focusing on a detective mouse named Pipsqueak. Rather than serving up a full menu of puffery, many productions are aimed at interesting children in science and art. The folks at Polka also showcase traditional story-tellers, puppets, and mime. Other attractions include the Children's Playground, Mr. Punch's Toyshop, and an exhibition describing how the theatre's shows are created.

Polk Theatre for Children, 240 The Broadway, London SW19, 081-543 4888.


## Best Place For The Kids To See A Movie

ICA Children's Cinema Club

Talk about time warp! Many Britons fondly remember cinema clubs and childhood Saturday mornings spent yelling their lungs out at the serialised adventures of cowboys Hoppy, Gene, and Roy, space explorer Flash Gordon, and Britain's own Dick Barton, secret agent. Here's a latterday flick club for kids—in the most unlikely setting. The Institute of Contemporary Arts is an international haven for cutting-edge contemporary arts and culture, but on Saturday and Sunday afternoons, it more resembles a kids' clubhouse. While adults are enjoying the innovative and often-provocative exhibits, children can join the ICA's cinema club (inexpensive one-day memberships are available) for a variety of feature-length films, including the best Disney films, musicals, and young-adventure flicks. This can be an easy, entertaining way to keep the kids occupied while parents enjoy other exhibits at the ICA or various nearby attractions, perhaps taking time for some intense shopping without the kids in tow.

ICA Children's Cinema Club, Nash House, The Mall, London SW1, 071-930 3647.


## Best Place For Kids Who Never Want To Grow Up

Peter Pan statue, Kensington Gardens

It appeared just like magic—a delightful surprise for the children of post-Edwardian London, whom author J. M. Barrie cherished. In 1912, eight years after the debut of his classic play, *Peter Pan*, Barrie commissioned noted sculptor Sir George Frampton to create a statue of the play's famous boy-hero. The statue, which depicts Peter playing a pipe above a base showing scenes and characters from the play, was then placed in Kensington Gardens one night without fanfare. The next day—to the delight of the children who frequented the park—Peter Pan had appeared, as if by magic, to frolic with his playmates. Today, the statue still is a favourite spot for kids and their families (and/or their nannies) to gather; smaller tykes are often seen stalking the bronze rabbits near the statue's base. Not far from the memorial to the fictional eternal boy are two other popular spots for kids: the Children's Playground (in the northwest corner of Kensington Gardens) and the Round Pond, a favoured spot for sailing toy boats.

Peter Pan statue, Kensington Gardens, London W2; near Lancaster Gate Underground station.

## Best Spot To Fly A Kite And Sail A Model Boat
Hampstead Heath

Amidst the hills and ponds of Hampstead Heath (see separate listing) children (of all ages!) will find *the* perfect spot to fly a kite or sail a model boat. There is, in fact, a special pond for model boats where you'll find a flotilla of miniature craft ranging from crude models fashioned by small boys to sleek yachts built to scale with incredible detail, with somewhat older skippers at the helm. As for kite flying, this ranging, hilly expanse of woody heathland is full of spots where a simple kite or an elaborate flying contraption will rise on a steady breeze. One of the most popular kite-flying venues is 319-feet-high Parliament Hill (see separate listing). To outfit a kite-flying expedition, head first to one of the two locations of The Kite Store (see separate listing), for an incredible array of kites to build or buy ready to fly.

Hampstead Heath, London NW3; near Hampstead Underground station.

## Best Spot To Buy Before You Fly
The Kite Store

This is the perfect shop for both types of kite flyers: those who worry about fractured spars and how to keep their kites from "dragging back" rather than "driving through" turns, and those who (like most of the rest of us) simply enjoy the vicarious thrill of hanging onto a multi-coloured, swooping and spinning kite that seems to have a will all its own. For the basic buy-the-kid-his-or-her-first-kite shoppers, there are a variety of traditional flat kites with streamer tails. Displayed right alongside those sweet memories of childhood are more serious toys, including ultra-complex triangular, square, and hexagonal box kites, and kites that resemble bald eagles, bats, seagulls, and mallard ducks. Test your mettle with a Skynasaur Stunt Kite, or fly a fanciful space shuttle, shark, or even a giant, wind-inflated pair of flying legs. Parachuting spiders, flying discs of all types, miniature hot-air balloons, boomerangs, and flying vampire bats round out this exemplary collection of airborne toys. When you're ready to launch your kite, head to the hilly expanses of Hampstead Heath (see separate listing).

The Kite Store, 48 Neal St, London WC2, 071-836 1666. Mon-Fri 10 am-6 pm, Sat 10:30 am-5:30 pm.

## Best Park To Ask A Kid To Take You To
Coram's Fields City Farm

Youngsters feel important on a trip to this slice of bucolic life in the heart of the city. The sign makes it plain: "Adults are not admitted unless accompanied by a child." Kids enjoy a variety of farmyard animals, including ducks, geese, sheep, rabbits, goats, and chickens. Parents can buy fresh eggs— just like on a trip to the country. It is appropriate that kids feel especially welcome, since this was the site of the Foundling Hospital, built in 1745 to care for destitute children roaming the mean streets of London. With space limited, children were admitted or refused shelter by means of a heart-rending drawing of a white or black ball. The hospital was founded by ex-sea captain and philanthropist Thomas Coram, and adjoining the park is headquarters of the foundation that bears his name. Inside are paintings by Hogarth and Gainsborough, a Raphael cartoon, and a manuscript of *Messiah* (both Handel and Hogarth were benefactors of the hospital). Also on display is a heart-tearing collection of coins and tokens left with children by mothers forced to abandon them.

Coram's Fields City Farm, 93 Guildford St, London WC1, 071-837 6138. Apr-Oct daily 8:30 am-9 pm, Nov-Mar Mon-Fri 8:30 am-4:30 pm. Free. Thomas Coram Foundation, 40 Brunswick Sq, London WC1, 071-278 2424. Mon-Fri 10 am-4 pm.

## Most Creative Crypt
London Brass Rubbing Centre

It doesn't *have* to be a rainy day to introduce youngsters to the popular hobby of brass rubbing. But you might reason that if you're going to spend an hour or two in a church crypt, why choose to do it on a sunny day. This centre, in the crypt of the church of St. Martin in the Fields, an imposing classical church designed 1722-1726, has more than 75 replicas of medieval church brasses ready for visitors to use. Subjects range from monarchs, merchants, castles, and courtiers, to knights, bishops, animals, and intricate coats of arms. Admission is free, paper, rubbing materials, and instruction are provided, and you pay according to the size of your work—from 50p to £10.50. If youngsters take to this hobby, there are brass-rubbing kits for sale, plus guidebooks that can launch expeditions to outlying churches. A gift counter also sells posters, postcards, rubbings, and other cultural- and historical-themed mementoes. There is a restaurant alongside the centre.

London Brass Rubbing Centre, St. Martin in the Fields church, Trafalgar Sq, London WC2, 071-437 6023. Mon-Sat 10 am-6 pm, Sun noon-6 pm.

## Best Dining Spot With Kids For Lunch
Smollensky's Balloon

A steakhouse isn't necessarily the first place you'd think of to take kids for a family lunch...But Smollensky's Balloon is definitely not exactly your average steakhouse! Beside its regular menu of steak, chop, roast, and burger specialities, this restaurant also offers great family meals on Saturday and Sunday afternoons, from noon-3 p.m. The menu for these meals includes kids-size burgers, steaks, and ice cream sundaes, a special peanut butter cheesecake, and other desserts; for adults, the steaks are large and charcoal-grilled to order. Adding to the appeal of these lunches are shows by strolling magicians, free balloons, live music, and a scheduled puppet show near the end of the three-hour extravaganza. Smollensky's offers good, friendly service from a mostly young staff—overall, the family lunches provide a casual and upbeat good time for adults and kids alike. Reservations are necessary to guarantee inclusion in this popular event.

Smollensky's Balloon, 1 Dover St, London W1, 071-491 1199. Mon-Sat noon-midnight, Sun noon-10:30 pm.

## Best Dining Spots With Kids For Dinner
Pizza Express

Let's face it—franchised pizza chains are convenient and affordable, but rarely inspire any great passion among their patrons. London offers a number of interesting pizza places, among them Kettners and Bob Payton's pioneering Chicago Pizza Pie Factory (see separate listings)...but, when family situation or budget calls for the speed and price of a franchised pizza, this London chain offers a good, popular alternative to more upmarket pizza restaurants. Founded in 1965, Pizza Express has become London's leading pizza chain on the strength of its simple, affordable menu, offering a variety of pizza toppings, plus salads, wines and sodas, and ice cream. Each outlet includes the chain's trademark large red ovens, usually situated in the center of the restaurant, so the kids can watch pizza being made. This is a good spot for vacationing American families to take the kids when they want something familiar and can't bear the thought of eating a Big Mac in London! The Pizza Express location in Dean Street offers live jazz, attracting top musicians from the U.S. and the U.K.

Pizza Express, 30 Coptic St, London WC1, 071-636 2244. Daily noon-midnight. (Many other locations, including 10 Dean St, London W1, 071-437 9595. Daily noon-midnight.)

## Best Dining Spot With Kids For Dessert (And More)

Pappagalli's Pizza

A pizza joint for dessert? Well, consider that the Italians also are famous for *gelato*, and that this West End restaurant offers Italian dairy ice cream in a variety of flavours (including dark chocolate, coffee, pistachio, hazelnut, and strawberry)—and that you can top it with combinations of hot chocolate fudge, butterscotch, strawberry sauce, and fresh whipped cream. And that parents might pour on a measure of Tia Maria, Amaretto, Bailey's, or some other liqueur. Then there is a choice of half dozen sundaes, built with scoops of ice cream and smothered with rich fudge and fruit sauce, and studded with chocolate chips, strawberries, marshmallows, nuts, and a variety of other dressings. Or go for the chewy fudge brownies, laced with hot fudge sauce, topped with whipped cream, and paired with scoops of ice cream. Enough said! Except that this *is* a good spot to go for thin- and thick-crust pizza (wholemeal dough is the speciality), and a good selection of pasta dishes that are available in children's portions. Stuffed garlic bread is a popular side order. Beverages includes wine, beer, aperitifs, and various juices and soft drinks.

Pappagalli's Pizza, 7-9 Swallow St, London W1, 071-734 5182. Mon-Sat noon-11:15 pm.

## Best Dining Spot With Kids For Cowboys

Texas Lone Star Saloon

Since the demise of the Saturday-morning cinemaclub serials and the decline of the TV and movie Western, and with Autry, Cassidy, Rogers, et al, long disappeared from the scene, kids have become more interested in more contemporary heroes such as Rambo, Superman, and the Simpsons. But while this pseudo-cowboy saloon may be of more historical interest to parents, kids love the continuous videos of the wild west and the frontier feel of the place, with cowboy pictures, bales of straw, and a rough-timber interior. Kids also seem to enjoy the food at this Tex-Mex eatery—basic burgers, chili, ribs, and steaks, with pecan pie and blueberry ice cream for dessert. Mexican items include tacos, enchiladas, and burritos. There is live entertainment and soothing margaritas for parents with jangled nerves. Look for another branch on the western edge of Bayswater (117a Queensway).

Texas Lone Star Saloon, 154 Gloucester Rd, London SW7, 071-370 5625. Mon-Wed noon-11:30 pm, Thu-Sat noon-12:15 pm.

## Best Dining Spot With Kids For T-Shirts

The Hard Rock Café

Burgers, T-shirts, and loud rock 'n' roll—this is the winning combination that has attracted millions of visitors to this famous shrine to some of America's most famous exports. This, the original outlet of this lively worldwide chain, was the first to bring the mighty American version of the hamburger to England—in 1971, a full five years before McDonald's hit London's West End. The burgers, shakes, steaks, corn on the cob, chili, apple pies, and ice cream (typically in large portions) are still popular draws here, as are the displays of rock memorabilia, such as guitars, gold records, photos, etc., including Elvis Presley's will and a guitar once played by Jimi Hendrix. And, while adults marvel at the artifacts of the '60s, their kids will likely be more interested in photos and belongings of such modern rockers as Billy Idol and INXS. Hard Rock Café attracts the occasional film, music, or sports stars, who get to avoid the legendarily long queues that snake in front of the restaurant and around the corner. And, while the Johnny-come-lately-in-London McDonald's may outsell this restaurant in burgers, the Hard Rock makes it up in clothing—this branch sells an estimated 750,000 T-shirts and sweatshirts each year.

The Hard Rock Café, 150 Old Park Ln, London W1, 071-629 0382. Sun-Thu noon-12:30 am, Fri & Sat noon-1 am.

## Most Amusing Amusement Parks

Chessington World of Adventures and Thorpe Park

The big attraction at Chessington—for kids of all

ages—is Europe's first hanging roller coaster—claimed to be the world's first that flies above the treetops and dives underground. Add a colourful indoor water ride known as Professor Burp's Bubble Works, and about 200 other rides and attractions, including Safari Skyway Monorail and the Runaway Minetrain, and you have Britain's top theme park. Also in Surrey, Thorpe Park is a popular family leisure park with more than 70 rides and attractions. Both parks offer unlimited rides for a single admission fee.

Chessington World of Adventures, Leatherhead Rd, Chessington, Surrey KT9, 0372 727227. Thorpe Park, Staines Rd, Chertsey, Surrey KT16 8PN, 0932 562633. Both parks are open from about Easter to October; phone for exact dates, times, and rates.

## Nicest Nannies For A Night
Childminders

It's fun to explore London with youngsters in tow. But there also are times when it is desirable, more fun, or absolutely essential to leave the kids at home—or at the hotel. Then, the ideal would be to call upon someone akin to P. L. Travers' incomparable fictional nanny. But failing being able to summon Mary Poppins to float down on her umbrella, the next best thing probably is to summon a babysitter from Childminders. This company has been dispatching short-term nannies throughout London and parts of Bucks, Berks, Middlesex, Surrey, and Kent for more than three decades and they most assuredly know that, just as a spoonful of sugar helps the medicine go down, you'll have a better time out on London Town knowing your children are in solid, caring hands. Childminders' nannies are culled from a group of more than 1,000 nurses, infants' teachers, and well-trained mothers available for babysitting on short notice. Phone as far in advance as possible, and be prepared to pay a membership fee as well as the hourly rate the first time you use the service.

Childminders, 9 Paddington St, London W1, 071-935 2049; 071-935 9763. Evening babysitters, Sun-Wed £2.45 per hour, Thu-Fri £3.25 per hour; day babysitters Mon-Sun £3.75 per hour.

# SHOPPING

## Best London Department Store With A Latin Motto

Harrods

Harrods' motto, "Omnia Omnibus Ubique"—All Things For All People, Everywhere—speaks volumes (albeit with a bit of hyperbole) about this, the undisputed king of London department stores. Now one of the most famous department stores in the world, Harrods began, rather humbly, as a neighbourhood grocer in 1849. Through growth, remodelling, and adaptation to shopping needs, it began to emerge as a department store around 1880, and now sprawls across a full block in Knightsbridge. Its 20 acres of shopping space on five floors attract approximately 30,000-50,000 customers each day, who are served by a staff of around 5,000. All things for all people? Perhaps not, but it does offer a wide variety of clothing and accessories for men, women, and children; furniture, toys, books, housewares, silver, china, glassware, and the huge Toy Kingdom; Harrods world-famous Food Halls offer meats, fruits, vegetables, bakery goods, wines, flowers, and much more (see separate listing); the store also has its own bank, shoe-repair shop, travel agency, barber and beauty salon, dry cleaners, and even its own in-store pub, The Green Man, located in the basement. Harrods is a great place to browse even if you're going to keep your pocketbook holstered; this could be as easily listed as a sightseeing attraction as a shopping destination! Attention bargain-hunters: The famous Harrods sales are held in January and July; these events draw huge crowds (especially the post-holidays sale in January).

Harrods, Knightsbridge, London SW1, 071-730 1234. Mon & Tue, Thu-Sat 9 am-6 pm; Wed 9 am-7 pm.

## Harrods' More Glamourous Neighbour
Harvey Nichols

If Harrods is the Rolls Royce of department stores, Harvey Nichols is the Lamborghini! This Knightsbridge neighbour of Harrods is smaller, but definitely more glittery and most decidedly *au courant.* It is the place to go for high fashion and designer labels—in women's, men's, and children's apparel. It, too, is a destination store. You can take afternoon tea at its roof-garden café, stop for a slice of quiche or coffee and a rich pastry at its basement restaurant, and get a perm and a facial at a hair and beauty salon. As for those labels, you'll find the likes of Ralph Lauren, Byblos, Calvin Klein, Nicole Farhi, Bruce Oldfield, Helen Storey—and just about any other high-fashion designer that comes to mind. There are designer floors, a basement menswear department, and a young-fashion department that's as hot as pink neon. You'll find a wide range of handbags, costume jewelry, and other accessories, plus kitchenware, bed and bathroom linens, glassware, and china.

Harvey Nichols, Knightsbridge at Sloane St, London SW1, 071-235 5000. Mon-Fri 10 am-8 pm, Sat 10 am-6 pm.

## Best London Department Store Founded By A Chicagoan
Selfridges

Around the turn of the century, the oft-repeated slogan at Chicago's legendary Marshall Field's department store was "Give the lady what she wants"—and what she wanted was multiple departments in a single store, catering to all of her shopping needs. Field's employee Harry Gordon Selfridge decided to import this American concept of a full-service store to London, and, in 1909, opened this store. Taking up a whole block, Selfridges is the largest store on Oxford Street. Its more than 500 departments generally stock a good selection of items at good prices (Selfridges promises to refund the difference on any item found for less at another store). The store attracts huge crowds shopping for housewares (including good china and glassware departments), clothes (designer and other styles, priced decently, if not at bargain-basement levels), furniture, toys, cosmetics, and a popular "Miss Selfridge" department, carrying young women's and "working girl's" fashions (this department has separate stores throughout London). Selfridges also offers a large food hall (although not on par with Harrods'—see separate listing), nine restaurants, a theatre-ticket outlet, and a bureau de change; there is a London Tourist Board office in the basement, offering helpful directions, maps, and sundry advice to visitors.

Selfridges, 400 Oxford St, London W1, 071-629 1234. Mon-Wed, Fri & Sat 9:30 am-6 pm; Thu 10 am-8 pm.

## Best-Looking Department Store
Liberty

If you're looking for a singular silk tie or an entire bolt of fabric, you probably won't find a wider and more distinctive selection than at this store founded more than a century ago by a Midlands' draper. Although it remains justifiably famous for its Liberty prints, created in-house and sold as fashion and upholstery fabrics or made up into items that make perfect gifts—scarves, aprons, napkins, tablecloths, etc—this really has grown into a department store. And it probably is London's best-looking and most charming department store, full of wonderful carved woodwork, handsome oak staircases, thick carpeting, and specialised galleries and boutiques-within-a-store. The building has a half-timbered faux-Tudor facade featuring an intriguing mechanical St. George-and-the-dragon clock. Check out the beautiful quilts, Persian carpets, extensive housewares, good-quality bed linen, and antique and contemporary jewelry that includes unusual pieces from the Orient. (In fact, it is the variety of imports from the East that continue to help set this store apart).

Liberty, 210-220 Regent St, London W1, 071-734 1234. Mon-Wed, Fri & Sat 9:30 am-6 pm; Thu 9:30 am-7:30 pm.

## Best Department Store To Find Pearly Queens
Marks & Spencer

Popular throughout Britain, with branches on High Street in most major towns (and outlets in many Commonwealth countries), this department store is known for reliable quality and moderate prices. In the idiom, it is "Marks & Sparks." Its St. Michael's brand has become synonymous with middle-class Britain, with generations of men, women, and children outfitted in shirts, skirts, sweaters, jackets, coats, socks, robes, and pajamas from what has been Mr. Everyman's store for more than a century. And while you can't try it on, you can take it back—for a cash refund, if you wish. This is the place to shop for a cashmere sweater—or for a selection of Marks' store-brand cosmetics and toiletries. When an Englishman takes off his trousers, he'll likely be wearing St. Michael's-brand underwear; when his wife sets the table to entertain, chances are the pâté, smoked salmon, pickles and chutney, jelly and blanc-mange came from Marks' food hall. The well-stocked food department offers a wide range of goods from fresh fruit and vegetables to fish, poultry, and meat. You'll find crumpets and scones, tinned soup and fresh mushrooms, plus St. Michael's-brand jams, jellies, and preserves. This flagship store has four floors.

Marks & Spencer, 458 Oxford St, London W1, 071-935 7954. Mon-Fri 9 am-8 pm, Sat 9 am-6 pm.

## Best Department Store That Casts Pearls Before Royalty
Asprey

If the only thing you do when you visit this shop is to admire the crystal chandeliers and sweeping staircase—keep an eye out for British and foreign royalty, and try to look as though you belong—you'll have an idea what it feels like to be rich and famous (supposing that you're neither). Perhaps London's most status-conscious store, with a royal warrant since the 19th century, this is the kind of place where if you have to ask how much it costs you probably can't afford it. It is a virtual department store of luxury goods: exquisite leather, silver tableware, candlesticks, and sconces, cutlery suitable for the most elegant dinner parties, luggage that makes a statement as it carries the laundry, pearl necklaces, art deco and Victorian jewelry, antique clocks, and business gifts appropriate for the most valued customer or most remote prospect. Royalty, jet-setters, and movie stars shop here regularly. Pick up a catalogue to display on your coffee table, and friends will think that you do, too.

Asprey, 165-169 New Bond St, London W1, 071-493 6767. Mon-Fri 9 am-5:30 pm, Sat 9 am-1 pm.

## Best Shopping District (Old Money)
Jermyn Street

Forget about baggies, floral ties in hothouse

colours, and anything funky! Jermyn Street, laid
out toward the end of the 17th century, is the bul-
wark of traditional British dress. Along this street
of charming mid-Victorian shopfronts you'll find
London's best shops for gentlemen's clothing.
There's Turnbull & Asser (see separate listing),
who made shirts for Winston Churchill and still do
for Prince Charles, and Hilditch & Key, shirtmakers since before the turn of the century. There is
Alfred Dunhill (at the intersection with Duke
Street—see separate listing), full of quality clothing
and luxurious leather accessories, Poulsen &
Skone, maker of bespoke shoes, and even a shop,
Czech & Speake (see separate listing), to make
sure that a gentleman's bathroom is properly
turned out with the right toiletries, brushes, and
fittings. The street was named after the Earl of St.
Albans, Henry Jermyn, depicted in a relief at
No.73 receiving deeds to the street from Charles II.

Jermyn Street, London SW1; near Piccadilly Circus
Underground station.

## Best Shopping District (Nouveau Riche)
South Molton Street

This short, trendy street off Oxford Street attracts
camp followers of the celebrated designers, trailing
eagerly in the wake of each new season's fashions.
They head for shops such as Brown's (see separate
listing), with three floors full of the latest clothing
and accessories by the cream of contemporary
designers, including Christian Lacroix, Jean-Paul
Gaulthier, Romeo Gigli, Franco Moschino, and
Rifat Ozbek. And they go to shops such as Butler
and Wilson (see separate listing) for a nonpareil
selection of costume jewelry and some fine pieces
of antique jewelry. The mod upmarket flavour of
South Molton Street continues directly across
Oxford Street with a cluster of shops on St.
Christopher's Place that includes Mulberry (see
separate listing), with raincoats and beautiful
bags, belts, and other accessories, and Nicole
Farhi, with elegant tailored clothes.

South Molton Street, London W1; near Bond Street
Underground station.

## Best Budget Shopping District (Ain't It A Bitch!)
Petticoat Lane (Middlesex Street)

In today's economy, London doesn't offer the shopping bargains it once did, but its famous street
markets still yield some good buys (amid a lot of
junk!). Most of all they can be fun—particularly

watching the chirpy cockney stallholders hawk their wares. Nowhere is this more evident than at (or "down" in cockney parlance) Petticoat Lane. Officially known as Middlesex Street (and collectively including a number of connecting streets), Petticoat Lane is a Sunday-morning tradition. Look for good buys on ladies' fashions, household items, and leather goods. You'll also find that souvenir T-shirts are cheaper here, as are ties (three for £5, but don't expect Italian silk!). Two musts: A container of jellied eels or cockles or whelks seasoned with pepper and malt vinegar from Tubby Isaacs stand at the Aldgate end of the market, and a pint of ale at Dirty Dick's pub (est. 1745), which anchors the Bishopsgate entrance to Petticoat Lane near Liverpool Street station (see separate listings).

"Petticoat Lane," Middlesex St, London E1. The market is open Sundays 9 am-2 pm.

## Best Market For Watching Buskers And Tourists

Covent Garden

Kids love the clamour and colour of Covent Garden, while young Londoners from nearby offices and shops meet there after work. But this sprawling pedestrian street market isn't for everyone. Many view it as crowded and tacky, purveying cheap souvenirs, dubious crafts, poor-quality clothing, and indigestible food. These naysayers have a point. Certainly, Covent Garden can become noisy and boisterous—particularly as closing time for the pubs draws near. Yet there are quiet backwaters in a maze of adjoining lanes where you can sip an espresso at an outdoor café, and find interesting little shops. And there is a mystique about the market, laid out by Inigo Jones in the style of an Italian piazza. It served London for more than three centuries and attracted such famous personages as diarist Samuel Pepys and George Bernard Shaw, who researched there the Cockney speech patterns he would ascribe to Eliza Doolittle. When the world-famous fruit-and-vegetable market moved south of the river in 1974, the glass-roofed buildings with their graceful iron pillars and arches were renovated and became a major London tourist attraction. The main floor is jammed with street-market stalls, flanked by brick-fronted shops that generally offer good quality merchandise. Popular activities are watching people and street performers—mimes, jugglers, acrobats, and assorted musicians. The balcony of the Punch & Judy (see separate listing) is a good spot to sip a pint and observe performers on the piazza below.

Covent Garden, London WC2; near Covent Garden Underground station.

## Classiest Shopping In Out Of The Rain
Burlington Arcade

Shop-until-you-drop types, tired of being hurried by disinterested companions, will find refuge in this fashionable galleria. It operates under its original code that prohibits running, whistling, singing, and even the unfurling of umbrellas. These ancient rules are enforced by liveried "beadles," ushers resplendent in top hats and black-and-yellow uniforms who also ring a ceremonial hand bell to announce the close of the day's business. Originally built in 1818 and renovated in the 1930s and 1950s, this Regency-style covered arcade has beneath its elegant glass roof London's richest concentration of fashionable shops and boutiques. Among its three dozen or so *expensive* shops, you'll find lots of antique jewelry—jade, turquoise, and garnet pins and rings, and fine Victorian and Georgian pieces—antique pocket watches, Irish linens, cashmere, conservative women's clothing (check out the exquisite silks at James Drew) and men's wear (especially shirts and paisley dressing gowns at Lords), tobacco, and toiletries. This ornate, gilt passage is a delightful spot to escape a sudden shower—but do remember to keep those umbrellas in check!

Burlington Arcade, off Piccadilly, London W1; near Piccadilly Circus Underground station. Mon-Sat 9 am-5:30 pm.

## Most Entertaining Shopping Arcade
The Trocadero

Kids love it; teens can wander here for hours. This glittery, garish—albeit fun—arcade complex can provide light family diversion, especially when young tourists have overdosed on pomp and ceremony. Here is where you can dress up in vintage clothing for a 19th-century-style family portrait—and where the kids can have made on the spot a T-shirt or button featuring their pictures. Then there's the Guinness Book of World Records Museum with its representations of those records of the superlative, the diminutive, and the incredibly trivial. All of this, plus a passel of stores selling cheap souvenirs and imitation gold, and a Far East food emporium, can be found here. Admittedly, the Trocadero isn't for the serious shopper or the serious sightseer, but, all the same, this gaudy tourist-trap can be worth a look-see, especially as a family-oriented diversion.

The Trocadero, Piccadilly Circus, W1, 071-287 4224.

## Best Antique Market
Alfies Antique Market

What's it all about, Alfie? In this case it's about more than 200 antique dealers trading at 370 stalls in the largest covered antique market in England—a total of more than 35,000 square feet of floor space on five floors. The dealers at this modern, attractive, purpose-built market have a heavy concentration in 18th- and 19th-century furniture and accessories; plenty of modern items are also available in all price ranges. Here, you'll find specialist dealers offering dolls, toys, pens, sporting memorabilia, books, cameras, gramophones, records, radios, watches, jewelry, silver, luggage, furniture, toys, and much more. The market's scenic highlight is its three-story sky-lit atrium, with a unique waterfall forming a curtain of falling water along one side of the bright open area. For a meal or snack while shopping, try the market's rooftop restaurant, which has an attractive terrace with a panoramic view.

Alfies Antique Market, 13-25 Church St, London NW8, 071-723 6066. Tue-Sat 10 am-6 pm.

## Best Antiques By Torchlight
New Caledonia Market

Serious antique enthusiasts arrive at this Bermondsey market by dawn and conduct some of their most intense dealings by the light of a torch. Offically, the Friday-morning market opens at 7 a.m. and by mid-morning most of the heavy trading has been concluded, with any bargains that might have been going snapped up by 9 o'clock or earlier. Several hundred stalls offer a wide variety of antiques, including china, clocks and other timepieces, silver, jewelry (especially Victorian), military collectibles, prints, inkwells, bottles, and various vintage writing implementalia, and an array of antique furniture. Part of the experience is to enjoy some early browsing and then retire for breakfast to one of a cluster of nearby cafés such as the Rose Dining Rooms. To sustain you as you wander the market are stalls with coffee, tea, rolls, and snacks such as jacket potatoes. The market overflows into adjoining streets, such as Long Lane, site of a covered area known as the Bermondsey Antique Market.

New Caledonia Market, Bermondsey Sq, London

SE1; near Borough Underground station. Fri 7 am-1 pm.

## Best Bet For Bedsteads, Beads, And Beatles Records

Portobello Road Market

A horse-and-cart loaded with used furniture? On the streets of modern London? If we're talking Portobello Road, why not? It has just about everything else—punks and poodles, buskers and barrows, skinheads and purple heads. You'll find a variety of antiques, junque galore, and an incredible assortment of bric-a-brac, from ink-squirting fountain pens to wind-up gramophones. An antiques market, noted for silver, is held on Saturdays; weekdays, there's a fruit-and-vegetable market, flea-market, and permanent shops, such as Alice's corner store with ancient musical instruments and authentic pub signs, and Blues with good-quality T-shirts and sweatshirts. Entering near the Notting Hill Gate tube station, you'll progress from reliable antique shops, through the produce market, to an enclave of nondescript flea-market stalls close to Ladbroke Grove station. Off the main thoroughfares, a network of arcades contains shops with high-ticket European and Oriental antiques, from Victorian inkwells to Chinese bronzes. Stalls are crammed with weapons, kitchenware, used books, records, dogeared postcards, cigarette cards, vintage jewelry and items of clothing that looks as though they might walk away unassisted.

Portobello Market, Portobello Rd, London W11. Mon-Wed & Fri 8 am-4 pm, Thu 8 am-1 pm, Sat 8 am-6 pm.

## Best Bet For Collectibles And Quiche

Camden Passage

If Portobello Road is the beer and bangers of street markets, Camden Passage is the wine and quiche! Tucked away in a labyrinth of streets, alleys, arcades, and passageways off Islington High Street, it is known for its good-quality antiques and collectibles and for the satellite wine bars and upmarket restaurants and bistros that make this a popular destination for yuppies and such. On Wednesdays and, particularly, on Saturdays, the market is crowded as hordes of stallholders hawk their wares. On other days, the market is not as hectic, although there still are scores of permanent shops and galleries to browse. Among an incredible variety of good-quality antiques and expensive bric-a-brac you'll find old china, books, paintings, prints, glassware, sculptures, and a selection of period furniture. There also are stalls selling second-hand clothing, records, books, furniture, and other recycled goods.

Camden Passage, Islington High St, London N1; near Angel Underground station. Mon, Tue, Thu, Fri 9 am-6 pm; Wed & Sat 8 am-4 pm.

# Best Place Where It Takes Money To *Buy* Money

Spink & Sons

If you're a collector, it takes money to buy money. And lots of it! Especially if you're in the market for Greek or Roman coins or for early-English currency. Numismatists from around the world out to expand their coin collections head to this big, rambling department store of art and artefacts. This historic establishment, dating from the 17th century, is equally known for its medals. It not only mounts and displays decorations, and publishes a guide about them, it *creates* medals—for Britain and for dozens of foreign governments. But, in addition to medals and orders, banknotes and coins, this dealer is known for its antique silverware and jewelry, exquisite paperweights, textiles, English watercolours, and Oriental and Islamic art.

Spink & Sons, 5-7 King St, London SW1, 071-930 7888. Mon-Fri 9:30 am-5:30 pm.

# Best Place To Buy An Old Master

Wildenstein

While you may be able to only wistfully gaze at a multi-million-pound Van Gogh on the auction block at Sotheby's or Christie's, you can buy museum-quality works by other top-name artists at this classy (as you'd well expect) art gallery. (A brief explanation of terms for U.S. visitors—art museums often are called "galleries" in England; Wildenstein, however, is a gallery according to the common U.S. definition: A business dealing in fine art.) Wildenstein is one of the top names in international art galleries, and has branches in New York, Tokyo, and other cities around the world. Even if you aren't in the market for a Rembrandt, Turner, or Picasso, the changing collection on display here (usually including heavy concentrations of Old Masters and Impressionist works) is fun to browse, especially during the gallery's two well-attended annual exhibitions (one held in summer, the other in autumn). Wildenstein is housed in an historic building which once was the home of Lord

Nelson.

Wildenstein, 147 New Bond St, London W1, 071-629 0602. Mon-Fri 10 am-5:30 pm.

## Best Toy Shop Not To Lose Kids In
Hamleys

Parents who let their kids loose in the world's largest toy store (according to *Guinness*) may have trouble retrieving them and probably will find the experience expensive. You can shop for cricket bats and baseball bats, footballs and snooker balls, Snoopy and the Simpsons, farmyards full of livestock, parade grounds full of famous regiments, battlements bristling with medieval knights, garages full of metal cars and taxis, and goods yards full of trains. Americans will find Rambo, Superman, and other kid heroes, along with the dulcet Barbie, and her British counterpart, Amanda Jane, quite proper in gymslip and school uniform. There are books and games galore, hobby kits for making models of Jaguar jets and Jaguar cars, the very latest state-of-the art electronics, and dolls that reproduce Britain's historic monarchs. There's Corgi, Matchbox, Mechano, and Lego, and Hamleys' perennial bestsellers, cuddly teddy bears.

Hamleys, 188-196 Regent St, London W1, 071-734 3161. Mon-Wed, Fri & Sat 10 am-6 pm, Thu 10 am-8 pm.

## Best Toy Shop Impossible To Lose Kids In
Toddler Toys

Here it is impossible to lose even the littlest of kids (for whom this shop was designed). In fact, this diminutive toy store is the antithesis of the rambling, multi-leveled toy emporium of Hamley's (see separate listing). The emphasis is on handcrafted wooden toys, such as a hand-carved, stylised Noah's Ark, painted in bright primary colours with its own rainbow, that carries a hefty price tag of £85. But you'll find less expensive items here, too, selling for a pound or two, among an inventory that ranges from simple building shapes to elaborate forts, rolling trains, cars, and carts, and various puzzles. Here's where you'll find a selection of so-called "educational toys" along with simple, durable, colourful playthings that are pure fun. The store has a second location across from Harrods (in the Knightsbridge Arcade), offers a mail-order catalogue, and ships internationally.

Toddler Toys, 4 Harriet St, London SW1, 071-245

6316. Mon & Tue, Thu-Sat 9:30 am-6 pm; Wed 9:30 am-7 pm.

## Best Place Say "Tanks, I Needed That!"
Beatties of London

Anyone who thinks that models are only for kids should see all the dads and uncles hunched over the offerings at this store on any given Saturday afternoon. As many of their purchases likely end up being worked on at dad's basement workbench as they do being presented as gifts. No wonder, considering the array of fascinating toys and models: Cars (vintage and new), boats (destined for the den desk or the yacht ponds in Hampstead Heath and Kensington Gardens), spaceships (from the realms of both NASA and *Dr. Who*), and a variety of military hardware, most notably sleek jet warplanes and sturdy tanks. Kits range from easy snap-together projects to intricately detailed replicas of the real things, requiring glue, paint, and plenty of patience. Beatties also stocks a huge range of model train sets (including all the little accessories—such as crossing gates, trees, station houses—that make a layout realistic), radio-controlled toys (dune buggies, race cars, yachts, etc.), the latest in electronic games, and other toys and dolls—ranging from crying, wetting infants to stylish dress-up Barbies from the U.S.

Beatties of London, 202 High Holborn St, London WC1, 071-405 6285. Mon 10 am-6 pm, Tue-Sat 9 am-6 pm.

## Best Place To Buy A Toy Soldier
Under Two Flags

Rank upon rank they stand, colourful armies of little soldiers, ready to march off into imaginary battles. Toy soldiers have been popular in England since the 1890s, when a toy version of Queen Victoria's guards was created by William Britain & Company in honour of the queen's Diamond Jubilee. These first sets and many other mini-regiments fashioned by Britain & Company are available at this store (for as much as £100)—as well as more affordable modern toy soldiers for new collectors or for kids. Under Two Flags also offers kits of make-'em- and paint-'em-yourself soldiers in lead, wood, tin, and other materials. Fanciers of these amusements will also find military books and magazines, war-themed board games, as well as statues, models, and other soldier- or military-oriented decorative items (a toy-soldier chess set is particularly popular).

Under Two Flags, 4 St. Christopher's Pl, London W1, 071-935 6934. Mon-Sat 10 am-6 pm.

## Best Toy Store For Adults
Just Games

While London still contains a few of the "naughty" adult shops that once dotted the streets of Soho, this particular "toy store for adults" is quite innocuous! Located in Soho (coincidentally or not), this shop specialises in a variety of games and toys, some geared for kids, but as many (or perhaps more!) that adults will enjoy. The stock here tends toward games, ranging from such classics as chess, checkers, mah-jongg, dominoes, and backgammon to such longtime favourites as Monopoly (using London locales instead of the original Atlantic City properties) and Clue to the latest set of update cards for Trivial Pursuit. For those who are challenged in multiple languages, check out the foreign Scrabble sets (in which the frequency of letters—and therefore the amount of each—differ from the English version). Just Games' name belies its stock a bit—in addition to the above games (and various card and electronic games), it also offers puzzles, books, and other toys. A popular recent trend (which is also reflected among the stock here) has been toward the executive "stress" or gag gifts, such as inflatable punching bags for the office or tongue-in-cheek trophies (e.g., "World's Worst Golfer").

Just Games, 62 Brewer St, London W1, 071-734 6124. Mon-Sat 10 am-6 pm.

## Best Bet To Do Your Bidding
Sotheby's and Christie's

From a masterpiece by Van Gogh to the guitars of famous rock stars (and a wide range of collectibles in between), nearly anything that someone wants to buy can be sold at these two world-famous auction houses. Sotheby's is the oldest (dating from 1744) and largest antique and auction house in the world. It offers regular weekly auctions for silver, furniture, glass, clocks, paintings, rugs, and other categories of desirable collectibles, as well as publicity-attracting events when everything from museum-quality art to cases of vintage wine to celebrity memorabilia are put under the gavel. Although the younger of the two, Christie's is no Johnny-come-lately, having been founded in 1766. Its main branch specialises in fine artworks, and holds more than 350 auctions a year, mostly of art, wine, furniture, and jewelry. The South Kensington branch in Old Brompton Road is a little more casual, often offering small lots of various collectibles (dolls, toys, photographs, clothing) not usually found in the tonier auctions at the main branch. Neither house accepts credit cards, so, if you want to participate in an auction, be prepared with cash—and steely nerves! Even if your budget does not allow bidding on some of the goods offered at these auction houses, an auction can be an entertaining way to spend an hour or two!...Just be sure to keep your hands in your lap, lest you find yourself the inadvertent owner of a painting, antique chair, or the love letters of Joan Collins!

Sotheby's, 34-35 New Bond St, London W1, 071-493 8080. Mon-Fri 9 am-4:30 pm, and other times for special auctions or viewings. Christie's, 8 King St, London SW1, 071-839 9060. Mon 9 am-7:30 pm, Tue-Fri 9 am-5 pm, and other times for special auctions or viewings. (Also at 85 Old Brompton Rd, London SW7, 071-581 7611.)

## Best Shopping Centre

Whiteleys

Among the new breed of high-tech shopping arcades popping up across Britain is Whiteleys, a dazzling new shopping mall in the Bayswater district. Housed in an Edwardian building occupying an entire block on Queensway, this new mall owes its beginnings to the now-defunct Whiteleys department store, which occupied this building from 1863 to 1981. Today, the beautifully-renovated building (featuring tall Greek columns, ornate brass railings, bubbling fountains, intricate plasterwork, and a grand staircase) contains an inviting array of shops, including such well-known establishments as Marks & Spencer, the Body Shop, Benetton, and Laura Ashley. The mall also offers patrons an eight-screen cinema (see separate listing), an entire floor of casual eateries, and a restaurant catering to more formal dining.

Whiteleys of Bayswater, Queensway, London W2, 071-792 3324.

## Best Men's And Women's Clothing Department Store

Simpson

Housed in a landmark building (which once was a geological museum), this store offers seven floors of time-honoured English fashions. Simpson was founded by tailor Simeon Simpson nearly a century ago, and was revolutionised into a one-stop market for buying clothes and accessories by his

son Alex in the early decades of this century—
making it the only store at the time where a gentleman could be outfitted from head to toe under
one roof. (Women were able to shop here for their
own fashions by the late 1930s, although it wasn't
until the last few decades that Simpson has
offered full-service selections in women's wear.)
Simpson is known as the home of DAKS clothing—
a somewhat-expensive, but well-made line of
casual-to-slightly formal clothes and accessories,
available in a vast array of styles and colours.
Prices can be on the high end, but the quality of
goods is also high. Simpson has Royal Warrants as
outfitters to Queen Elizabeth, Prince Philip, and
Prince Charles; its staff is knowledgeable, polite,
and helpful (but not hovering). The store has
recently added an excellent sushi bar to its traditional English restaurant on the lower level—it is
open Monday-Saturday noon-2:30 p.m.

Simpson, 203 Piccadilly, London W1, 071-734 2002.
Mon-Wed, Fri & Sat 9 am-5:30 pm; Thu 9 am-7 pm.

## When Only The Right Name Will Do
Gucci

This toney boutique is world-famous for its accessories and for its distinctive signature colours.
This shop offers Gucci bags, wallets, key rings,
briefcases, luggage, and scarves, as well as a line
of expensive, but well-made shoes. Some people
say the Gucci name has more lustre than the
goods—and look down on consumers who are
"duped" into carrying monogrammed advertisements for an already-famous retailer. Others
swear by the quality of the Gucci line, blithely and
proudly carrying items branded with the ubiquitous Gucci "G." The debate rages—but one thing is
certain: The prices definitely reflect the generally
sky-high reputation of this chain.

Gucci, 27 Old Bond St, London W1, 071-629 2716.
Mon-Fri 9 am-5:30 pm, Sat 9 am-5 pm.

## Best Stop For Womenswear From Young Designers
Whistles

If you were to head for London's hottest new clubs,
trendiest new restaurants, and most fashionable
wine bars, you'd probably run into young professional women (of the upwardly mobile variety)
stylishly attired in clothes from this small chain of
fashion boutiques. On the cutting edge of the cou-
turiers' craft, Whistles introduces to Londoners
trendsetting clothes and accessories by up-and-

coming young international designers. It also carries a line of established labels. The store's in-house lines offer good value on ultra-fashionable designs. Also stocked are leather and suede shoes and other components of a complete ensemble. Although many of these avant-garde fashions have hefty price tags, the chain also has a good selection of moderately priced clothes.

Whistles, 12-14 St Christopher's Pl, London W1, 071-487 4484. Mon-Wed, Fri & Sat 10 am-6 pm; Thu 10 am-7 pm.

## Best High Temple Of Womenswear From Top Designers
Browns

The fickle finger of high fashion probably will most often point the chicest of chic to this temple of designer labels. One word sums up the price range of these in-vogue fashions and accessories: expensive! However, in-the-know shoppers with champagne tastes and beer budgets make a point of checking the racks of the "Labels For Less" department, where last season's styles are marked down by 50 percent or more. This can be especially good news for tourists from the United States, where European trends generally tend to filter down a season or two later. This three-floor headquarters store (with branches elsewhere, including on Sloane Street), carries the lines of such well-regarded British and Continental designers as Christian Lacroix, Jean-Paul Gaulthier, Romeo Gigli, Franco Moschino, and Rifat Ozbek. It also offers a range of correspondingly pricey shoes, swimwear, costume jewelry, earrings, and other accessories.

Browns, 23-27 S Molton St, London W1, 071-491 7833. Mon-Wed, Fri & Sat 10 am-6 pm; Thu 10 am-7 pm.

## Best Bet For Bargain Designer Fashions
Constant Sale Shop

Women looking for designer clothing at mass-production prices should head to this friendly shop, found among the upmarket boutiques and other stores of Fulham Road in Kensington. Designer-at-a-discount is the game here, where once-top-of-the-line (if a little behind-the-times) frocks by such famous names as Armani, Ungaro, Valentino, and others are offered at prices up to 60 percent lower than originally asked. This is a unique sort of a "bargain basement," with the designer houses themselves sharing in the managing and stocking of the shop, meaning that these are guaranteed to be the real thing and not counterfeit knockoffs. And, particularly for visitors from the United States, a point to remember is that just-out-of-fashion in London can mean up-to-date (or even *ahead* of the fashion) in most other places—especially in all but a few cutting-edge areas of the States.

Constant Sale Shop, 56 Fulham Rd, London SW3, 071-589 1458. Mon-Sat 10 am-6 pm.

## Best Bets To Dress Like Princess Di

Emanuel & Belville-Sassoon

Since that day of pageantry and celebration in 1981, when Prince Charles married Lady Diana Spencer, fashions for young Englishwomen have never been the same! Since then, the Princess of Wales has set the standard for trendy and stylish womenswear. Although she has yet to issue any Royal Warrants, some of her favourite shops and designers are well-known, and attract the well-heeled followers of Di's fashion dictates. One of her longtime fancies has been the work of designers David and Elizabeth Emanuel (who designed the Princess's wedding gown). These in-demand designers now operate a shop on trendy and fashionable Beauchamp Place, offering smart daytime suits and dresses, and elegant fairy-tale-style evening gowns. The Emanuels used to do private designing, by reference only...now it's merely by appointment only—and better bring your sturdiest charge card: These fashions are priced from £800 and up! Another shop favoured by the trend-setting Princess is Belville-Sassoon on Pavilion Road, not far from the young-socialite stomping grounds of Sloane Street. Diana is a loyal supporter of designer David Sassoon's styles. The attractive day and evening wear found here range in price from £250-£1,250; special custom creations (such as wedding gowns) can be had for up to £2,000.

Emanuel, 10 Beauchamp Pl, London SW3, 071-584 4997. Mon & Tue, Thu-Sat 10 am-6 pm; Wed 10 am-8 pm. Belville-Sassoon, 73 Pavilion Rd, London SW1, 071-235 3087. Mon-Fri 9:30 am-5:30 pm.

## Best Fashions If You're A Woman Over 5'10"

Long Tall Sally

It used to be that tall women were stuck finding whatever clothing was available in their sizes off the rack (as out-of-style as it may have been) or were forced to pay the high price of custom-tailored clothing. But shops like this one on Chiltern Street (just a block off of Baker Street) answer the problem. Long Tall Sally offers a wide variety of elegant, designer (and everyday) fashions for tall women—from around 5'10" and up—in sizes ranging from 12 to 20. These items run in a range of styles and colours aimed at nearly all ages, tastes, and budgets, and include casualwear, lingerie, evening gowns, running/exercise clothes, and coats. (A sociological note: Princess Di is 5'10", and it's probably at least partially due to the influence of her relentlessly glamourous looks that women in England have realised that you can emphasize and glory in height, rather than downplay it.)

Long Tall Sally, 21-25 Chiltern St, London W1, 071-487 3370. Mon-Wed, Fri 9:30 am-5:30 pm; Thu 9:30 am-7 pm; Sat 9:30 am-4 pm.

## Best Men's Shop For The Young Professional

Review

The latest trends in menswear can be found at this fashionable clothing store located on Oxford Street. Review caters to upmarket tastes on blue-collar budgets; it offers a large selection of the latest suits from English and Italian designers, as well as more affordable imitations inspired by these designs. The store also stocks an enormous collection of custom-made ties (which can be a little pricey) and a large selection of casual clothing. The sales staff is friendly and helpful, and there's a full-time tailor on the premises, meaning alterations usually are completed quickly. On any given day, you'll likely find sales in progress (sometimes store-wide, sometimes within specialty departments), making bargains easy to find for discerning and patient shoppers. Especially recommended for the younger crowd.

Review, 326 Oxford St, London W1, 071-491 7141. Mon-Sat 10:30 am-6:30 pm.

## Best Suits (Outside Of The Old Bailey)

Savile Row

It was back in 1969 that the Beatles gave their last public performance on the roof of the building at 3 Savile Row which housed their Apple Corps. But that's *recent* history. Since the 1850s this street has been synonymous with fashionable bespoke tailoring—as it so remains. Alistair Cooke likes the cut of the cloth at Hawes & Curtiss while Leslie Charteris' fictional character, The Saint, was a patron of the staid premises of Anderson & Sheppard, where you may need an introduction. Other top tailors along this most famous of fashion streets are Kilgour, French & Stanbury, Gieves & Hawkes, makers of fine blazers, and Henry Poole, court tailor to Napolon II. Those who'd like a suit with the imprimatur of a Savile Row tailor can count on paying anywhere from £500 to £1,200 for a two-piece suit (extra for a waistcoat), depending upon the fabric. They also can expect to go for three fittings, but might reasonably anticipate the best-fitting suit they've ever owned—a suit with a life-expectancy of 20 years.

Savile Row, London W1; near Piccadilly Circus Underground station.

## Best Bet To Hire A Tuxedo

Moss Bros

This multiple-outlet family business, open since 1860, is the place to go throughout London (and the rest of England) to hire formalwear for a variety of occasions. The choices include smart morning wear (for members of wedding parties—and even wedding guests—or for wear at such daytime social events as the Royal Ascot and Derby race meetings), formal evening wear (for such "black tie" outings as dinners, parties, and receptions), and even full Highland outfits for either category. (According to rules of etiquette and custom, any subject of the U.K. may opt for kilted Highland wear for situations that call for either morning or evening dress.) Each outlet offers thousands of suits in various styles; prices range from £28-£39 for morning and evening wear, with Highland outfits starting at £43 (a deposit of £50 is also required with each hire). And, to complete the picture of elegant savoir faire, these stores also provide accessories to complement ensembles— including top hats, shirts, ties, shoes, scarves, gloves, and more. Moss Bros also offer hunting and riding outfits and women's formal gowns for hire, as well as suits and used tuxes for sale. (Some outlets of the chain are known as The Suit Company.)

Moss Bros, 88 Regent St, London W1, 071-494 0665. Mon 8:30 am-7 pm; Tue, Wed, Fri 9 am-7 pm; Thu 9 am-8 pm; Sat 9 am-6 pm. Also many other Moss Bros or The Suit Company outlets throughout London and England.

## Best Shop To Dress For A Country Weekend

Hackett

One can't help but imagine that Leslie Howard

would have shopped at Hackett. And *Mr.* Minniver. It's a traditionalist sort of place that Sloane Rangers popularised in the early 1980s. That is when the store started out by selling high quality second-hand clothes—tweeds, hacking jackets, corduroys, and such that were the vogue in the 1930s, '40s, and '50s. The small Fulham shop of Jeremy Hackett and Ashley Lloyd Jennings has grown into a full-fledged men's department store housed in a striking 18th-century building full of splendid marble and mahogany (plus two other branches). It also is full of these conservative, timeless styles that sold so well as used clothes that the store now reproduces them as new. In this staid establishment, men will find just about everything they need to dress like a Sloane Ranger, from fine cotton singlets and Argyle socks to cable-knit pullovers and cashmere waistcoats. There's the tweedy look for a weekend in the country and a full line of riding apparel. There is even a for-hire department with formal wear from Moss Bros (see separate listing).

Hackett, 27 King St, London SW6, 071-497 9383. Mon-Wed, Fri & Sat 9 am-6 pm; Thu 9 am-7 pm.

## Top Shop For Trenchcoats

Burberrys

Conservative, unfashionable, predictable. Trendy shoppers might eschew Burberrys as they pile on pejoratives (although Burberrys' clientèle considers these to be *pluses!*), but there is no denying that this British institution makes a nonpareil waterproof—as it has been doing since 1856. Their signature trenchcoats with the distinctive red-black-and-fawn plaid lining, along with matching accessories, now are obtainable across the globe, and even in mid-air and mid-Atlantic. But you'll find an unmatched variety at this original store (and at its Regent Street sister), including the famous trenchcoat itself in a half-dozen or so shades. Matching accessories include scarves, hats, umbrellas, watch bands, luggage, sweaters, and shawls. There's a children's department to help ensure propagation of the Burberrys' tradition.

Burberrys, 18-22 Haymarket, London SW1, 071-930 3343. Mon-Wed, Fri & Sat 9 am-5:30 pm; Thu 9 am-7 pm.

## Best Place To Find A Cashmere Jumper

Berk

From crisp, button-down shirts to colourful soft

sweaters—thus can be described the manufacturing and retailing journey of this shop's founder and namesake. David Berk started out as a men's shirtmaker in the early 1950s, but after he tried his hand at fashioning ladies' cashmeres, he changed his focus. Now, Berk is one of England's largest makers and retailers of cashmere jumpers. These classic cardigans and pullovers are available in a range of attractive styles and in a virtual rainbow of colours from muted to bright, including navy, emerald, camel, wine, pink, charcoal, red, yellow, and brown. In addition to what probably is the largest selection of cashmeres in all of London (and perhaps in the world, according to some sources), Berk also sells shoes and even cashmere kilts. However, bargain-seekers from out of the country should be forewarned that recent increases in cashmere prices have pushed the classic English sweater out of the "buys worth visiting London for" category. There *is* a terrific selection here, but the prices are high (although not as high as in the United States, for example). Berk has many locations throughout London, as well as stores in New York, Houston, and Boston in the States.

Berk, 46-50 Burlington Arcade, Piccadilly, London W1, 071-493 0028. Mon-Fri 9 am-5:30 pm, Sat 9 am-4:30 pm. Also many other locations.

## Smartest Sweaters In A Rainbow Of Colours

Benetton

Sure, you can get sweaters from this successful worldwide chain in any number of cities—but you should also remember that the once-desirable bargains on many types of British woollens aren't exactly what they used to be...and, besides, these are nicely made, mostly affordable sweaters, which are popular both with residents and visitors. Head to any number of London outlets—Benetton has *many* London locations, including more than a dozen on Oxford Street alone (there's a large one at 328 Oxford)—for famous Italian sweaters, sweatshirts and pants, leggings, jackets, accessories (stockings, gloves, hats), and other colourful casualwear and mix-and-match separates; these are available in the chain's trademark bright purples, greens, reds, blues, and other colours. There are also shrunk-down versions of these comfy, yet stylish clothes for kids. In general, the quality is good and the prices are decent (if not outright bargains).

Benetton, 328 Oxford St, London W1, 071-491 2016. Mon-Wed, Fri & Sat 9 am-6 pm; Thu 9 am-8 pm. Also many other locations.

## Best Bet For The Shirt On Your Back

Turnbull & Asser

Among famous figures (literally and figuratively speaking) there may be no more telling example of disparate forms than the portly profile of the late Winston Churchill and the angular frame of the present Prince of Wales. Sir Winston had his shirts custom-made on these august, wood-panelled premises. Prince Charles still does. So, on occasion, does actor Robert Redford, who wore shirts from this royal shirtmaker in the film *The Great Gatsby*. Founded in 1885, the shop originally made hunting apparel. Today, it specialises in ready-made and (with an order of six or more) bespoke shirts. You'll also find a line of distinguished ties, braces, robes, and other accessories, plus ready-to-wear and tailor-made suits on adjoining premises. Churchill had his trademark one-piece wartime siren suits designed by Turnbull & Asser. One is on display for posterity.

Turnbull & Asser, 71 Jermyn St, London SW1, 071-930 0502. Mon-Fri 9 am-5:30 pm, Sat 9 am-4:30 pm.

## Best Bet For A Blazer

Gieves & Hawkes

Lord Nelson and Captain Bligh of the Bounty patronised this men's tailors that now is presided over by a fifth-generation Gieve. So does the United States Commander-in-Chief, President George Bush. The prestigious No.1 address on the most famous street for men's tailoring is assigned to a handsome townhouse that dates from 1731-32 when Savile Row was originally laid out. This elegant tailors' and haberdashery shop has an atrium, ceiling fans, and chandeliers, and still supplies tailoring to the Royal Navy. For civilian customers it offers bespoke and ready-made suits, shirts, and formal wear. It is noted for its well-cut blue blazers, perhaps the most versatile of men's wear. There are silk ties, handmade according to the shop's centuries-old designs, and such accessories as suspenders, socks, waistcoats, cashmere sweaters, and even gold watches. Customers in the market for a two-piece custom-made suit should be prepared to spend upward of £800 and wait up to 60 days for the finished product.

Gieves & Hawkes, 1 Savile Row, London W1, 071-434 2001. Mon-Fri 9 am-5:30 pm, Sat 9 am-1 pm.

## Best Bet For Bags & Belts

The Mulberry Company

That fashion buzz word, "accessorising," is epitomized here—but with a most decidedly English accent. Shop at Mulberry for exquisitely crafted traditional-style bags, satchels, sports totes, and various distinctive luggage in leather, rubberised cotton, and other stylish fabric. A wide range of belts includes leather, leather trim, and various printed fabrics. The store (with another branch in Harvey Nichols—see separate listing) also carries men's and women's casual clothing, knitwear, and waxed-cotton raincoats.

The Mulberry Company, 11-12 Gees Ct, St. Christopher's Pl, London W1, 071-493 2546. Mon-Wed, Fri & Sat 10 am-6 pm; Thu 10 am-7 pm.

## Best Bet For A Brolly
### Swaine, Adeney, Brigg & Sons

When it rains in London (as it frequently does) you can buy a made-in-Taiwan folding umbrella from one of the street hawkers who sprout on street-corners on rainy days like mushrooms in a hedgerow. Or you can go to the family business that's been in Piccadilly since 1750 and received a royal warrant to make riding crops for George III. Handmade of the finest silk taffeta with handles embellished with silver, gold, ivory, or soft leather, these are the brollies that won an Empire and which definitely should not be left at the Empire. Shop, too, for top-drawer, understated luggage, Barbour waxed cotton jackets, tweeds, sweaters, picnic hampers, and fine leather goods including whips (strictly for gentlemen!). If you're into riding, hunting, or shooting—or need outfitting for a weekend in the country—you'll want to come here for the very best—as does British royalty.

Swaine, Adeney, Brigg & Sons, 185 Piccadilly, London W1, 071-734 4277. Mon-Wed & Fri 9 am-5:30 pm, Thu 9 am-7 pm, Sat 9 am-5 pm.

## Oldest Shop For Staying Dry
### James Smith & Sons

The stately sign and Victorian shop-front of Europe's largest and oldest umbrella- and walking stick-emporium have been landmark sights to Londoners and travellers-in-the-know since 1830. Step inside and you will be whisked back to an era when brilliant, sturdy craftsmanship was prized in manufacturing above all else. Most of the items in stock have been hand-crafted in England out of native woods, from crook chestnuts and sturdy ash to apple and maple and such rare and valuable woods as ebony, rosewood, partridge cane, and all-bark malacca. The shop's best-known and most-versatile offering is the so-called "solid stick," a hand-made umbrella mounted on a walking stick specially designed both for support and protection from the elements. More-exotic items include sword sticks (made to order) and sticks with all manner of animal-head handles cast in bronze or resin, including bears, apes, badgers, eagles, bulldogs, airedales, labradors, tigers, otters, basset hounds, horses, and ducks. The shop's staff is able to fill special orders, cutting sticks to exact size and supplying treasured ceremonial umbrellas and maces to collectors and even African tribal chiefs. (An American collector once asked Smith's to make walking sticks of every English wood, and the total exceeded 70!) You can buy a basic umbrella here for as little as £9, but the luxurious Polished Real Rosewood Crook with rolled gold collar will set you back a tidy £145.

James Smith & Sons, Hazelwood House, 53 New Oxford St, London WC1, 071-836 4731. Mon-Fri 9:30 am-5:25 pm.

## Best Hats At The Birthplace Of The Bowler

James Lock

If you enter this shop is search of a Coke, they'll be more than happy to oblige. They'll know you're not in need of a soft drink (nor anything illegal), but simply want to see that traditional British headgear, the bowler hat. The bowler was invented here in 1850, when a William Coke requested a hard, round-shaped hat to protect his gamekeepers in the field. The hat was made by the firm of Bowler, but "coke" remains the preferred name at Britain's oldest hatters. Since the company opened its doors in the mid-18th century, it has supplied hats to the Duke of Wellington ("something with plumes, if you please"), to Lord Nelson (incorporating a special eye shade), to Beau Brummel, as well as to such contemporary hat fanciers, as Frank Sinatra and Harrison Ford. You can order a fishing hat, Panama, grey silk hat for Ascot, and a felt job for the fox hunt, as well as a wide range of hats and caps that you can wear on High Street, Main Street, or Threadneedle Street.

James Lock, 6 St. James's St, London SW1, 071-930 5849. Mon-Fri 9 am-5 pm, Sat 9:30 am-12:30 pm.

## Top Spot For A Tweed "Titfer"

Herbert Johnson

The English have a penchant for headgear, at work and at play, from the plebian cloth cap of the working man lining the terraces at Chelsea, Spurs', and Queen's Park Rangers' football matches, to the cream of society outfitted in silk top hats at Ascots. The Royals lead the way with hats for all occasions and this shop has held a royal warrant since catering to the headgear needs of Edward VII as Prince of Wales. Founded in 1889, the shop carries hats for men and women, ranging from berets, bowlers, and boaters to peaked caps and panamas. If you're looking for just the thing to go with a new sports car, traditional tweed caps are a speciality.

Herbert Johnson, 30 New Bond St, London W1, 071-408 1174. Mon-Fri 9:15 am-5:30 pm, Sat 9:30 am-4 pm.

## Best Place To "Tie" One On

T. M. Lewin & Sons & The Tie Rack

Men may seem to have it easier than women when it comes to accessorising—but what a wide variety of choices there are simply among ties! Colour, style, pattern, even the way you tie it—these all must be weighed carefully. To help men put that finishing touch to a suit or other ensemble, these two disparate tie shops offer different approaches. Lewin takes the high road, selling "exclusive" ties, including more than 6,000 club, university, and other special-pattern ties (but there's a caveat: You must be able to prove your membership or association with any particular group or club to be able to purchase a tie bearing its insignia). Lewin also stocks a fine selection of ties with no purchase requirement (save, perhaps, good taste!), including bespoke ties of various fabrics and styles and fine, ready-made ties (and shirts). Treading more populist ground is The Tie Rack, a ubiquitous chain of affordable tie shops (located in many shopping centres and blocks, as well as in some tube and rail stations). The choices here include a cornucopia of different colours, fabrics, and patterns for all tastes and budgets. (The Tie Rack can be a good stop if you're in need of a last-minute gift.) Also, many of the Jermyn Street men's shops—especially shirtmakers such as Turnbull & Asser and Hilditch & Key—sell a fine selection of bespoke and ready-made ties.

T. M. Lewin & Sons, 106 Jermyn St, London SW1, 071-930 4291. Mon-Fri 9 am-5:30 pm, Sat 9:30 am-5:30 pm. The Tie Rack, 15a Kensington Shopping Mall, Kensington High St, London W1, 071-937 5168. Mon-Sat 9 am-6 pm. Also at many other locations.

# Best Shop To Find The Right Shoes (Upmarket)

Bally & Charles Jourdan

You needn't cross the Channel to find the best European shoes in which to attire your feet. These two outlets of famous Continental manufacturers offer some of the best selections of toney shoes to be found in London. Bally has long been one of the biggest names in shoes, and its imported-from-Switzerland styles are available at nine outlets on London's major shopping streets. Bally's conservative, well-made shoes in up-to-date women's styles (as well as men's classic loafers and oxfords) range from about £50-£100. Another great spot for fine footwear is Charles Jourdan, on Brompton Road. This French boutique offers well-regarded men's and women's shoes in a large variety of styles, as well as clothing, bags, ties, scarves, and other accessories for men and women. Jourdan's shoes are in the £75-£150 range—but the best (and busiest) time to shop here is during the annual January sale, with savings of up to 50 percent. (Jourdan's is conveniently close to Harrods, should you wish to combine both stores' January sales in one potentially exhilarating and exhausting—and money-saving—shopping foray.)

The Bally Shop, 30 Old Bond St, London W1, 071-493 2250. Mon-Sat 9:30 am-6 pm. Also many other locations. Charles Jourdan, 39-43 Brompton Rd, London SW3, 071-581 3333. Mon Sat 10 am-6:30 pm.

# Best Shop To Find The Left Shoes (Budget)

Bertie & Dolcis

Not all of the footwear to be found in London stores carry budget-busting price tags. Primary among affordable shopping for shoes is the Bertie chain, with locations on prime shopping streets throughout London, such as Sloane Street, Oxford Street, and King's Road. These stores feature a nice variety of good-quality shoes at affordable prices. Most of these are casual- and work-wear rather than dressing-up-and-going-out sort of shoes (with some exceptions); the selections include very good choices of styles, sizes, and (especially) colours. The mostly Italian-made designs offered here range from around £25-£50. Another popular bargain shoe stop are the stores of the Dolcis chain (especially the main store on Oxford Street). The selections can be limited at times, but the prices are right—around £20-£40.

Bertie, 15 The Market, Covent Garden, London WC2, 071-836 9147. Mon-Sat 9:30 am-8 pm. Also many other locations. Dolcis, 350 Oxford St, London W1, 071-629 5877. Mon-Sat 9:30 am-6 pm. Also many other locations.

## Best Shop To Find Right And Left Shoes Made Expressly For *Your* Right And Left Feet

John Lobb

If money is no object when it comes to clothing your body (with top-notch designer fashions or smart bespoke suits), why not devote that kind of attention—and money!—to your feet? Founded by John Lobb in 1850, this is perhaps the finest shoemaker in the world. It is a very atmospheric shop—smelling richly of leather, with cobbler's tools strewn about, Royal Warrants on the wall, and lovingly made examples of shoes on display. Lobb's makes shoes and boots for members of the royal family (it holds warrants for Queen Elizabeth, Prince Philip, and Prince Charles), as well as the rich and famous from across England and around the world. But it's not a place to go if you're in a hurry for a pair of shoes. A master shoemaker will meticulously measure your foot and inquire as to the style and type of shoe you desire (examples are on hand to ease this process, if necessary). Then follows a wait of six months to a year while a pair of perfectly made-to-order shoes are painstakingly crafted (the good news is if you want additional pairs in the future, they can be ordered by mail and will only require a wait of three months). Not quick...and not cheap, either: Prices start at around £600-£800, depending upon the style. If these pricey shoes seem as if they should be a once-in-a-lifetime extravagance, they might well be: Lobb's shoes have been known to outlive their owners! (With proper care, Lobb shoes often last 25-40 years.)

John Lobb, 9 St. James's St, London SW1, 071-930 3664. Mon-Fri 9 am-5:30 pm, Sat 9 am-1 pm.

## Best Place To Go If You Have Cold Feet

The Sock Shop

What can you say about socks—after you've acknowledged that they keep your feet warm and that men, when they cross their legs, look a lot more attractive with than without? Well, you might say that this store has about 2,000 different kinds—in stripes, plaids, polka dots, diamonds, and concentric circles, in garish, bright neon colours, in athletic white, and in conservative black and grey. If you want socks that make a statement—literally, as well as figuratively—you'll find them here inscribed with slogans both witty and whimsical. There is also a selection of plain and patterned tights and other women's hose, plus some underwear and umbrellas. This specialty store also offers convenience, with shops around London, especially at Underground stations.

The Sock Shop, 89 Oxford St, London W1, 071-437 1020. Mon-Sat 8:30 am-7 pm.

# Best Bet For Whimsical Socks

Paul Smith

Funky and conservative coexist surprisingly well at this shop where garish socks in bright colours inscribed with just about anything that strikes the designer's fancy—from bunches of cherries to famous autographs to seasonal weather maps—have become a signature best seller at around £12 a pair. Flamboyant silk ties, staid woollen cardigans, eye-catching scarves, well-cut suits, extravagantly bold boxer shorts, and traditional tweeds run point and counterpoint through this attractive showcase of one of England's most successful and internationally renowned designers of menswear (Harrison Ford and Paul McCartney are clients). Along with the wit and whimsy, you'll also find a fine selection of shirts, shoes, sweaters, sports coats, cashmere blazers, corduroy and other casual trousers, raincoats, and conservative business suits, as well as a variety of watches, pens, lighters, and assorted knick-knacks. The shop, with handsome bare wooden floorboards, is housed in an old Victorian chemist's.

Paul Smith, 41-44 Floral St, London WC2, 071-379 7133. Mon-Wed, Fri 10:30 am-6:30 pm; Thu 10:30 am-7 pm; Sat 10 am-6:30 pm.

# Best Bet For Babying Baby

Mothercare

Americans familiar with U.S. branches of this chain are surprised at just how more expansive the British versions are, particularly this flagship store on Oxford Street. And while they won't find any apple pie, they will find just about everything to do with motherhood, that other staple traditionally claimed as all-American. A wide range of clothing and other merchandise spans the decade or so from the need for maternity clothes to fashions for early teens. In addition to prenatal essentials and baby equipment such as bottles and plastic feeding dishes, the store carries such items as christening gowns, strollers, swimsuits, and Wellington boots—the ubiquitous shiny "Wellies" familiar to generations of British school children. Kids love the radiant primary colors and the cartoon characters featured on T-shirts, sweatshirts, jackets, pants, dresses, and hats. The store has baby-changing facilities and offers a mail-order catalogue.

Mothercare, 461 Oxford St, London W1, 071-622 6621. Mon-Sat 9:30 am-6 pm.

# Best Shopping For Children's Clothes

## British Home Stores

Generations of British families have depended on this large nationwide chain of department stores (with 17 stores in London alone) for a wide selection of reliable, modestly priced goods. Geared to locals rather than tourists (and somewhat akin to a combination of the familiar Woolworth's and the U.S. chain of K mart stores), British Home Stores is known for offering good values and low prices on a variety of household goods. BHS outlets offer home furnishings, kitchenware, linens, lighting, and clothing for women, men, and, especially, children. Its range of children's clothes includes a wide variety of colours, styles, and sizes, with a reputation for being sturdy and long-lasting. BHS also offers a good-priced restaurant in its Oxford Street location (and also at the Kensington High Street branch).

British Home Stores, 252-258 Oxford St, London W1, 071-629 2011. Mon-Wed, Fri & Sat 9 am-6 pm; Thu 9 am-8 pm. Also many other locations.

# Best Jeweler To The Royal Family

## Garrard

When those recent royal bridegrooms, Charles and Andrew, got their engagement rings, they did not just pop into *any* jewelers' shop. They left the matter up to Garrard, the official Crown Jewelers since 1843. (Rumour has it that the royal rings in question were custom-designed at a cost of more than £30,000 apiece!) Founded in 1735, Garrard is responsible for the care (and occasional repair) of the Crown Jewels; they have also provided crowns and jewelry for many of the world's other royal families, and trophies for many sporting events. Beyond its royal responsibilities, Garrard carries fine jewelry and gift items for a range of budgets—from around £25-£40 all the way up to £1 million! Here you'll find fine antique silver—candlesticks, bowls, vases, coffee pots, figures—crystal, china, desk sets, decorative items and knickknacks, exquisite jewelry, colourful pins, charms, cuff links, tie clips, classic watches (Rolex, Patek Philippe, Piaget), wallets, date and address books, and clocks (in models from ornate antiques to spare, modern designs). And, if you spot Prince Edward in Garrard, poring over cases of ring models, there may be another royal wedding in the offing!

Garrard, 112 Regent St, London W1, 071-734 7020. Mon-Fri 9:30 am-5:30 pm.

## Best Costume Jewelry Fit For A Princess

Butler & Wilson

On trendy South Molton Street this glitzy jewelry shop probably has London's paramount selection of costume jewelry, as well as a good selection of antique pieces. Whatever jewelry you need to accessorise whatever outfit you have in mind, you'll probably find it here, including fashionable earrings, clips, pins, brooches, bracelets, necklaces, and even tiaras suitable for a coming out party. There are striking reproductions of art deco and art nouveau pieces, and antique jewelry that attracts such patrons as Princess Diana and entertainment celebrities. Butler & Wilson also carries its own designs, eagerly anticipated by the cognoscenti season-by-season. The shop has a second branch near Sloane Square (189 Fulham Road).

Butler & Wilson, 20 S Molton St, London W1, 071-409 2955. Mon-Sat 10 am-6 pm.

## Best Jeweler If You *Don't* Happen To Be A Monarch

Sanford Brothers Ltd.

Not every jewelry shopper can afford to employ the custodians of the Crown Jewels as their diamond merchant. Happily, those bound by such budgetary constraints can find quality counsel and a good selection at this family-run business (the current proprietor is the grandson of one of its founders). Established in 1923, this shop is located in the Staple Inn Building, a tourist destination in its own right—dating from 1586, it is the only half-timbered building of its type to survive from Elizabethan London. The Sanford Brothers store deals in an extensive variety of jewelry, loose diamonds and precious stones, new and second-hand silver, watches, clocks, pewter, leaded crystal, and other valuable items. In general, it offers a

wide range of goods in a wide range of prices. This
shop also offers repair services for jewelry, clocks,
and watches, and can arrange estate sales of gold,
silver, and jewelry.

Sanford Brothers Ltd., 3 Holborn Bars, Old Elizabeth
Houses, London EC1, 071-405 2352. Mon-Fri 10 am-
4:30 pm.

## Best Shopping Bet For Anything That's Left

Anything Left-Handed Ltd.

Pity the poor southpaw! Unless you're a lefty, you
probably can't appreciate how tough it is to live in
a right-handed world. This shop does, and here
you'll find left-handed scissors, a corkscrew that
turns anticlockwise, knives serrated on the left-
hand side of the blade, and a variety of other
kitchen and garden equipment, plus pottery
(including mugs with slogans that face out for left-
handed folk), novelty clocks (where three-o'clock is
on the left!), and a variety of books, and posters, T-
shirts, and greeting cards for and about left-hand-
edness. How about a left-handed boomerang, an
address book with left-handed index insetting,
playing cards identified on all four corners, or gen-
uine Swiss Army knives adapted to left-handed
usage? This shop, below an attractive brick-
fronted building with foliage sprouting from window boxes, offers a catalogue and a left-handers'
club with its own newsletter.

Anything Left-Handed Ltd, 65 Beak St, London W1,
071-437 3910.

## Best Use Of Hot Air (Outside Of Parliament)

The Glasshouse

While some may claim that the House of Commons
is London's leading producer of hot air, this glass
studio and gallery also puts out a lot of hot air,
and to much better—and practical—use than the
MPs. Located just around the corner from the
Royal Opera House, the Glasshouse has been open
since 1969, and is the only gallery in central London devoted to the creation and exhibition of contemporary glass. Glasshouse is run by a collective
of four individuals (all well known among British
glass artists) who act as the studio's directors—
Annette Meech, David Taylor, Fleur Tookey, and
Christopher Williams. In the studio's hot workshop, broken glass is melted and blown into various shapes (some easily identifiable, some more
fanciful). Visitors can observe these processes from

inside the studio through an observation window. In the basement is a cold workshop, where cutting, engraving, and polishing of semi-finished pieces takes place. Glasshouse produces both functional items (goblets, bowls, pitchers, perfume bottles, paperweights, vases), as well as purely artistic works that are shown in their own gallery and abroad. This is a good spot not only to see glass artworks, but also for kids to watch glass being made.

The Glasshouse, 65 Long Acre, London WC2, 071-836 9785. Mon-Fri 10 am-6 pm, Sat 11 am-5 pm.

## Most Sensible Scents

Floris

There is an English-country-garden-full of fragrances right in the heart of London at this perfumer that set up business at this location back in 1730. Since Minorcan Juan Floris first began extracting fragrances from English flowers, this shop has been selling such traditional scents as lily of the valley, violet, rose, lavender, sandalwood, jasmine, geranium, carnation, and extract from the fragrant white flowers of stephanotis. The shop has held royal warrants since the 18th century to supply its perfumes, toilet waters, cologne, soaps, and bath oils to royal households. Shop here, too, for shaving brushes with badger bristles, toothbrushes with mother-of-pearl handles, alabaster soap dishes, powder puffs, combs, brushes, and mouthwashes fit for royal breath. Handsome mahogany showcases that stretch floor-to-ceiling were salvaged from the Great Exhibition of 1851.

Floris, 89 Jermyn St, London SW1, 071-930 2885. Mon-Fri 9:30 am-5:30 pm, Sat 9:30 am-4 pm.

## Best Bet For "Making Scents"

Penhaligon's

Soft flowery fragrances, bold woodsy bouquets, and invigorating citrus aromas—these are a mere sampling of the pleasing scents to be found at this perfumery. Founded by barber William Henry Penhaligon in 1870, this shop was big with socialites in Victorian London, but fell into decline after passing from Penhaligon family ownership early in the 20th century. After being taken over and revived by Sheila Pickles in 1975, this has, once again, become a top provider of gentlemen's and ladies' scents and toilet accessories—including by Royal Warrant to Prince Philip and Prince Charles. Here you can find a wide variety of exotic, specially made scents for men and women such as Hammam Bouquet, Victorian Posy, Elisabethan Rose, English Fern, and Jubilee Bouquet. These are available in eau de toilette, cologne, bath oils, soap, shampoo, after shave (in some varieties) or body lotion (in others), and talcum powder—all in bottles and containers that harken back to Penhaligon's halcyon days, including classic, Victorian-era labels. This gracious shop also stocks shaving and grooming accessories, gift packages of scents, items for the home (such as room spray, potpourri, and scented candles), and even scented diaries, photo albums, address books, and other personal books.

Penhaligon's, 41 Wellington St, London WC2, 071-836 2150. Mon-Fri 10 am-6 pm, Sat 10 am-5:30 pm. Also many other locations.

## Best Bet For The Very Best Of British
Naturally British

You'll find the expected here—Scottish woolens, Irish linens, English knitwear, and Welsh lace. But you'll also find the unexpected, such as jars of blackberry-and-apple jam, damson preserves, and coarse stone-ground mustard, traditional games such as skittles and shove-'alfpenny that have disappeared from pubs, and fine examples of cabinetry and one-of-a-kind pottery. This is a showcase of the work of artisans from across the British Isles. Shop for unique jewelry, wicker, woodcrafts, hand-made puzzles, games, and toys, hand-woven tablecloths, glassware, and ironwork. You'll find items price-tagged with multiple zeros, as well as souvenirs you can buy for a few pennies, all beautifully displayed on handsome antique furniture.

Naturally British, 13 New Row, WC2, 071-240 0551. Mon-Sat 10:30 am-7 pm.

## Bonniest Shop To Buy A Tartan
Scotch House

Even if there is not a *Mac* in your name, or in your entire family tree, you may find this emporium of things Scottish a fun place to browse. If you *do* have a *Mac* or a *Mc* in your name, there are charts and books here to help you trace your clan and choose exactly the right dress tartan. That established, you may wish to select a finely-made, leather-trimmed kilt from the largest selection in London. Or, if yours is an obscure tartan, they'll make it to order for you. This, too, is the place to shop for cashmere, mohair, lambs'-wool, and Shetland sweaters and scarves, for fine, nubby tweed garments that outlast fads (and maybe their owners), for Argyle socks, and for tartan ties, tammies, blankets, jackets, vests, skirts, and other garments that'll declare your heritage (or simply look nice and wear well). There's a fine children's department with a selection of junior kilts.

Scotch House, 2 Brompton Rd, London SW1 (and several other locations), 071-581 2151. Mon & Tue, Thu-Sat 9 am-6 pm; Wed 9 am-7 pm.

## Best Bet For A Bit Of The "Auld Sod"
Irish Shop

There's more than a bit o' the begorrah and blarney to be found in the goods sold at this Duke Street shop, just off Oxford Street, around the corner from Selfridges. As its name indicates, the focus is on things Irish, especially fashions and gifts, including china, crystal, linens, and a wide range of handmade woollens. At this family business opened in the mid-1960s, you'll find the "big names" of Irish products—Waterford and Galway Crystal, Belleek China (in both dishes and decorative ware), Donegal tweeds, and the distinctive Aran fishermen's sweaters, rugged and warm. Also stocked are linen damask cloths, placemats, and serviettes in an assortment of sizes and patterns, and various Irish souvenir-type items, including books, records and tapes of Irish music, leprechaun dolls, and shamrock-adorned shirts, hats, etc. (The Irish Shop also has a second London outlet, at 80 Buckingham Gate.)

Irish Shop, 11 Duke St, London W1, 071-935 1366. Mon-Wed, Fri & Sat 9:30 am-5:30 pm; Thu 9:30 am-7 pm. Also at 80 Buckingham Gate, London SW1, 071-222 7132. Mon-Fri 9 am-5 pm, Sat 9:30 am-3 pm.

## London's Loveliest Linen
The Irish Linen Company

As you might expect from the name, the fine linens in this shop come from the legendary looms of Ireland—although some of this lovely linen is much more extensively travelled than the short passage across the Irish Sea. The exquisite hand-embroidery on many of the items on sale in this specialty shop is done in Madeira, China, and other far-flung points of the globe. If these seem like circuitous routes to this West End shop, consider that this firm has been in business since 1875 and definitely should have it down pat by now. Shop for beautiful tablecloths, dainty handkerchiefs, as well as placemats, napkins, guest towels, and, of course, fine linen sheets. Given the quality of the goods and the cachet of the store's location in the upmarket Burlington Arcade (see separate listing), you know you can expect premium prices.

The Irish Linen Company, 35-36 Burlington Arcade, London W1, 071-493 8949. Mon-Fri 9 am-5:30 pm, Sat 9 am-4:30 pm.

## Best Taps For Your Tub
Czech & Speake

On fabled Jermyn Street, the mecca of men's bespoke clothing shops and the literal lap of luxury, is the ultimate bath shop. This is where you come when you feel that your bathroom is deserving of a touch of class. The specialities here are peerless bathroom fittings and exquisite toiletries. The fittings are faithful reproductions of Edwardian and Victorian originals, fashioned in gleaming, decorative brass. Czech & Speake's own line of old fashioned toiletries for men and women includes bath oils and soaps in such traditional fragrances as rosemary and thyme.

Czech & Speake, 39c Jermyn St, London SW1, 071-439 0216. Mon-Fri 9 am-6 pm, Sat 10 am-5 pm.

## Best Bet For Mystical Merchandise
Davenports Magic Shop

If you've an unfulfilled longing to declare that you've nothing up your sleeve while producing a rabbit from a hat or correctly identifying a playing card chosen by a willing victim, then this long-standing shop is the place to indulge your prestidigitational fantasies. Davenports offer a full range of mystifyingly magical material, from simple sleight-of-hand tricks for a pound or two to expensive set-ups for more elaborate illusions. (This shop is patronised by both amateur conjurers and professionally performing magicians.) In addition to the basic ring, rope, and card tricks—not to mention the saw-a-lady-in-half props—Davenports also offers a variety of puzzles, masks, costumes, books, "gag" gifts, and literally hundreds of practical jokes (most of which are of the exploding cigarette, black-foaming soap, and plastic vomit variety). Kids love this shop—but parents not wishing to wake up with a rubber snake in their bed should keep an eye on what the little nippers buy!

Davenports Magic Shop, 7 Charing Cross Underground Shopping Arcade, London WC2, 071-836 0408. Mon-Fri 9:30 am-5:30 pm, Sat 9:30 am-4 pm.

## Best Shops For Fine Stogies

Davidoff Of London & Robert Lewis

A word of warning to U.S. citizens preparing to visit these two shops, perhaps the leading importers of cigars in all of Europe: The good news can be summed up in two words—Cuban cigars!; the bad news, in five—you can't take them home! So, enjoy these fine smokes while you're in London, but don't bother trying to smuggle them back to the States. (Yet another advantage to living in London!) Davidoff is a modern, elegant shop offering a fine selection of both house brands and Havanas—this store features what seems to be the largest collection of Havana cigars east of Cuba and west of the offices of certain Politburo members in Moscow. Davidoff also offers varieties of cigars from Denmark, the Caribbean, and the Netherlands; a good collection of accessories (cutters, humidors, and ashtrays), and pipes and tobaccos; as well as a special house cognac—for the ultimate indulgence of soaking a fine cigar. Robert Lewis dates from 1787, and is thought to be the oldest cigar shop in England. This is where Churchill bought his Cuban Romeo Y Julietas— Winnie had an account here for more than 60 years. Lewis has a wide selection of Havanas, and offers good bargains on its fine house brands; it also carries pipes, tobacco, snuff, and handmade cigarettes. The staff is attentive and friendly.

Davidoff Of London, 35 St. James's St, London SW1, 071-930 3079. Mon-Sat 9 am-6 pm. Robert Lewis, 19 St. James's St, London SW1, 071-930 3787. Mon-Fri 9 am-5:30 pm, Sat 9 am-12:30 pm.

## Best Tobacco Agent For A Secret Agent

Alfred Dunhill

James Bond had his cigarettes specially made elsewhere, but he did ignite them with one of Dunhill's famous lighters. The fastidious 007 also favoured shirts fashioned from silk-like Sea Island cotton (originally harvested on the Sea Islands off the coast of Georgia, U.S.A.), also sold here. The famous tobacconist has been at this location since 1907 and has vastly expanded its line to include soft, hand-tooled leather luggage and a variety of other leather goods, men's clothing and accessories, watches, toiletries, and an array of adult toys that make good gifts. The emphasis is on top quality (with prices to match). For smokers, the shop still custom-blends pipe tobacco (and stocks an extraordinary variety of pipes) and keeps its inventory of cigars in top shape in a humidor that has private lockers for favoured customers. Americans come here for Cuban cigars—but must remember to puff them before they return to the States (where they are banned). The prized lighters come in a variety of styles and prices.

Alfred Dunhill, 30 Duke St, London SW1, 071-499 9566. Mon-Fri 9:30 am-6 pm, Sat 9:30 am-5:30 pm.

## Best Bet To Provision A Perfect Picnic
Harrods Food Halls

Sausages in every conceivable taste, shape, and texture hanging in front of the tiled walls of a *charcuterie;* a fish department that stocks such smoked exotica as *three* kinds of kippers, smoked sprat fillets, and Arbroath smokies; showcases crammed with golden-crusted pies stuffed with ham, veal, chicken, game, and a variety of other savoury fillings, along with the famous Moulton Mulberry pies; a colourful melange of pâtés and terrines; dignified help in crisp white aprons and straw boaters. These—and much, much more are what you'll find in Harrods' remarkable food halls. Opened in 1849, the legendary Harrods department store (see separate listing) grew out of merchant Henry Charles Harrod's modest London grocery and tea shop, and the company has never forgotten its roots. A total of 16 of the store's 300 departments are part of the beautiful and renowned food halls, which are decorated with the famous Daulton tiles. The impressive depth of selection includes more than 500 varieties of cheese and 130 types of fresh breads and scones baked on the premises. Add freshly made pasta, fresh meat, poultry, and game, jams, jellies, preserves, chutneys, pickles, fruit, confectionery, wines, and spirits, and you create endless possibilities for provisioning picnics and, of course, for elegant entertaining.

Harrods Food Halls, Knightsbridge, London SW1, 071-730 1234. Mon & Tue, Thu-Sat 9 am-6 pm; Wed 9 am-7 pm.

## Best Place To Say "Cheese"
Paxton And Whitfield

This is the shop that John Cleese, as a beleaguered and eventually belligerent patron of a cheeseless cheese shop in a famous *Monty Python* sketch, *should've* repaired to when he "suddenly came over all peckish." This store offers more than 300 British and European varieties of cheese, and traces its history back to 1740 as a partnership between the Cullum and Paxton families (the Whit-

field of the firm's current name joined in 1837).
You'll find a good variety of classic Stiltons, Ched-
dars, Wensleydales, Cheshires, Roqueforts, and
Camemberts. Especially popular are gift combinations of port wine and Blue Stilton cheese (in distinctive black earthenware jars), and special
"cheeses of the month" subscriptions, which bring
a selection of three different cheeses each month
by mail. Paxton and Whitfield also offers pre-
packed hampers for picnics or special occasions
(containing cheeses, wine, pâtés, biscuits, nuts,
jams, sauces, and sweets), as well as hams,
smoked salmon, Christmas puddings, truffles, tea,
and a variety of sauces and condiments. This store
has been suppliers to the royal family since 1870
(it currently holds a warrant from the Queen
Mother).

Paxton And Whitfield, 93 Jermyn St, London SW1,
071-930 0250. Mon-Fri 8:30 am-6 pm, Sat 9 am-4 pm.

## Best Bet In London To Shop For French Groceries

Boucherie Lamartine

Outside the smart, canopied storefront are legions
of vegetables—baskets of lettuce, leeks, mushrooms, blushing red tomatoes. Inside the bright
airy shop that is decorated with Tiffany-style
lamps are racks laden with battalions of bread—
pale white and golden brown crusty loaves—and
shelves neatly stacked with jars of French delicacies: herbs, spices, mustard, cornichons, flavoured
vinegars, brandied fruit, jams, jellies, and preserves—an Aladdin's cave of ambrosial delights.
The selection of French cheeses, stylishly laid out
on rattan, is spectacular. This elegant food store
was opened in 1982 by Marc Beaujeau and his
partner, the celebrated Albert Roux, whose restaurant, Le Gavroche (see separate listing), was the
first in the United Kingdom to earn the coveted
Michelin three stars. Much of the stock is
imported twice weekly from markets in France,
such as poultry, farmhouse cheese, and fresh
fruits and vegetables. Meats may be French or
English, but are cut the French way. Freshly-
baked breads and patisserie are available, as are
many prepared meals.

Boucherie Lamartine, 229 Cherry St, London SW1,
071-730 4175, 071-730 3037 (answerphone after 7
pm). Mon-Fri 7 am-7 pm, Sat 7 am-4 pm.

## Best Bet For Bushels Of Oysters

Bentley's Oyster Shop

Planning an oyster bash! Bentley's is the place to

find fresh, plump oysters ready to be shipped any-where in the United Kingdom. Famous for its seafood restaurant and oyster bar (see separate listings), Bentley's annually buys more than 50 tons of oysters—about half a million individual oysters. They are farmed from Bentley's own beds at the Cuan Oyster Farm on the shores of Strang-ford Lough in Northern Ireland, and are flown in daily to the London shop. Strangford Lough—part of a designated marine nature reserve—is noted for the variety of marine life which thrives in its clean, clear waters. The shop also has supplies of oysters from Poole, in Dorset, and from the Duchy of Cornwall. A 24-hour answering service is pro-vided for the convenience of customers. Native oys-ters range from £60 to £85 per hundred, Pacific oysters are priced at £32 per hundred (prices, of course, subject to fluctuation).

Bentley's Oyster Shop, 11 Swallow St, London W1, 071-734 4756, 071-734 0431 (24-hour answering ser-vice).

## London's Poshest Grocery Store

Fortnum & Mason

It started as a grocery store—and it still is Lon-don's poshest grocery story, where the wait staff wears tails. But, since its founding in 1707, it has evolved into much more. It is the Fountain Restau-rant, really more of an old fashioned tea room, which is the spot for Devonshire cream teas, stylish sandwiches, and light evening meals (ideal for pre-theatre). It is a soda fountain that delights kids with its sundaes and other ice-cream concoc-tions, it is a wine merchant, and it a department store with upper floors devoted to clothing, leather goods, home furnishings, and even antiques. But most of all, it is those marvellously indulgent food halls, with shelves full of epicurean exotica, rows of marvellous, jams, jellies, preserves, mar-malades, pickles, and chutneys, chocolates and confectionery, tea and coffee, pot-upon-pot of pâté, and incredible imports (such as the storied Sacher torte from Vienna). Queen Victoria is said to have dispatched a consignment of beef tea to Florence Nightingale in the Crimea, while generations of English gentlefolk have purchased hampers to take to Ascot, Henley, and other venues that call for elegant alfresco dining. Kids love the entertain-ing mechanical clock, where Messrs. Fortnum and Mason appear on the hour to greet one another.

Fortnum & Mason, 181 Piccadilly, London W1, 071-734 8040. Mon-Fri 9 am-5:30 pm, Sat 9 am-5 pm.

## Best Shop That Has It Down To A Tea

R. Twining & Co.

As amazing as it may seem, when Thomas Twining purchased his coffee and tea house in 1706, tea was highly taxed and little regarded in England. It wasn't until 1784, when Twining's grandson Richard convinced Prime Minister William Pitt to reduce the tax on tea, that England really became a land of tea drinkers (until then, coffee and even ale had been the prevalent breakfast drinks). Dating from the original coffee and tea house, the London branch of Twinings on The Strand is the oldest ratepayer in the City of Westminster—and its shop is the oldest business on the same site with the same name and owned by the same family selling the same product in all of London! Lest you think this merely is a record-book type of curiosity, rest assured that this shop still stocks the best China, India, and Sri Lanka (Ceylon) teas; the quality and selection offered has made it a mecca for tea lovers. Earl Grey is the most popular blend, but more adventurous fanciers of a good cuppa can opt for a more fruity or spicy blend. The shop also has a small museum tracing the history of the Twining family and its tea business over the past 280-plus years. And, as only seems fitting, Twinings holds a Royal Warrant as tea and coffee merchant to the Queen.

R. Twining & Co., 216 The Strand, London WC2, 071-353 3511. Mon-Fri 9:30 am-4:30 pm.

## Best Chocolatier At Which To Eat Your Words

Charbonnel et Walker

"Darling, forgive me!" Have that message spelled out on what many—including the Royals—claim are the world's best chocolates, and you may quickly receive the grace you seek—especially if the loved one you may have wronged has a sweet tooth. You can buy a box of chocolates already assembled, or create a custom assortment by selecting your own favourite centres—perhaps violet, orange, or raspberry cream, mocha crisp, walnut swirl, or Turkish delight. Your special message of love, thanks—or forgiveness—is written right on the chocolates. You can order animal-shaped chocolates for children, and choose from a variety of presentation boxes, some appropriately frilly and lacy for that Significant Someone. This chocolatier, where you quite literally might eat your words, holds a royal warrant and includes prominent residents of the Palace among its clientèle.

Charbonnel et Walker, 28 Old Bond St, London W1,

071-491 0939. Mon-Fri 9 am-5:30 pm, Sat 10 am-4 pm.

## Best Place To Lift Your Spirits
Berry Bros. & Rudd Ltd.

Look for ancient premises with a gilt sign depicting a coffee mill and you'll find one of London's preeminent wine-and-spirit merchants. The sign once marked a grocer's store opened here by a Widow Bourne in 1699. (The first building on the site was a farmhouse next to a hospital founded in 1100 for the care of "leprous maidens," later rebuilt by Henry VIII as a trysting place for Anne Boleyn.) As for the building's current tenants, no other family has been selling wine from one building for so long. The shop has changed little in 200 years, with its uneven floor, high wood-panelled walls dark with the patina of time, a Victorian high desk, and original wheelback Windsor chairs, where aristocracy once sat to deliberate its choices—and where it still does. The shop looks more like an old counting house, where you almost expect to see quill pens and morocco-bound ledgers. Look for the beam scales that have kept track of famous weight watchers since the time of Byron and Beau Brummel. Wines, kept in cool cellars, include a wide range of still and sparkling wines from France, Germany, Australia, Spain, Portugal, Hungary, Italy—in fact, from just about anywhere you'd expect wines to originate. The firm has long produced its own brands of Scotch Whisky, which have evolved into the popular Cutty Sark blends.

Berry Bros. & Rudd Ltd., 3 St. James's St, London SW1, 071-930 1888. Mon-Fri 9:30 am-5 pm.

## Best Bet For Vera Lynn And Cox's Pippen
Berwick Street Market

With the historic fruit-and-vegetable market long gone from Covent Garden, this popular open-air market could be the spot where a latterday Henry Higgins might run into a contemporary Liza Doolittle. Certainly, it is one of the best spots in London to buy fresh produce—and perhaps the best spot to get the *best buys* on fruit and vegetables, in the most unlikely location. This busy, clamourous street market is slap in the middle of the somewhat dubious enticements of Soho. You'll find the best seasonal produce from British orchards and farms and a variety of more exotic fruits and vegetables imported from Britain's EEC partners—

plus cheeses, fresh fish, and meat. The lively
Berwick Street Market (which also incorporates
Rupert Street to the south) also is the spot you'll
most likely find such potential collectibles as an
old Vera Lynn 78, a Lonnie Donegan LP, a vintage
copy of *Picture Post,* or an early edition of Dylan
Thomas poetry, at a clutch of stalls offering a variety of used tapes, records, magazines, and books.

Berwick Street Market, London W1; near Tottenham
Court Road & Oxford Circus Underground stations.

## Best Market For (Hungry) Early Risers

Smithfield Market

To experience this famous city meat market at its
busiest, you'll need to set your alarm alarmingly
early—well before dawn, since it opens at 5 a.m.
Then you'll need to be alert for burly men in soiled
white aprons toting massive sides of beef. By the
time most city workers are thinking about lunch,
the Smithfield porters are ready to go home. If you
elect to have an early breakfast, Smithfield pubs
and coffee shops open early. A good choice is the
Fox & Anchor (see separate listing), for a gour-
mand's meal of meat, eggs, chips, and all the trimmings (and also a good spot for lunch). The Victorian Italianate-style market, built in the late 19th
century, occupies about 10 acres and reputedly is
the world's largest meat market. Historically, it
was the site of the Bartholomew Fair dating back
to the 12th century and of gruesome executions
up until the middle of the 17th century. Worth
noting—and perhaps photographing—is London's
only statue of Henry VIII.

Smithfield Market, Charterhouse St, London EC1;
near Farringdon and Barbican Underground stations. Mon-Fri 5 am-noon.

## Best Bet To Remedy A Headache (And More!)

Boots The Chemist

Brits call them chemists, Yanks call them drug-
stores; either way you describe these handy combination pharmacies and notions stores, Boots is
*the* name in London, with more than 90 outlets
within the city. The Regent Street branch of Boots
is one of the chain's largest, offering three floors of
notions, medicines, and other sundry items. Of
course, you can get a prescription filled here, but
you can also find health and beauty aids, appliances, housewares, film (and developing services),
and much more; some even have a small food
department or take-away counter. The different

branches of Boots' vary in size and in hours open. (In an emergency, the local police station can direct you to a late chemists; different ones take turns staying open late on different nights.) Underwoods is another widely represented chain in London; its Queensway branch is open daily until 10 p.m., including Sundays.

Boots The Chemist, 182 Regent St, London W1, 071-734 4934. Mon-Wed, Fri & Sat 9 am-5:30 pm; Thu 9 am-6:30 pm. Also many other locations. Underwoods, 75 Queensway, London W2, 071-229 9266. Daily 9 am-10 pm. Also many other locations.

## Best Place To Shop Before You Sail
Captain O. M. Watts

Generations of sailors, before setting sail on the open seas, have set a course to this shop to stock up on all varieties of nautical equipment. The store was founded in 1928 by its namesake Captain Watts, a former merchant seaman, and its slogan is "Everything for the Yachtsman and his Yacht." Here you'll find inflatable rafts and boats, charts, books, maps, safety and navigation equipment, and clothing and accessories—even for non-salt sorts who would never dream of venturing out onto the water, but who still favour stylish and protective nautical rain slickers. There are a variety of decorations and adornments—such as nameplates, signs, and other personal touches— for boaters to trim their crafts. The store produces a great, fun-to-read catalog of its stock of marine equipment and accessories; the staff mostly consists of boating enthusiasts who offer knowledgeable and friendly service and advice.

Captain O. M. Watts, 45 Albemarle St, London W1, 071-493 4633. Mon-Wed, Fri 9 am-6 pm; Thu 9 am-7 pm; Sat 9 am-5 pm.

## Top Shop For Underground Posters
London Transport Museum Shop

Those ubiquitous, indispensible maps of the London Underground that decorate the subways and the tourist literature of London were designed in the 1930s by Henry Beck, an electrical engineer (note the map's similarity to a wiring diagram), to replace a more geographically literal but almost impossible to follow earlier map. The colourful, stylized maps (with an angular representation of the River Thames) also make good wall art and are available in poster form at the shop of this engaging museum of transportation (see separate listing) located in Covent Garden. This is a great shop for unusual and nostalgic posters, particularly copies of vintage London Transport posters promoting trips into the country by tube, red double-decker bus, and Green Line coach. The shop also carries a good range of books celebrating British transportation, the London Underground, and other transportation subjects, plus cards, T-shirts, souvenir mugs, trays, and other related memorabilia.

London Transport Museum Shop, Covent Garden, London WC2, 071-379 6344. Daily 10 am-5:45 pm.

## Best Shop That's Always In Good Voice

HMV Record Store

For a compact disc of hot reggae sounds from UB40, a cassette of evergreen Beatles hits to play in your car, or a classic LP of classical music—a little Mozart or Chopin, perhaps—this store, which bills itself as the largest in Europe, has music for just about every taste. Within its massive inventory spread over four warehouse-like floors, you'll find plenty to watch as well as listen to, with videos of such hit movies as *Pretty Woman* and *Henry V* and vintage television fare such as popular episodes of *Upstairs*, *Downstairs* and *Fawlty Towers*. There's another branch on Oxford Street near Marble Arch and a third in the Trocadero (see separate listing) at Piccadilly Circus.

HMV Record Store, 150 Oxford St, London W1, 071-631 3423. Mon-Wed, Fri & Sat 9:30 am-7 pm; Thu 9:30 am-8 pm.

## Jazziest Record Shop

Ray's Jazz Shop

Looking for the latest Wynton Marsalis compact disk? Or maybe a few of Charles Mingus' classic sides, or even a hard-to-find early Billie Holliday record? Since the 1950s, this store has been the best place in London to find jazz music in all of its recorded forms. Ray's offers new and used, mainstream and "out there" jazz music on CDs, vinyl albums, cassette tapes, and, in some examples, even on original 78 r.p.m. records. Occasionally, rare records are available, which are bid on by interested parties. Ray's also stocks books, magazines, posters and other jazz-oriented memorabilia. And this is more than just a record store—it can be an invaluable resource: A bulletin board of upcoming events can clue you in to the latest jazz happenings in and around London (especially free performances at clubs, pubs, and student organisations). The stock here is extensive and the staff knowledgeable. They'll even spin a few cuts for you if you want to check out a new release or an unfamiliar oldie.

Ray's Jazz Shop, 180 Shaftsbury Ave, London WC2, 071-240 3969. Mon-Sat 10 am-6:30 pm.

## Best Place To Shop If Your Name's Bond, James Bond

The Counter Spy Shop

This discreet-looking shop on South Audley Street, near Grosvenor Square, is the sort of place that Q, the Secret Service dirty-tricks-meister, might send 007—were it not for the name. There is nothing covert about either its name or its line of merchandise. Blatantly called The Counter Spy Shop, it is an incredible source of espionage-oriented equipment for wannabe Bonds—with the serious purpose of providing security and safety for individuals, corporations, and property in this age of wanton crime and terrorism. Shop here for "bug" sweepers, telephone scramblers, homing devices in pens (and cigarette packs, watches, and hearing aids), night vision equipment, mini-microphones and listening devices, bullet-proof clothing, bomb detectors, x-ray scanners, and cameras disguised as sprinkler heads, clocks, smoke detectors, and even car antennas. For the ultimate in surreptitious surveillance that no businessman should be without, there is the video-recording briefcase. The store also stocks instructional videotapes on such security topics as detecting bugs and wiretaps, foiling bomb attempts, using bullet-proof vests, and methods of surveillance. SPECTRE agents and wayward spouses beware!

The Counter Spy Shop, 62 South Audley St, London W1, 071-408 0287. Mon-Fri 9:30 am-5:30 pm.

## Best Place To Shop If Your Name's Kerr, Graham Kerr

David Mellor

As a gourmet, whether you gallop or merely trot, this is the shop to which you should run to stock the perfect kitchen. This was the first of three British kitchenware shops set up by famed designer David Mellor, winner of many design awards and recipient of an Order of British Empire (OBE) in 1981. The store offers a wide range of useful and smart cooking and dining products, including an award-winning line of cutlery designed by Mellor himself and manufactured at his factory just outside of Sheffield. A staggering array of items includes pots, pans, pottery, glasses, bowls, platters, knives, graters, slicers, openers, corers, peelers, juicers, whisks, measuring cups and spoons, scales, scoops, strainers, spatulas, turners, colanders, baking dishes, rollers, moulds, woks, steamers, baskets, and other kitchen utensils, equipment, and appliances. (Where possible, the stock primarily includes items produced in Great Britain.) Mellor also offers a good selection of cookbooks, and produces an attractive *Cook's Catalogue*, which depicts items available in the store and by mail order, imparts advice as to their use, and includes a checklist of suggested essential kitchen equipment for the first-time homemaker.

David Mellor, 4 Sloane Sq, London SW1, 071-730 4259. Mon-Sat 9:30 am-5:30 pm. Also at 26 James St, London WC2, 071-379 6947.

## Best City Souvenirs Made In Taiwan

Yes, London is one of the finest shopping cities in the world...but, like any other major city that attracts an abundance of visitors—and, perhaps even *more so* than other cities—London has a staggering number of tourist-trap shops selling souvenirs of dubious quality. Sometimes, flush with the moment and their surroundings, people have been known to succumb to the lures of impulse purchases at these shops. However, the bottom line is this: Do you really need a beach towel emblazoned with the Union Jack or a Big Ben coffee mug or a Di and Fergie T-shirt? And do you want to lug whatever it is you buy of this nature along with you until your return home? Probably not. But, for those who can't resist—or even relish in—an occasionally kitschy purchase, we suggest shopping trips to some of the more touristy shops that can be found on Oxford Street, Leicester Square, Piccadilly Circus, and Carnaby Street, as well as a sizable number of the stalls in the Portobello Road and Bermondsey street markets. And, for souvenir-shoppers with a higher purpose, we direct you to the next entry...

## Best City Souvenirs *Not* Made In Taiwan

### Covent Garden General Store

This large gift bazaar on two floors offers a large range of gifts and souvenirs in all price ranges. And while some of these items can be of the junky-kitschy quality of the material to be found in the sorts of shops mentioned in the previous listing, many are of a higher quality and can make good keepsakes of a visit to London. A section of the store is set aside as the "British Shop," with a good selection of souvenirs. Here you'll find pottery, decorative items, T-shirts and other clothing, toys, posters, glasses and mugs, soaps, scents, a large selection of housewares, chocolates, greeting cards, etc.; in general, there are thousands of items at reasonable prices. The General Store has a good range of hours and is open late. It also offers a restaurant downstairs featuring such light fare as salads, soups, jacket potatoes, and sandwiches. Other good spots for a variety of unique souvenirs in London are the Old Curiosity Shop on Portsmouth Street, the shops of the Museum of London and the London Transport Museum, and the Hard Rock Café (see separate listings).

Covent Garden General Store, 111 Long Acre, London WC2, 071-240 0331. Mon-Sat 10 am-midnight, Sun 11 am-7 pm.

## Most Curious Souvenirs
Old Curiosity Shop

In Charles Dickens' time, London was full of so-called "curiosity shops." Whether this is the particular one that he fictionalized in *The Old Curiosity Shop* as the home of the ill-fated Little Nell is a matter of some dispute. It is said to be the oldest shop in London and, since it dates from 1567, is one of the few surviving examples of Tudor architecture. Today, the attractive building brims with souvenirs of all sorts, ranging from china, pewter, and glassware, to first editions and mugs and bookmarks inscribed with quotations from the famous author's work. You'll find some antiques in the historic shop, along with such items as prints, brassware, and silhouettes of Dickensenian characters that are suitable for framing and make nice gifts.

Old Curiosity Shop, 13-14 Portsmouth St, London WC2, 071-405 9891. Mon-Fri 9 am-5 pm, Sat & Sun 9:30 am-4:30 pm.

## Best Buttons With Your Bows
Gallery of London

Need a badge or buttons to go with the old school or regimental tie? This shop, just off Jermyn Street, London's bastion of traditional men's furnishings, is the retail outlet of the London Badge and Button Company, specialising in military, college, and school insignia in a variety of forms. You can choose a hand-embroidered crest, meticulously hand-burnished reproductions of Edwardian and Victorian buttons, and accessories such as enameled tie clips and cuff links. American shoppers will find the crests of Ivy League and other major U.S. universities such as Yale, Harvard, and Princeton. And even though it may seem a little caddish, some shoppers buy intricately wrought regimental patches, school emblems, and buttons simply as fashion accessories to dress up blazers, sweaters, T-shirts, and other casualwear—without ever having come within hailing distance of the subject regiment or school.

Gallery of London, 1 Duke of York St, London SW1, 071-925 2082. Mon-Sat 9 am-6 pm.

## Best Bet For Button Gluttons

Button Queen

For anyone who likes to sew, or who knows anyone who likes to sew, this is a great shop to stock up on unusual buttons or to find an uncommon gift. A stock of thousands of buttons includes modern, old, and antique buttons, with prices ranging from a few pence to £200 or more. You'll find buttons made of cloth, mother of pearl, wood, glass, papier-mâché, china, silver, and horn, with some intricately embroidered and others handpainted. Collectors' items include prized 18th-century Wedgwood buttons. Also in stock are buckles and a selection of unique cuff links and earrings fashioned from buttons.

Button Queen, 19 Marylebone Ln, London W1, 071-935 1505. Mon-Fri 10 am-6 pm, Sat 10 am-1:30 pm.

## Best Enameled Boxes

Halcyon Days

When you are in need of a little inspiration for a unique gift for someone special, consider this beguiling boutique of boxes. We're talking exquisite hand-painted enameled boxes, both antique and new. The latter you might choose for a collector, selecting perhaps a vintage snuff box or an ornate antique jewelry box. If you order a custom-made box, you can have it inscribed with a message of thanks, love, or friendship. The range and variety of these decorative boxes is enormous. Selections include reproductions of old-English designs, pretty flora and fauna, seasonal scenes, sporting motifs such as boating, hunting, fishing, and riding, verse and quotations from literature, and various commemorative themes. These ornamental, eye-appealing boxes are ideal for storing pills, pins, clips, jewelry, and whatever else comes to mind.

Halcyon Days, 14 Brook St, London W1, 071-629 8811. Mon-Fri 9:15 am-5:30 pm, Sat 9:30 am-4:30 pm.

# Best Places To Get A Reel Deal

House Of Hardy & C. Farlow

These two London shops are angler heavens, full of the latest in rod-and-reel gadgetry, custommade lures and flies, and a variety of accessories and clothing for the avid fisherman (and -woman). Hardy specialises in handmade reels and, especially, rods, made of graphite, cane, and fiberglass materials, that are considered some of the finest in the world, and are priced to reflect it (you're paying for quality and very good service). Hardy also offers all sorts of general fishing tackle, a line of country/sporting clothing, and even a compact fishing rod to stuff into a briefcase for handy usage on a business trip—or for just a day in the country when you claim to be out of the office on meetings! Farlow is a modern-looking shop with roots in the past (it was founded in 1840). It offers a good stock of equipment and supplies (especially for trout and salmon fishing), and houses one of the largest collections of fishing flies in London. (The handsome Wheatley fly box, containing about 50 flies, is a nice gift for Izaak Walton types at about £30.) The shop carries a good selection of sporting and casual clothing—for hunting or fishing (or just to *look* like you do either). When members of the royal family decide to drown a worm or two, they usually do it with supplies from this shop.

House Of Hardy, 61 Pall Mall, London SW1, 071-839 5515. Mon-Fri 9 am-5 pm, Sat 9 am-4 pm. C. Farlow, 5 Pall Mall, London SW1, 071-839 2423. Mon-Fri 9 am-5 pm, Sat 9 am-4 pm.

# Best Place To Chase Paper

Paperchase

Need a ream of plum-coloured foolscap typing paper? Or how about decorations for a birthday party or maybe a leather-bound address book? Head to this chain of stores to fill these or any other stationery needs. Paperchase features a literal rainbow of fine writing papers, cards for nearly all occasions, wrapping paper, notebooks and address books (including popular Filofax brand books), pens, pencils, posters, prints, art materials, and art books. These stores also offer a good selection of party-oriented items, including serviettes, tablecloths, signs, and balloons, all available with matching messages, either joyful or mocking. Holiday-themed decorations are available too, such as skeletons and witches for Halloween, and elves and Father Christmas for Christmas. There are good prices on most of these items.

Paperchase, 213 Tottenham Court Rd, London W1, 071-580 8496. Mon-Sat 9 am-6 pm. Also other locations.

## Best Stationery Fit For A Queen

Smythson of Bond Street

If you were lucky enough to get a hand-written note from Queen Elizabeth, it's very likely that it would be on a thick, engraved, pale blue piece of stationery from this upper-crust shop. Founded in 1887 (and the holder of a Royal Warrant), Smythson offers top-of-the-line, very proper stationery. The store's signature paper is light blue (if it's good enough for the Queen...), but white, cream, and other colours also are available. Smythson is also a good spot to find high-quality handmade envelopes, Christmas cards, diaries and appointment books, and desk accessories. These items are generally expensive—but, American tourists please note, cost less than the same items would run in the United States. (And, in an etiquette-oriented note, if the Queen *does* write you, this is how you would address your reply to her: Her Majesty Elizabeth, Queen of England, Buckingham Palace, St. James's Park, London SW1. Your letter's salutation should be "May it please Your Majesty" or simply "Madame.")

Smythson of Bond Street, 54 New Bond St, London W1, 071-629 8558. Mon-Fri 9:15 am-5:15 pm, Sat 9:15 am-12:30 pm.

## Best Place To Become Your Own Personal Tailor

Clothkits

Even if you feel a bit lost with a needle and thread, you can become your own tailor with some help from this innovative shop. As its name implies, Clothkits offers kits of ready-to-make clothes that you assemble and sew yourself. Some of these kits feature already-cut patterns, ready to be sewn; others are a little more challenging, with cutlines marked on pieces of fabric. In either case, you needn't be an accomplished seamstress or tailor to make these items—each package includes simple, step-by-step instructions, and are designed for people with little or no previous sewing experience. The kits feature both adult's and children's styles (the children's kits yield particularly nice, colourful outfits) in a range of different colours and fabrics; the kits also include matching threads, buttons, and any other accessories needed to make the particular piece (or pieces) of clothing. You can try on samples to help determine necessary sizes for certain patterns. Clothkits also sells a limited selection of ready-made clothing and accessories.

Clothkits, 39 Neal St, London WC2, 071-240 7826. Mon-Sat 9:30 am-6 pm.

# Best Shop That Accepts No Bull

## Lawley's

Brides-to-be head to this plush, blue carpeted store, along with friends and relatives shopping for brides-to-be, and anyone else who is planning to set up house and may be in need of fine English bone china. You'll find the royalty of fine china beautifully represented—the likes of Royal Doulton, Royal Worcester, Crown Derby, Aynsley, Minton, and Wedgwood—as well as the aristocracy of crystal—Waterford, Edinburgh, Brierly, and Stuart. Collectors come here shopping for Lladro figurines and David Winter cottages. And if that nuptial-bound lady is all set for china, there is a wide range of cutlery.

Lawley's, 154 Regent St, London W1, 071-734 3184. Mon-Wed, Fri & Sat 9:30 am-6 pm; Thu 9:30 am-7 pm.

# Best Shop More Kindly To Bulls

## Reject China Shop

So-called "reject shops" and stores specialising in "seconds" are something akin to those duty-free shops at airports. It sounds like a good idea, you *can* find some bargains, but you should approach them warily, knowing what you're looking for and with a good idea of what it typically costs. That said, it can be worthwhile inspecting the mountains of bone china, crystal, glassware, and pottery, and the array of cutlery on display at these warehouse-like stores (this one on Regent Street and a grouping of others on Beauchamp Place in Knightsbridge). Although the selection is more limited than at some of the other china specialty stores, many of the famous makes and patterns are represented, and you may find some bargains in discontinued lines and second-quality goods. Much of the stock, however, is mint stuff at prices similar to elsewhere. A mail-order catalogue is available, and a shipping department to help tourists get their purchases home.

Reject China Shop, 134 Regent St, London W1, 071-434 2502. Mon & Tue, Thu-Sat 9 am-6 pm, Wed 9 am-7 pm.

# Best Shop To Spice Up Your Life

## Culpeper Herbalists

Named after a pioneer herbalist, this shop is full of herbs and spices designed to make you feel better, look better, and smell better, and to make your food taste better. The fragrance is tempting, as is the array of creams, essences, bath salts and oils, soaps, sachets of potpourri, scented pillows, shampoos, talcum powders, toilet water, and a variety of sweets, such as barley sugar. Most of the herb-based cosmetics are made from plants grown by Culpeper. The store carries close to 200 varieties of dried herbs, including many medicinal herbs favoured by homeopaths. For the cook are culinary spices as well as vinegars, mustards, honey, teas, ginger, and herbs in pots ready for the kitchen garden. Culpeper offers a mail-order catalogue and has a branch in Covent Garden (8 The Market).

Culpeper Herbalists, 21 Bruton St, London W1, 071-629 4559. Mon-Fri 9:30 am-6 pm, Sat 10 am-5 pm.

## Best Place To Find Sports Of All Sorts

Lillywhites, Ltd.

Alpine ski equipment, bowling balls, and cricket stumps, rugby uniforms, shuttlecocks, and tennis rackets—you'll find equipment for sports of all sorts at Europe's largest sporting-goods shop. Established in 1863, this is a department store devoted to athletic supplies, with floor after floor of equipment, clothing, footwear, books, and videos. For the super-fit—or those with aspirations to be— are departments devoted to tracksuits, exercise equipment, and rackets sports. For those who prefer more sedentary pursuits, there is a wide selection of equipment for snooker, billiards, and darts. There is a dazzling selection of sports shoes for every imaginable occasion—and some that you probably couldn't even guess at—plus equipment for riding, shooting, fishing, and water sports. If you can't find a particular item of sporting paraphernalia within Lillywhites' six floors, they'll order it for you!

Lillywhites Ltd, Picacadilly Circus, SW1, 071-930 3181. Mon, Wed, Fri & Sat 9:30 am-6 pm; Tue 9:45 am-6 pm; Thu 9:30 am-7 pm.

## Best Shop That Won't Send You Packing

The Packing Shop

Some people have a way with parcels, causing brown paper, string, and tape to serve them with orderly folds, neat corners, and well-executed knots. Others? Well, a package ends up looking like so much rumpled laundry bundled in wrapping paper. And when it comes to packing and shipping something valuable, perhaps an antique china dish, a delicate cameo, or a treasured piece of pottery, even those who are handy with string and paper might want to defer to experts. These particular experts specialise in custom packing and shipping fragile items. They'll get your package to its destination safely, using protective injection-applied foam where appropriate, and on time—across Britain and around the world (same day in Britain, for example, and to the United States within 48 hours). They can make a gift look pretty, too, with a wonderful array of decorative paper, ribbons, and bows. They'll pick up from a shop or a hotel.

The Packing Shop, 19 George St, London W1, 071-486 0102. Mon-Fri 9 am-6 pm, Sat 9:30 am-3:30 pm.

# ROMANTIC

## Most Romantic Spot Of Tea In A Royal Park

Richmond Park

At this large, meandering park, you can get a peek at wildlife, get an idea of what England's forests of hundreds of years ago looked like, and, perhaps most pleasantly, relax with a cup of tea on a breeze-kissed terrace overlooking the splendour of the park. Established by Charles I in 1637 as royal hunting ground, Richmond Park spreads out for more than 2,000 acres, making it the country's largest Royal Park. Much of the acreage is still in its natural state—for example, huge, sturdy oaks that date from the dense medievel forests that once covered this area. The park also offers a wide variety of native flora and fauna. Most notable among the latter are the herds of deer that still roam wild (some of the deer are used to people and have been known to creep close to curious gawkers). The gardens of Isabella Plantation are especially popular from about mid-April to late May, when their beautiful azaleas and rhododendrons are abloom. The park also contains the King's Observatory (now a meteorological station), the White Lodge (George I's hunting lodge—now the Royal Ballet Junior School), and Pembroke Lodge, once the childhood home of philosopher Betrand Russell and now a wonderful destination for a spot of tea in the park.

Richmond Park, Richmond, Surrey, 081-940 0654.
Daily 5 am-dusk. Near Richmond Underground station. Pembroke Lodge, 081-940 8270. Daily Jan-Oct,
weekends Nov & Dec (hours vary).


## Most Romantic Restaurant For Dinner

Julie's

Going one better than a restaurant that serves fine
food in a romantic setting, Julie's offers a choice of
*several* cosy and intimate settings. Opened more
than two decades ago, this labyrinthine Holland
Park restaurant and wine bar is known for constantly changing the interior design of its many
elegant rooms. Start your evening in the Champagne Bar, with canapés, bubbly, and Cole Porter
tunes around delicately latticed partitions and
tables; or in the plush Sitting Room, where you
can relax in overstuffed couches and chairs
around an open fireplace or in a quiet alcove.
When it is time for dinner, your romantic journey
continues with a stylish Anglo-French menu. Try
medallions of venison with brandied black cherries
in the soft pink surroundings of The Forge, featuring the original bellows. Dine on roast pheasant
with hazelnut stuffing and wild Rowan jelly around
the Moroccan tables and palms of the honeysuck-
le-filled Garden Room, complete with an antique,
cast-iron spiral staircase. Or tempt your palate
with Kent duck with apricots and tawny port
sauce in a private eating area of the Gothic Room,
resplendent with original gothic mouldings from
the old School of Paul's. Whatever your choice of
meal and seating—and there are several others—
Julie's provides a memorable romantic and gastronomic excursion.

Julie's, 135 Portland Rd, Holland Park, London W11,
071-229 8831 or 071-727 4585.


## Most Romantic Alfresco Dining— Indoors!

Odette's

Request a table in the conservatory of this
Regent's Park restaurant, with light filtering in
through the overhead glass, and you'll create the
feeling of an alfresco meal—without need to worry
about the weather. This multi-level, plant-filled
French restaurant has a room lined with gilt-edged
mirrors and a downstairs wine bar with intimate
booths. The menu is French-based with an eclectic
mix of English and international dishes. Start with
duck terrine or ginger-accented duck salad, and
continue with terrine of lobster and sweetbreads,

saddle of venison with chestnuts, or turbot baked with an herb crust. Other unusual creations might include pigeon with bacon and lentils and duck with wild mushrooms and chicken mousse. The adjoining wine bar offers a list of more than 50 French, Italian, Spanish, Australian, and Californian wines, including a good selection of champagnes. A chalkboard menu offers salads, sandwiches, and such selections as venison sausage.

Odette's, 130 Regent's Park Rd, London NW1, 071-586 5486. Mon-Fri 12:30-11 pm, Sat 7:30-11 pm.

## Most Romantic Restaurant In Kensington
Launceston Place

With pretty flowers, light filtering through a skylight, and cosy Victorian rooms full of fetching mirrors, art nouveau prints, and watercolours, this is a romantic spot for lunch or dinner. Nor will you necessarily need arrange a bank overdraft in order to eat here, especially if you take advantage of reasonable prix fixe lunches and dinners and a quite acceptable house wine. The creative cuisine includes such dishes as pheasant casserole with wild mushrooms, fricassee of sole with langoustines, calves' liver with onion marmalade, and filet of sea bream complimented by ratatouille. Starters include ham and melon and mushroom-filled ravioli; recommended desserts are pineapple fritters and bread-and-butter pudding. After leaving the restaurant, it is pleasant to stroll around this stylish Kensington residential neighbourhood that seems as if it might belong in a fashionable country town rather than in the heart of London.

Launceston Place, 1a Launceston Pl, London W8, 071-937 6912. Mon-Fri 12:30-11 pm, Sat 7:30-11 pm, Sun noon-3 pm.

## Best Romantic Hotel
Blakes Hotel

If 60 of the most exquisite sets created in Hollywood's Golden Age were suddenly to break out of their celluloid prisons and burst to life in vibrant colour, they would almost equal the magnificence of the guest quarters at Blakes. *Almost.* This South Kensington hotel is the brainchild of designer Anouska Hempel, who set out in 1986 to create a set of fantastically stylised living spaces that challenge the imagination and lift the spirit. Here, you can live out your most opulent daydreams: Become a sultan by sitting under a triangle of gold-striped antique silk draperies on an ebonised and gilt, Empire-style daybed; or smell the jasmine of the Orient in the lavish Chinese Room, where white-plumed birds frolic on a large chinoiserie screen and lacquer-and-gilt Thai elephants trumpet greetings across the huge, high-gloss coffee table. Many of the pieces—superb Regency beds, Biedermeier lyre tables, and maplewood chairs—were created by Hempel's extensive network of craftsmen. Many others are fine antiques, such as the vintage Vuitton trunks in the reception area. Selections in the dining room—inkfish risotto, chicken and crab with garlic ginger sauce—complement this paen to the decorative arts. The only problem with staying at Blakes is that you might find it difficult to leave. When you do tear yourself away, a short walk along leafy streets leads to the new Brompton Cross centre of shops and a five-minute taxi ride takes you to Harrods and Hyde Park.

Blakes Hotel, 33 Roland Gardens, London SW7, 071-370 6701.

## Most Romantic Small Hotel

Mostyn Hotel

Unless a crown is a permanent part of your wardrobe, you won't be invited to stay in Buckingham Palace while visiting London. But you can choose what may be the next best thing, within the stately 18th-century confines of the Mostyn, where you will feel the reverberations of royalty past. Originally, it was the home of Lady Black, lady-in-waiting to the court of King George II. The lobby and other common areas retain many original features, including ornate ceilings and fire surrounds designed by John Adam, but each room has been modernised. Pastel fabrics and Impressionist prints leave the stylish suites awash in colour, from the king-size beds to the spacious and tasteful sitting rooms. Venture forth to the Tea Planter Restaurant, where, surrounded by memorabilia of the British Empire, you can sample prime Scottish meat grilled over hickory salts or roasted suckling pig. Beckoning guests is the nearby bustle of the West End—Marble Arch, the shops of Oxford and Regent streets, theatres, and the jewelers of Bond Street.

Mostyn Hotel, Bryanston St, London W1, 071-935 2361.

## Most Romantic Floating Cabaret

The Romance of London

This is one nightclub that really rocks and rolls!

As the luxury catamaran *Natica* slips away from Westminster Pier most Sunday evenings, couples cast off for a high-spirited romantic dinner-and-dancing tour of London along the Thames. As comperes point out such famous landmarks as St. Paul's Cathedral and the Tower of London, you can relax with an aperitif before your four-course, candelit meal. With after-dinner coffee comes magic of a quite literal kind provided by strolling prestidigitators with a little something up their sleeves. The upper deck balcony and the tables in the lower saloon surround a stage; in this cabaret setting, romantic and popular songs are performed as the *Natica* glides past the fabled clipper ship *Cutty Sark* (moored at Greenwich) and then continues on its way to the Thames Flood Barrier. On the return trip you can sway with the current and to the beat of the music on the dance floor or head up on deck for a stunning view of Tower Bridge and along the river's floodlit banks. The *Natica* is the largest catamaran on the Thames, so you'll likely find a secluded spot for a quiet moment alone!

The Romance of London, departing on the *Natica* Sunday evenings from Westminster Pier, 071-620 0474.

# Best Embodiment Of Love In Statue Form

Eros, the God of Love, Piccadilly Circus

Much like love itself, there's more than meets the eye when it comes to this famous fountain and statue surrounded by the traffic of Piccadilly Circus. Erected in 1893 (as London's first aluminium statue), it was meant to honour the philanthropic works of the 7th Earl of Shaftesbury by depicting the "Angel of Christian Charity." How this cherub eventually came to be known as Eros, the Greek god of erotic love, is not clear. Nevertheless, this winged, bow-and-arrow wielding statue has become a favourite mascot for London's lovers. The recently widened island plaza that contains this statue is a popular spot for young people to gather, some locked in embraces that have been no doubt inspired by the crafty machinations of (the alleged) Eros. This also is a favourite spot for meeting foreign visitors, who seem to congregate here with guidebooks, maps, drinks, and munchies.

Eros Statue, Piccadilly Circus, London SW1; near Piccadilly Circus Underground station.

# Most Languid River Ride

## Punting On The River Cam, Cambridge

It is well worth the drive (not much more than 50 miles—80 kilometers—from London) for a day's romantic outing to Cambridge, with perhaps a quiet luncheon for two at a village inn along the way, afternoon tea in town, and, of course, punting along the "Backs." There is something languid and peaceful about propelling a punt along the River Cam, with willows reflected in the water, timeless stone bridges, sweeping lawns that invite a picnic, grazing ponies, and cows folded in bucolic somnolence. Chauffeured punts are available for those who prefer to sit back and enjoy the sights while someone else (a boatman, perhaps complete with straw "boater" hat and blazer) worries about manipulating the long pole. When you get off the river, spend a quiet time exploring the ancient colleges of Cambridge, some dating back to the 13th century, many of which have beautiful gardens; the University Botanic Garden has formal lawns, flower beds, and greenhouses open to visitors. Cambridge has excellent pubs, many along the river, as well as wine bars, coffee houses, and restaurants.

Tourist Information Centre, Wheeler St, Cambridge CB2 3QB, 0223 322640.

# Most Immortal Kiss

## Rodin's "Le Baiser" sculpture, Tate Gallery

Offering an esteemed collection of fine art, the Tate Gallery (see separate listing) is a perfect place for a casual, romantic stroll. (And also for a delightful lunch and a glass of wine in the museum's well-regarded café—see separate listing.) But the most romantic spot in the gallery is just off its Central Hall, in the Sculpture Gallery (which is replete with works by such noted artists as Henry Moore). The focus of the gallery is its most beloved and identifiable piece, by French sculptor Auguste Rodin—a circa 1900 copy of his 1886 sculpture "Le Baiser," which is better known as "The Kiss." Today, this world-famous work, which depicts two stylised lovers wrapped in a tight embrace, is considered Rodin's masterpiece—a far cry from the Victorian days of its unveiling, when it was decried as being "obscene." Absorbing, yes; inspiring, probably (it depends on who you're with!); but obscene? Shows how far art appreciation—and societal mores—have come.

Rodin's "Le Baiser" ("The Kiss"), Tate Gallery, Millbank, London SW1, 071-821 1313. Mon-Sat 10 am-5:50 pm, Sun 2-5:50 pm. Free.

## Best Bet For Dinner, Dancing, The View—And You
Roof Gardens

Although Rank's flagship hotel, the Royal Garden, is not exactly a skyscraper, its sixth-floor rooftop restaurant/club does offer a panoramic view across Kensington. You can look out onto the pretty green swathes of Hyde Park and Kensington Gardens and across the royal residences at Kensington Palace to the distant twinkling lights of the West End skyline. This is a fitting spot for a romantic splurge, with dining by candlelight and dancing to live music in a garden setting. This fashionable upmarket nightspot, owned by music and airline impresario Richard Branson, attracts a small set of London clubgoers and a sprinkling of celebrities.

Roof Gardens, Royal Garden Hotel, 99 Kensington High St, London W8, 071-937 8000. Thu & Sat 7 pm-1 am.

## Most Regal Underthings
Bradleys

It is not just because the Royals are reputed to shop at this Knightsbridge specialty store that makes it so popular. It also is because of the large selection of lingerie—probably the largest in London—stylishly fashioned in the finest silk, satin, cotton, and lace. From captivating peignoirs and slinky teddies to comfortable cotton nightdresses and silky pajamas, this is the shop to find nightthings and underthings that are sophisticated and alluring—or simply plain and comfortable. Shop here for designer gowns, bras, foundation garments, fleecy slippers, and a small selection of beachwear. The store also carries a line of lingerie with its own label.

Bradleys, 85 Knightsbridge, London SW1, 071-235 2902. Mon & Tue, Thu-Sat 9:30 am-6 pm; Wed 9:30 am-7 pm.

## Most Sexy Underthings
Janet Reger

Glamour is the watchword at this lingerie shop on trendy Beauchamp Place. With a reputation for attracting models and show-biz folk, it stocks lingerie and nightwear that is the ultimate in frilly and fancy. As Marilyn Monroe might have commented, "dreamy." Wispy underthings, shimmery satin teddies, the sheerest nightdresses, beguiling peignoirs, and comely camisoles are available in frilly, lace-trimmed satin and silk, in polycotton, and in simple cotton that never looked so alluring. Colours range from shades of delicate lavender, pink, and peach to seductive reds and blacks. Americans might view this sophisticated, pricey store as a British version of Victoria's Secret. A mail-order catalogue is available.

Janet Reger, 2 Beauchamp Pl, London SW3, 071-584 9368. Mon-Fri 10 am-6 pm, Sat 10 am-5 pm.

# Best Place To Let Love Bloom

Edward Goodyear

Whether your love for that special someone is a growing concern or a hardy perennial, this shop can provide the flowers and plants that can help those feelings blossom. Established in 1880 by its namesake, this is one of the oldest florists in London. It offers a garden of flowers, plants, and floral arrangements for use as gifts or as decorations at parties, banquets, and weddings. (In fact, Edward Goodyear provided elaborate floral displays, bridesmaid's headdresses, and bouquets for Charles and Di's wedding in 1981.) This shop is popular—it is estimated to sell more than 2,000 red roses on a typical Valentine's Day. Edward Goodyear is one of only 12 companies to hold all four currently issued royal warrants (from Queen Elizabeth, Prince Philip, Prince Charles, and the Queen Mother), and is owned by the Savoy Group of hotels, restaurants, and shops (as in the Savoy Hotel—see separate listing).

Edward Goodyear, 4 Brook St, London W1, 071-629 1508. Mon-Fri 8:30 am-5 pm. Also other locations.

# PARKS & GARDENS

## Best Short-Cut Between Buckingham Palace and Piccadilly

Green Park

This Royal Park's proper appellation is "The Green Park" (although the definite article is rarely included in common usage), a fitting name for perhaps the single greenest concentration of parkland in London, unbroken by either flowers or bodies of water. (It is the only Royal Park in town without either flowers or a lake.) The green expanses of this park are favourite spots for sunning and/or picnicking among area office workers; clement mid-days will find multitudes lounging throughout the park, both in the sun and under the park's many varieties of shade trees. (Canvas-and-wood deckchairs are available for hire.) The smallest Royal Park in London, Green Park was created in the 1660s from what had been a swampy burial ground for lepers and, later, the site of ice houses built for Charles II.

Green Park, London W1; near Green Park Underground station.

## Best Park That Is Forever

Hampstead Heath

To get away from the hectic pace, noise, fumes, and bustle of central London, it is not necessary to

travel hours (or even *one* hour) out into the surrounding countryside. You can get back to nature
and leave modern London behind merely by journeying some four miles north of the center of the
metropolis to the sprawling wilderness that is
Hampstead Heath. This 800-acre expanse of
wooded paths and open, rolling fields was loosely
established as first a manor common and then as
public parkland in the 1600s; Parliament issued a
decree protecting the park for "the use of the public forever" in 1872. It offers separate lakes for
swimming, fishing, and boating, a pond for model-
boat enthusiasts, horse paths, running and walking tracks, 10 tennis courts, and areas for cricket,
rugby, and football. The heath is a fine spot for
strolling, and is open 24 hours...But prudence dictates vacating before dark the remote parts of the
heath (particularly the dense and wild western
section). Hampstead Heath is also known for its
annual Bank Holiday fairs, which draw thousands
of revelers. Parliament Hill, in the southern section
of the heath, offers a splendid view of the City skyline (see separate listing).

Hampstead Heath, London NW3; near Hampstead
Underground station.


# Best Little-Known View Of The London Skyline

Parliament Hill, Hampstead Heath

To get a terrific eyeful of London (and, perhaps, to
stand in the footsteps of history), head to this hill
in the southern part of Hampstead Heath (see separate listing). Rising 319 feet (97 meters) above sea
level, the hill provides excellent panoramic views of
London, particularly of the skyline of the City.
Aside from purely aesthetic pleasures, the hill is
also a favourite spot for kite-flying, attracting
colourful squadrons of flying contraptions on
weekends. As for the hill's history, stories abound.
One tale claims that the hill owes its height to
piles of dead buried there during the Plague.
Another says that ancient British Queen Boadicea
and her tribe watched the Roman outpost of Londinium burn from here in the year 61 A.D. What
seems more definitely truthful is that the hill is
most likely to have gained its name due to the plan
of Guy Fawkes' fellow Gunpowder Plotters to meet
there to watch the Houses of Parliament be blown
sky high on the Fifth of November, 1605. As noted
by history (and by millions of schoolboys with fireworks to light), the plot was foiled and such devastating pyrotechnics avoided, but the name
remains.

Parliament Hill, Hampstead Heath, London NW3;

near Hampstead Underground station.

## Best Park Where Henry VIII Once Hunted Deer

Hyde Park

Just west of the West End spreads the most notable of the "green lungs" that make up the city's extensive park system. At 350 acres, Hyde Park is one of the largest urban parks in the world and is the largest Royal Park in London. (Kensington Gardens is contiguous to the west of the park, adding up to more than 600 acres of unbroken parkland.) The park is made up of one-time manor land that Henry VIII seized from the monks of Westminster Abbey and turned into his personal happy hunting ground, stocked with boar, bulls, and stag (deer hunting continued in the park until the 1760s). Beginning in the 1600s, the park was opened to the public, and today offers a pleasant urban oasis of rolling lawns, shady trees, ponds, and patches of flowery gardens; activities available include jogging, biking, boating, swimming, and fishing. Hyde Park became world famous as the site of the Great International Exhibition in 1851, which was a precursor to the modern world fair. Also in Hyde Park are the Serpentine lake, the sand horse path of Rotten Row, and the free-speech mecca of Speakers' Corner (see separate listings); Kensington Gardens contains a popular statue of Peter Pan (see separate listing).

Hyde Park, London W1; near Hyde Park Corner and Marble Arch Underground stations.

## Best Place To Row, Row, Row Your Boat

The Serpentine, Hyde Park

So named because of its gently curving, snake-like shape, this 41-acre manmade lake, created in 1730 by the damming of the river Westbourne, is central London's major water playground. Row boats (and even small sailing dinghies) are available for hire; the lake also hosts flotillas of model sailing boats and swimmers—the latter especially in the broad, southern-shore section called the Lido. The Serpentine has been popular and notable since its creation—occasionally for strange or sad reasons. For example, in 1814, an authentic recreation of the battle of Trafalgar was staged here as part of a festival celebrating the end of the Napoleonic wars...and, in 1816, poet Percy Bysshe Shelley's first wife drowned herself here. On a more pleasant, yet still-strange note, the Serpentine is also the home-base to the Serpentine Swim-

ming Club, the members of which take a traditional plunge into the lake's icy waters on Christmas Day. The section of the lake that curves from
Hyde Park into Kensington Gardens is called the
Long Water.

The Serpentine, Hyde Park, London W1; near Hyde
Park Corner and Knightsbridge Underground stations.

## Best Park For Family Fun
Battersea Park

In 1951, Britain was struggling with postwar austerity and London still was littered with debris
from the blitz and pockmarked with ugly bomb
sites gaping like missing teeth in a smile. Then
came the ambitious Festival of Britain, bringing
music, entertainment, and fairground fun to the
drab, grey London scene. Its legacy is the attractive Festival Gardens that were appended to this
riverside park opened in 1853. Prior to that, the
area was known as Battersea Fields, the haunt of
gypsies and river ruffians and the site of a duel
between the Duke of Wellington and Lord Win-
chilsea. Today, this delightful park that stretches
its woodlands and lawns along the river across
from Chelsea is enjoyed for its boating lake, deer
park, small children's zoo (see separate listing),
botanical garden, playing fields, and sculptures by
Henry Moore and Barbara Hepworth. You can
roller skate, play tennis and soccer, enjoy fun fairs
and parades and a football game under the lights,
and admire a serene Japanese buddhist pagoda
built in 1985 in the name of world peace.

Battersea Park, London SW11, 081-871 7530; near
Sloane Square Underground station (then bus).

## Best Bridle Path With A Corrupted Name
Rotten Row, Hyde Park

There's nothing rotten, really, about this straight
horse path in the south end of Hyde Park. The
name is just a bit of Cockney-mangled French
reflecting the path's heritage. From about the 16th
century, it was the royal path between Westminster and Kensington—thusly, it was called "La
Route du Roi," French for "the king's way." A few
years pass, and, *voilà!*, the name becomes corrupted into "Rotten Row." This straight sand path
stretches about 1½ miles along the park's southern edge. It's a popular site for horseriding; horses
are available for hire nearby (see separate listing).
And, in a bit of trivia, Rotten Row is believed to be
the first street in England to be illuminated at
night—the path's propensity for attracting

marauding highwayman caused William III to order in 1689 that a row of lamps be strung along the path.

Rotten Row, Hyde Park, London W1; near Hyde Park Corner and Knightsbridge Underground stations.

## Best Botanic Garden That Happens To Be The Birthplace Of A King

Royal Botanic Gardens, Kew

Planted in 1846, a mere nine years into the reign of Queen Victoria, the Royal Botanic Gardens' Chilean Wine Palm has grown into what is believed to be the world's tallest greenhouse plant, at more than 58 feet tall. When this giant palm tree was a seedling, these venerable gardens (known informally as Kew Gardens) already were 115 years old and *they* have grown into the leading botanical garden in the world. The 300-acre site (located near the river Thames, southwest of London) was begun in 1731; much of its finest areas were laid out in the 1770s by legendary landscape architect "Capability" Brown (nicknamed for his constant observations that areas showed "capabilities" for improvements). The garden's huge flowerbeds (a stunning sight during spring and summer blooming) and vast greenhouses (warm, lush, and beckoning during inclement months) are home to approximately 50,000 different plants. Buildings on the grounds include the Dutch House mansion (dating from 1631 and also known as the Kew Palace), birthplace and summer home of King George III; the Orangery, an attractive 1761 building now housing a museum; and the Temperate House, an acre in area, which houses a large collection of greenhouse plants, including the towering ancient palm. As a research and cataloging institution, the garden handles a wide variety of inquiries from professional horticulturalists and green-thumbers.

Royal Botanic Gardens, Kew Rd, Richmond, Surrey, 081-940 1171. Daily 10 am–dusk. £1.

## Best Shakespeare In The Park

Open Air Theatre, Regent's Park

The sun goes down, the stage lights come up, and it's time for Shakespeare under the stars. This delightful seasonal theatre presents mostly the works of the Bard, often in elaborate period costume. (As you might imagine, this sylvan setting is perfect for performances of *A Midsummer Night's Dream!*) Founded in 1933, and currently housed in a 1,200-seat auditorium constructed in 1975, this theatre boasts better sightlines and acoustics than are usually found at outdoor venues. Head here for an entertaining night of theatre and refreshments (served from the longest theater bar in the entire city), but don't fear the weather—if it rains on you and Hamlet (or Macbeth or whomever is trodding the boards that night), you'll receive make-good tickets for a subsequent performance. Adjoining the theatre is the lovely Queen Mary's Rose Garden, offering a stunning array of blooms in more than 40,000 bushes and beds.

Open Air Theatre, Inner Circle, Regent's Park, London NW1, 071-486 2431. Jun-Sep Mon-Sat 7:45 pm; Wed, Thu, & Sat matinées 2:30 pm. £5-£12. Near Baker Street Underground station.

## London's Oldest Royal Park

St. James's Park

Each of London's Royal Parks has its individual charms—such as Hyde's famous landmarks, Green's sunny grasslands, and Regent's theatre and garden—but this smallish (93-acre) park may just be the city's overall most attractive and pleasant park. It was laid out by Henry VIII in 1532 as the first Royal Park in London, and was once inhabited by a royal menagerie of wild animals. Today, its most notable inhabitants are birds, especially the ducks that flock to its five-acre lake. (Until 1988, it was also known for its flock of five to six pelicans, which were descended from a pair presented to Charles II by the Russian ambassador; these have since been moved to the London Zoo because they used to chase and eat the park's pigeons, much to the delight or horror of observers.) A bridge offers one of the least-known, but best-appreciated views from any park in London—to the east are the rooftops and spires of Whitehall, to the west is Buckingham Palace. A band plays on summer days (except Sundays).

St. James's Park, London SW1, 071-930 1793. Daily 5 am-midnight. Near St. James's Park Underground station.

## Best Place To See More Than 8,000 Animals In 36 Acres

The London Zoo, Regent's Park

Although the panda and the penguins, the giraffes and gorillas attract most of the attention at London's venerable zoo, perhaps some of its less-desirable residents—such as the bird-eating spiders or the 15-foot python—better symbolize the history of this pioneering zoo: The London Zoo has the world's oldest collection of insects and was once the home of the world's largest poisonous snake. But, admittedly, it's probably the more cute-and-cuddly animals that have helped to make this one of London's most popular attractions. Opened in 1828 as one of the first urban zoos in the world, it occupies a large triangle in the northern section of Regent's Park. One of the zoo's highlights is its Clore Pavilion, which contains both the world's largest collection of small mammals, and, in its basement, Moonlight World, which offers a black-lit look at such rarely seen nocturnal animals as giant fruit bats and kiwis. Feeding times for the various animals are posted near the entrance of the zoo and are a very popular spectacle (especially among the comical penguins and sleek, splashing seals). The zoo also offers the Children's Zoo with a farmyard, baby animals, and daily cow-milking demonstrations; camel and pony rides are available.

The London Zoo, Regent's Park, London NW1, 071-722 3333. Apr-Oct daily 9 am-6 pm, Nov-Mar daily 10 am-dusk. Adults £4.30, students and OAPs £3.50, children 4-16 £2.60, children under 4 free. Near Camden Town Underground station.

## First Zoo Without Bars

Whipsnade Park Zoo

This zoo is the wildest place around! Located approximately 35 miles northwest of London, it covers 580 acres, with much of its space given over to large, open expanses containing free-roaming wild animals, mostly grouped by their native geographic areas. (Those animals not roaming free are displayed in barless, enclosed habitats.) Whipsnade Park, which serves as the breeding park for the London Zoo in Regent's Park (see separate listing), was the first open-air zoo in the world. Among its highlights are many rare species (including white rhinos, cheetahs, and cranes), demonstrations of trained birds of prey, a seal show, and a recently added Discovery Centre, offering a black-lit nocturnal world and a manmade tropical rain forest. You can drive through the wide-open areas, safari-style, or ride a steam train. A picnic area offers a great view of animals roaming the plains; be sure to bring binoculars and/or cameras.

Whipsnade Park Zoo, Dunstable, Bedfordshire, 0582 872171. Oct-Apr Mon-Sat 10 am-6 pm, Sun 10 am-7 pm; May-Sep daily 10 am-sunset. Adults £4.50, children 4-16 and students £2.70, children under 4 free; driving own car through park £5; free parking.

## Best Place To Cultivate A Green Thumb

Syon Park

The gorgeous gardens of this 55-acre park are the envy of visitors given to tending small patches of green behind their houses. Highlights of its dazzling array of greenery and blooms include a six-acre rose garden, a wide variety of trees ringing large lawns, still-fruit-bearing mulberry bushes planted here in the 1500s, a landscaped path around a man-made lake (perfect for strolling), and the 1827 Great Conservatory, which displays flowering bushes and a notable collection of orchids (the Conservatory is said to be the model for the much larger Crystal Palace from the Great International Exhibition of 1851). The park was mostly designed in the 18th-century by noted landscape architect "Capability" Brown and opened to the public in 1968. It is on the grounds of the Duke of Northumberland's Syon House, which dates from the 1500s, and was remodelled extensively by architect Robert Adam in 1762 (it is considered by many to be his masterpiece); this elaborate jewel-box of a house is open to the public. The park also contains the British Heritage Motor Museum (see separate listing) and the London Butterfly House, exhibiting a large collection of butterflies from around the world (and where, especially during summer, live butterflies flit among visitors in recreated natural scenes).

Syon Park, Brentford, Middlesex, 081-560 0882; near Gunnersbury Undergound station. Daily 10 am-6 pm. Adults £1.50, children and OAPs £1.

## Oldest Botanical Garden In London

Chelsea Physic Garden

It wouldn't be too farfetched to say that the roots of the U.S. Civil War (1861-1865) can be traced back to this walled, four-acre garden. Cotton seeds were sent from here to the American colonies in the early 1700s, helping to establish the cotton industry in the Southern states, which led to large cotton plantations, the demand for slaves, and, eventually, war! On a more peaceful note, this garden dates from 1673 and was only recently (1983) opened to the public. It was originally laid out by the Society of Apothecaries of London—explaining why many of its approximately 5,000 plants are therapeutic and medicinal herbs. This pleasant oasis also offers a large variety of trees, bushes, shrubs, and flowers from around the world; the oldest rock garden in England (including stones from the Tower of London); and a 30-foot olive tree—by far the tallest in this far-from-the-Mediterranean country. It's not open long hours (although it *is* open daily during May's Chelsea Flower Show), but the garden is worth a visit, especially for dedicated green-thumbers.

Chelsea Physic Garden, 66 Royal Hospital Rd, London SW3, 071-352 5646. Apr-Oct Wed & Sun 2-5 pm. Adults £2, children £1. Near Sloane Square Underground station.

# Best Park Laid Out By Louis XIV's Gardener

Greenwich Park

This is a Royal Park with a touch of a French accent. It was laid out by André le Nôtre (Louis XIV's gardener and landscape architect) for Charles II in the late 17th century. Its 200 acres consist mainly of rolling grasslands and rows of trees bordering paths. Its notable high spot (literally *and* figuratively) is Greenwich Hill, which offers excellent views of Greenwich, the Thames, and the surrounding Docklands and East London. Greenwich Park is also world famous for a line running through it: This is the home of the Old Royal Observatory, the site of the Prime Meridian (0 degrees longitude) and the establishing spot of Greenwich Mean Time, accepted around the world as the benchmark from which time is measured. Another notable structure in the park is the brick Ranger's House (dating from 1688), which contains the famous Suffolk Collection of royal portraiture. To the south of the park is Blackheath Common, the site of the world's first golf club (founded in 1608 and no longer extant).

Greenwich Park, Charlton Way, London SE10, 081-858 2608. Daily 5 am-dusk.

# Best Park To Mingle With The Horsey Set

Clapham Common

While considered below the Horse of the Year Show and Derby Day (see separate listings) on the social-calendar/horsey-set Richter Scale, the Greater London Horse Show can be a nice introduction to the English equestrian scene (for those inclined to be interested). This gathering is held annually on Clapham Common over the August Bank Holiday Weekend. Located south of the Thames, Clapham Common is a 220-acre triangular park, ringed by some handsome 17th- and 18th-century homes. This park has its own Speaker's Corner (inspired by the original in Hyde Park—see separate listing); besides the Horse Show, it also hosts a variety of small fairs and festivals.

Clapham Common, London SW4; near Clapham Common Underground station. Greater London Horse Show held Aug Bank Holiday Weekend.

# SIGHTSEEING

## Best Spot For The Old Guard...And The New

### The Changing of the Guard, Buckingham Palace

While some say the pomp and spectacle of this long-standing ceremony is best left to tourists, we suspect that more than a few British breasts swell with pride watching the Changing of the Guard. Presented daily at 11:30 a.m. in summer (11:30 a.m. every *other* day the rest of the year)—and called off during inclement weather or during certain special state events—the changing takes approximately 30 minutes and usually attracts a large crowd. (It seems as if every tour coach circling London stops here and disgorges its charges around 11:25 a.m., adding to the crush.) Marching to the accompaniment of their own band, the new guards approach the palace forecourt with military precision and rousing pageantry. Garbed in crisp uniforms of scarlet and blue, with bearskin hats, the ranks of guards pass each other, symbolizing the passing of the responsibility of guarding the palace. Pomp, to be sure, but very photogenic pomp. The best view of this popular spectacle is from directly in front of Buckingham Palace, which has been home to Britain's reigning monarch since Queen Victoria took residence in 1837. The royal standard is flown on the flagpole when HRH, The Queen is in residence. But, whether she's home or not, the palace remains closed to the public.

Buckingham Palace, St. James's Park, London SW1, 071-930 4832. Apr-Jul daily 11:30 am, Aug-Mar alternate days 11:30 am.

## Best Spot To Sing "I Aint Got Nobody"
The Tower of London

It's best to visit what is one of the most fortified buildings in the world (begun in 1078 by William the Conqueror) with a bit of lore firmly in mind: If you don't see the clipped-wing ravens preening about this superb example of Norman architecture alongside the Thames near Tower Bridge, legend suggests you should leave the Tower at once. It is said that if the ravens disappear, the Tower will fall and the Kingdom with it. (Which explains the ravens' clipped-wing condition; officials aren't taking any chances!) But try not to lose your head here (as Anne Boleyn did in 1536 on Tower Green), because there are plenty of sights to set it awhirl. After you watch the morning changing of the guard, find a red-suited Yeoman Warder at the Middle Tower to lead you through the complex that has served as a palace, prison, treasury, arsenal, mint, even a zoo. Exhibits range from The Crown Jewels—including the exquisite bejewelled and fur-fringed Imperial State Crown worn by Her Majesty The Queen only at her coronation and on major State occasions—to the rack in the room housing the Instruments of Torture and Punishment. In the Royal Armouries, you'll find artillery, weapons, and royal suits of armour spanning the history of the Kingdom. On the second floor, the Chapel of St. John stands as a powerful testament to Norman church architecture. Stand at the ramparts of The Wall Walk or in the yard facing the high, arched windows of the Chapel Royal of St. Peter and Vincula and you might feel the spirit of another age pass through you, wafted on a gentle London breeze.

The Tower of London, London EC3, 071-709 0765. Mar-Oct Mon-Sat 9:30 am-6 pm, Sun 2-6 pm; Nov-Feb Mon-Sat 9:30 am-5 pm. Adults £5.90, students & OAPs £4.50, children £3.70.

## Best Spot That You Can Visit (But The Queen Can't)
House of Commons

At times, debates on the floor of the House of Commons are the greatest show in town, full of acerbic wit, cutting repartee, and measured insults.

Although a procedural handbook outlaws such rank accusations as "liar," "vulgar," and "corrupt," quick-thinking MPs often slip barbs by the Speaker, who acts as referee—such as when Winston Churchill avoided "liar" in favour of "terminal inexactitude." Sir Winston's most famous retort was to Lady Astor's remark that were she his wife she would poison his coffee. "And if I were your husband," he rejoined, "I'd drink it." To watch the fireworks (which often fizzle into yawns), join the queue outside the St. Stephen's entrance to gain admission to the Strangers' Gallery (more formally, the gallery for "Distinguished and Ordinary Strangers"). Waits can be long—especially during crises—but you can get to the head of the queue with a pass from your MP, Embassy, or High Commissioner (although only four each are allocated daily). The austere late-Gothic-style building opened in 1950 after destruction of an earlier building by World War II bombing. Visitors should feel privileged if they gain entrance to this august body, since the Queen herself is not permitted to enter the House of Commons.

House of Commons, Westminster, London SW1, 071-219 4272. Mid-Oct-late Jul, Mon-Thu after 2:40 pm, Fri after 9:30 am.

# Timeliest Spot To Check Your Watch
## Big Ben

Nearly everyone knows that the famous name "Big Ben" refers not to the clock—or even its 320-foot tower, which rises above the Houses of Parliament—but rather to the 13- to 15-ton (estimates vary) bell *inside* London's unofficial "official" timekeeper. But here are four facts about Big Ben (and its clock and tower) that you may *not* know: 1. It is not known exactly for whom the bell received its popular moniker, but the leading candidate is Sir Benjamin Hall, who was commissioner of works when the clock was built in 1859 (other logical nominees include Benjamin Vulliamy, the queen's clockmaker at the time, or perhaps even Big Benjamin Caunt, a hulking boxer of the era); 2. The bell was cast in the same foundry as America's Liberty Bell; 3. The clock's minute hands are 14 feet long, made of copper, and are hollow; and 4. The famous eight-note toll that the clock's chimes sound hourly—which is used to lead off BBC news broadcasts—is from a passage of Handel's Messiah.

Big Ben (at the Houses of Parliament), London SW1; near Westminster Underground station.

# Best Place To "Bone Up" On British Monarchy

Westminster Abbey

As the site of every British Coronation since that of William I in 1066, this most famous of abbeys is known as the "birthplace of monarchies," but it also serves as the final resting place for countless royalty and nobility. Elizabeth I is buried in the North Aisle of the 1519 Chapel of Henry VII under the grand vaulted roof (Henry VII himself lies behind the Altar). Five kings and four queens lie near the shrine in the Chapel of St. Edward the Confessor. In the Gothic Nave (the tallest in England), the Monument to Sir Issac Newton, with an intricate effigy of the man best known for conceiving the law of universal gravitation, beckons followers of science. Poets' Corner, in the South Transept, is frequented by lovers of the arts who come to see the tomb of Geoffrey Chaucer, as well as monuments to the fanciful Lewis Carroll, John Milton, and, of course, William Shakespeare. Stunning statuary memorialising great citizens past fill the Abbey. But you can take a break from such grave matters by viewing the oak Coronation Chair made for King Edward I by Master Walter of Durham, and by visiting Westminster Abbey Museum in the vaulted Norman Undercroft beneath the former monks' dormitory. The High Altar of The Sanctuary is the focal point of the Abbey's architecture as well as of its regular services and celebrations.

Westminster Abbey, at Broad Sanctuary and St. Margarets St, London SW1, 071-222 5152. Mon-Fri 9 am-4:45 pm, Sat 9 am-2:45 pm. Adults £2.60, students & OAPs £1.30, children under 16 60p.

# Best Cathedral To Whisper Its Praises

St. Paul's Cathedral

Attacked by early critics, Luftwaffe bombs, and modern encroachments of steel and glass, London's Anglican cathedral remains a focal point of the City. There have been churches on the site since the 7th century, with an even larger cathedral destroyed by the Great Fire of 1666. This stone, baroque masterpiece of Sir Christopher Wren took 35 years to complete and a translation of his Latin epitaph in the cathedral says it all: "Reader, if you seek his monument, look around you." Kids love the Whispering Gallery, worth the 259-step climb to test marvelous acoustics that enable them to communicate in a whisper across the gallery. Visitors from the United States stop at the American Memorial Chapel, honouring 28,000

U.S. service personnel stationed in Britain who gave their lives during World War II. And everyone is curious to see photographs of the 1981 wedding of Prince Charles and Lady Diana Spencer—and the dramatic photograph of London aflame around St. Paul's during the blitz. Nelson and Wellington have tombs in the crypt, as does architect Wren and Turner, Reynolds, and other famous artists interred in Painters' Corner. The dome, uncharacteristic of English churches, is second in size only to the one found at St. Peter's in Rome.

St. Paul's Cathedral, Ludgate Hill, London EC4, 071-248 2705. Varying hours and prices for admissions and guided tours.

## Best Bet For Legal Eagles With Poseys Of Roses
Old Bailey

In the middle ages it was a short journey from courtroom to prison—and for the odours that would rise up from the cells into the courtroom. To counteract the foul smells, judges adopted the practice of carrying nosegays. Although the dreaded Newgate Prison is gone and the building on its site no longer has a connected jail, judges maintain the tradition of carrying poseys and court officers symbolically sprinkle dried flowers on the courtroom floor. Apart from these traditions, the public gallery of the Old Bailey—officially the Central Criminal Court—is the place to see the big trials presided over by judges and barristers in wigs and robes. The present baroque stone building, with its gilt Lady of Justice holding scales and sword atop its copper dome, is the third on the site, built around the turn of the century.

Old Bailey (Central Criminal Court), Newgate St, London EC4, 071-248 3277. Mon-Fri 10:30 am-1 pm, 2-4 pm. Free.

## Best Spot To See Chuck & Di When They're In Town
Kensington Palace

Although London's most famous royal residence, Buckingham Palace, draws the big crowds, they are kept at a distance, outside the gates. This London home of the Prince and Princess of Wales and of Princess Margaret is a palace that you can go into! Visit the Royal Apartments, see where Queen Victoria and Queen Mary were born, view Princess Diana's wedding dress, and admire such art and artifacts as paintings by Van Dyke and Rubens, Queen Victoria's dollhouse and other childhood playthings, and a writing cabinet from the 17th century with an exquisite tortoise shell inlay. The palace was built as a country house around the beginning of the 17th century. In 1689, King William III and Queen Mary II commissioned Sir Christopher Wren to redesign it. George II was the last reigning monarch to make the palace his residence. The stunning Court Dress Collection spans several centuries in displaying finery worn at court. After visiting the palace, inspect the pretty gardens and the Orangery built by Queen Anne.

Kensington Palace, Kensington Gardens, London W8, 071-937 9561. Mon-Sat 9 am-5 pm, Sun 1-5 pm. Adults £3; OAPs, students £2.50; children £1.50.

## It Was The Best Of Places...

The Dickens House

It was the best of times and the worst of times. This was the house where Charles Dickens, then in his mid-twenties, secured his reputation. And it is the house where his beloved sister-in-law, 17-year-old Mary Hogarth, collapsed and died in his arms. Later, he used this tragedy as a model for the death of Little Nell in *The Old Curiosity Shop.* Here, he wrote *Nicholas Nickleby,* worked on *Oliver Twist,* began *Barnaby Rudge,* and finished *Pickwick Papers*—even though he lived here only from April 1837 to December 1839. On a private road attended by porters in mulberry-coloured livery, the house was Dickens' first sign of upward mobility. Today, it is a museum with an exhaustive collection of books, manuscripts, letters, portraits, illustrations, personal effects, and other memorabilia. In his study are such items as his favourite china monkey and the desk at which he worked the day before he died in 1870. The dining room, where he loved to entertain, has a handsome mahogany sideboard and the grandfather clock that belonged to coach proprietor Moses Pickwick, whose name Dickens appropriated. A shop has rare editions, prints, stationery, Toby jugs, first-day stamp covers, busts of Dickens, and various souvenirs.

The Dickens House, 48 Doughty St, London WC1, 071-405 2127. Mon-Sat 10 am-5 pm. Adults £1.50, students £1, children 75p, families £3.

## Best Spot To Insure Your Legs—And Other Valuables

Lloyd's of London Tours

Movie stars' legs and breasts, movie-production delays, vacation weather, and ships and their cargoes are all fair game for the underwriters at Lloyd's as they make good on their claim to insure anything, but anything—just as long as the insured is willing to pay the premium. Edward Lloyd began doing business in a coffeehouse in the 17th century. Its latest successor, the gleaming glass-and-steel building opened by The Queen in 1986, speaks more of computerised big business than of city merchants sipping java as they exchange information about shipping. Ride an outside glass elevator to the visitor centre, where exhibits unfold the colourful story of the world's largest insurance company. Below is the Underwriting Room, the nerve centre of worldwide underwriting; above is a soaring, 200-foot-high atrium. On display is the ship's bell salvaged from HMS *Lutine* that went down in 1799 with a cargo of bullion. Traditionally, the bell was sounded to tell of a disaster at sea. Guides explain how Lloyd's took a bath on the *Titanic* sinking and on the San Francisco earthquake and fire of 1906. Tours are free, and there's even a coffeehouse—1990s-style.

Lloyd's of London, 1 Lime St, London EC3, 071-623 7100. Mon-Fri 10 am-2:20 pm. Free.

## Best Place To See Where Winnie Spoke And The World Listened

Cabinet War Rooms

For the 15th consecutive night Airmarshall Goering's vaunted Luftwaffe has London under siege. Your warm underground shelter seems suddenly chilly as you hear the muffled sounds of the one-sided battle. The three-foot slab of reinforced concrete overhead doesn't entirely shut out the steady drone of heavy bombers, the rumble of exploding bombs, and the punctuating bark of antiaircraft guns. You wonder how well these Cabinet War Rooms, cloistered below a steel-framed government building, would stand up to a direct hit. London during the blitz of 1940-41? For sure. But this scenario also applies to London of the 1990s when the blitz is pretty much limited to onslaughts upon British sterling. Special effects at the mesmerising Cabinet War Rooms relive an air raid on England's capital, while tours allow visitors to inspect the Spartan underground office and makeshift bedroom that are part of an underground warren of bunkers from which Winston Churchill and his cabinet conducted the war during bombing raids on London. Inspect the map room, the cabinet room, and the small room from which Winnie made transatlantic telephone calls to FDR—all frozen in a 1940s time warp. You can rent headphone sets for an audio tour and buy stirring

WWII posters—"Careless talk costs lives," "Dig for victory"—and other memorabilia at a gift shop.

Cabinet War Rooms, Clive Steps, King Charles St, London SW1, 071-930 6961. Daily 10 am-6 pm. £3.50 including headphones.

## Best Bridge Not Dismantled And Shipped To Arizona

Tower Bridge

Rumour has it that the multi-millionaire American who bought the old London Bridge thought he'd purchased the historic, landmark Tower Bridge instead! Of course the famous, familiar Tower Bridge is still here, providing great views of London and the Thames from an enclosed walkway spanning its two towers. Besides its scenic vistas, the bridge also offers a fascinating museum detailing history of the bridges on the Thames, a collection of models demonstrating how the bridge works, and a sparkling Victorian-era engine room housing the now-unused hydraulic mechanisms that raised and lowered the bridge before the operation was converted to electrical usage in the 1970s. The view from Tower Bridge is very popular with photographers and other sightseers. But it was once the *last* view that a number of distraught people saw—until the walkways were enclosed, this was a renowned site for suicides.

Tower Bridge, London SE1, 071-407 0922. Apr-Oct daily 10 am-6:30 pm, Nov-Mar daily 10 am-4:45 pm. Adults £2.50, children and OAPs £1. Near Tower Hill or London Bridge Underground stations.

## Best Statue That Is Spared The Adoration Of Pigeons

Winston Churchill statue

With apologies to one of Winston Churchill's most famous and stirring wartime speeches: Blood, sweat, toil, and tears, yes; pigeon droppings, no. Really, it just would *not* do for the likeness of the British bulldog of World War II to be desecrated by indiscreet birds. So, the top of this statue of Churchill is slightly electrified to keep pigeons from flocking around Winnie and "honouring" him the way they have Nelson for years. (Approximately a ton of pigeon droppings were recently cleaned off of the admirable Admiral and his soaring column in Trafalgar Square!) This 1973 statue depicts a resolute-looking Churchill in his greatcoat, cane in hand, surveying the streets of his beloved London. Fittingly, the statue is opposite the Houses of Parliament, where Churchill spent so much of his adult life—in fact, his run of just under 64 years as an MP is the longest in British history.

Winston Churchill statue, opposite the Houses of Parliament, London SW1; near Westminster Underground station.

## Best Spot Where There Is No Place Like Holmes'

"221b" Baker Street

London has long-since outlawed the coal-burning fires that created the pea-souper fogs that swirled around mysterious visitors arriving at 221b Baker Street. And, of course, the hacks that deposit latterday visitors no longer are horse-drawn. So it does take a stretch of the imagination to picture the rooms occupied by that deductive genius Sherlock Holmes and his blustering sidekick and chronicler, Dr. Watson. Particularly since the actual street address is fictional! However, Holmes' fans generally agree that the detective's quarters would be located on the site now occupied by offices of the Abbey National Building Society. Thus, the site has become hallowed ground to members of the Baker Street Irregulars and legions of other avid Holmes' followers. Reputedly, along with conducting its mortgage business, the building society keeps a clerk busy dealing with correspondence directed to the famous Baker Street address. Those who have seen any of the nearly 200 films about the detective may be interested in visiting the Sherlock Holmes pub (see separate listing), where Sir Conan Doyle once stayed and wrote about, and where there is a creation of the detective's Baker Street study.

Abbey National Building Society, at the site of 221b Baker St, London NW1.

## Best Misnamed Egyptian Monument

Cleopatra's Needle

It's a trivia-lover's dream, this eye-catching monument along the Victorian Embankment. First, it predates its namesake by several centuries (although it did stand in front of Cleopatra's palace). Second, the monument has a twin in Central Park, New York. Third, buried beneath it is a Victorian time capsule with a portrait of the monarch, a copy of *The Times*, and other memorabilia of the era, including pictures of a dozen Victorian beauties. Fourth, the sphinxes "guarding" the base were mistakenly positioned facing inward instead of outward, and so remain. The 68'-6"-tall, 186-ton pink-granite obelisk, fashioned in Heliopolis, Egypt, some 3,500 years ago, was a gift presented in 1819 to commemorate the defeat of the French in 1798 in the Battle of the Nile. Beset by problems, the monument finally arrived in England in 1878, following a journey of five months via a specially-built iron pontoon. Today, its hieroglyphics and symbols are a curiosity to visitors and photographers strolling beside the river.

Cleopatra's Needle, Victoria Embankment, London WC2.

## Best Spot To Ponder After You've Shooed The Pigeons

Trafalgar Square

Lofty in victory—even a pyrrhic one that cost him his life—Admiral Lord Horatio Nelson towers over London and faces south toward Portsmouth, the home port of his vanquishing fleet. Nelson's Column, a 170-foot Corinthian column, topped by a 17-foot statue of the Admiral, and erected in 1842, is one of London's most identifiable landmarks. The surrounding square is named after the 1805 naval battle where Nelson defeated Napoleon—but where Nelson was also mortally wounded by French fire. Bronze tablets at the column's base depict scenes from Nelson's famous battles; these were cast from melted-down cannons captured from Napoleon's forces. The four lions ringing the column (a popular spot for kids to gambol) were sculpted by noted animal painter Sir Edwin Landseer, and were added to the monument in 1867. This is the spot where the national Christmas tree is erected annually and where crowds turn out to hail the coming of the New Year. This is also a *very* popular spot for pigeons—the column and statue recently required an extensive cleaning to remove an estimated *ton* of pigeon droppings from its surface.

Trafalgar Square, London WC2; near Charing Cross Underground station.

## Best Place To See Where A Headstone "Marx" The Spot

Highgate Cemetery

This famous Victorian resting place of Karl Marx also contains the grave of George Eliot, the female novelist, buried in 1880 as Mary Ann Cross (née Evans). These graves are in the Eastern Cemetery, open daily to the public. The Western Cemetery, which may be visited only as part of a tour group, is an overgrown wilderness. Current restoration work is aimed at taming the tangle of undergrowth to reveal remarkable carved monuments, ornate tombs, ivy-covered gravestones, Egyptian catacombs, and a Gothic chapel. Marx died in 1883 and his grave, the object of pilgrimages from around the world, has a stone appropriately inscribed "Workers of the World Unite," as well as a monument erected in the 1950s. The cemetery was consecrated in 1839.

Highgate Cemetery, Swains Ln, London N6, 081-340 1834. Apr-Sep 10 am-5 pm, Oct-Mar 10 am-4 pm.

## Best Place To Bring Your Soapbox
Speakers' Corner, Hyde Park

"And what about Laplander independence and home rule for the reindeers?" railed the wild-eyed man to the bemused crowd gathered around him. His piece said, the man stepped off his makeshift stage of a wooden box and wandered off to wherever reindeer-supporting extremists go. Was he crazy, for real, or a try-out for a new Monty Python episode? Such is the attraction (and the heritage) of this famous spot. Located at the northeast corner of Hyde Park (near Marble Arch, the memorial celebrating the victories at Trafalgar and Waterloo), Speakers' Corner is specifically set aside for anyone who wishes to spew oratory on any subject—provided the subject isn't obscene and doesn't incite violence. These speeches have been going on here since 1872, when, in an attempt to mollify the masses after large-scale rioting in previous years, the right to free assembly was allowed by Parliament. (Contrary to common opinion, therefore, it is not the speakers, but rather the *groups gathered to listen* to them who are technically protected by law.) The most lively action is found on Sunday mornings; would-be orators who want to regale the masses with their theories, beliefs, or convictions should bring their own boxes.

Speakers' Corner, Hyde Park, London W1; near Marble Arch Underground station.

## Best Place To Pay Your Respects
The Cenotaph

This stark monument on a wide stretch of Parliament Street is the most sombre spot in London—every year on the second Sunday of November from 11 a.m. to 11:02 a.m. This is when two minutes' silence is observed during the annual service commemorating the fallen of two world wars and Londoners turn out to recall the poppy fields of Flanders and the beaches of Normandy. Usually, the Remembrance Sunday service is attended by the Queen and leading statesmen and other dignitaries from Britain and the Commonwealth. The stone monument, with its simple inscription, "To the Glorious Dead," was unveiled in 1920, designed by Sir Edward Lutyens to honour the dead of World War I. The simple, poignant inscription was added following World War II.

The Cenotaph, Parliament St, London SW1; near Westminster Underground station.

## Best "Circus" (Hold The Clowns And Elephants)

Piccadilly Circus

What once was considered "the hub" of the mighty British Empire is now regarded a bit less loftily...but is still the spiritual (if not quite physical) centre of one of London's busiest and most popular areas, Soho. This neon-lit, crowded jumble of a roundabout, long-favoured as a London meeting place, offers a variety of shops, restaurants, and other attractions, most notably in the restored centre of the Trocadero (see separate listing). It would be hard to say which there are more of around Piccadilly at any given time—Londoners, tourists...or pigeons. But, they all seem to be rushing to or from somewhere. Piccadilly is also home to a favoured fountain statue that is called Eros (for the god of love), but which was supposed to represent a decidedly less carnal figure—an angel (see separate listing). And the name? It comes from the 17th century, when the neighbourhood's most prominent resident had made his fortune manufacturing "picadils," stiff formal collars popular at that time.

Piccadilly Circus, London SW1; near Piccadilly Circus Underground station.

## Best Square Once Favoured By Duellists

Leicester Square

From Shakespeare to Rocky Balboa, from Charlie Chaplin to the Rolling Stones, this square has seen entertainers and entertainments of various stripes throughout its existence. In years gone by, it was the site of many a duel...today, it offers cinemas, music clubs, restaurants, and pubs. Leicester Square was originally laid out in the 1660s and was later converted into a garden square in the late 19th century. It offers a grudging oasis in this area's rushing tumult; among its stretch of well-trod greenery are notable statuary, including those depicting Shakespeare, Chaplin, and Sir Isaac

Newton. The area surrounding the square is home to a variety of entertainments—restaurants, pubs, dance clubs, and four large cinemas—making this one of London's top nightlife areas (see separate listing). Also here is the popular Leicester Square Half-Price Ticket Booth (see separate listing). And while you won't see duels here anymore, you may see a few unsavoury characters—this square's growing resemblance to New York's seedy Times Square makes it a place to take caution and not walk alone after midnight. A few blocks north of Leicester Square is London's popular Chinatown neighbourhood, centered around Gerrard Street.

Leicester Square, London WC2; near Leicester Square and Piccadilly Circus Underground stations.

## Best Site That Protects Other Sights
The Thames Flood Barrier

It may seem strange to list a public works site such as this as a prime sightseeing destination, but, then again, this is no ordinary facility. What looks somewhat like a sliced-and-diced version of Sydney's world-famous Opera House scattered across a stretch of the Thames is actually a £550-million flood protection system. The Barrier's nine gleaming, steel-hooded piers contain mechanisms that raise up to 3700-ton concrete barriers from the bed of the Thames; these barriers join to form a 65-foot wall in 30 minutes, completely damming the river to prevent it from bursting its banks. All told, more than 500,000 tons of concrete was used to construct the barrier walls and mechanism piers. Built from 1975 to 1982 (and officially opened in 1984), the Barrier is operated about once a month, to ensure that it can be quickly employed when necessary (you can inquire as to when testings are scheduled; they are impressive to watch). A Visitors Centre presents an audio-visual presentation about the construction and operation of the Barrier; cruises tour the piers for a closer look at the mammoth works.

The Thames Flood Barrier, Unity Way, London SE18, 081-854 1373. Mon-Fri 10:30 am-5 pm, Sat & Sun 10:30 am-5:30 pm. Adults £2, children under 16 and OAPs £1.20.

## Best Historic Spot In The Center Of It All
Charing Cross

With a recorded history reaching back to Roman times, you'd expect London to (collectively) have a long memory...And the modern re-establishment of this 13th century memorial is a perfect example of that memory. You see, in the southern end of Trafalgar Square (see separate listing) stands a statue of Charles I, who was beheaded after the English Civil War of the mid-1600s. But *originally* on this site was a cross, erected in 1291 by Edward I, marking the final stopping place of the funeral procession of his beloved Queen Eleanor. This became known as Charing Cross, "Charing" being a corruption of the French phrase *chère reine*, meaning "dear queen." This cross stood until 1647, when it was torn down during the anti-royal crusades of Cromwell's republican government. This is where the memory of London comes in— when a hotel was built nearby the original site, across from the Charing Cross railway station, in the 1860s, a new cross to Queen Eleanor was erected in front of the station. Dash through the busy traffic to visit Charles and the cross' original site, and you can truthfully claim to have been in the centre of London—all distances to and from the city are measured from this landmark (as noted by a plaque at the foot of the memorial to the unfortunate Charlie).

Charing Cross, London W1; near Charing Cross Underground station.

# Best Attraction With An Alcoholic Beverage Named After It

Cutty Sark

With trade winds billowing her canvas, the sleek, three-masted *Cutty Sark* was fastest of the famous clipper ships that raced to London with their precious cargoes of tea from China. Built on the Clyde in 1869, at the height of her power during the great clipper races, she covered 363 miles (580 kilometers) in a record 24 hours. The ship takes her name from *Tam O'Shanter*, a poem by Robert Burns. She later carried cargoes of Australian wool. Tours above and below decks include an outstanding collection of ships' figureheads and exhibits that chronicle the era of the great clipper ships that raced the China seas. After touring the clipper and her tiny neighbour, *Gipsy Moth IV* (see separate listing), head for the Trafalgar Tavern (see separate listing), a restored riverside pub built in the 1830s. With your pint, try an order of whitebait, the tiny, crisply fried fish that is a local speciality.

Cutty Sark, King William Walk, Greenwich SE10, 081-858 3445. Mon-Sat 10 am-5 pm, Sun noon-5 pm. Adults £2, children £1.

# Best Sight To Make You Appreciate Air Travel

## Gipsy Moth IV

Moored alongside the famous three-masted *Cutty Sark* (see separate listing), this tiny yacht looks like a model. It's only 54 feet (16.8 meters) long with cramped living quarters that make it difficult to imagine that the *Gipsy Moth IV* was able to successfully circumnavigate the globe in a mere 226 days—or that this feat was accomplished with a single sailor at the helm, and that this person was a sprightly 66 years old. William Chicester's 29,677-mile (47,483.2 kilometers) odyssey was completed in 1967, and made him the first Englishman to sail solo around the world. He was knighted by Queen Elizabeth II, who used the same ceremonial sword that Elizabeth I had used in 1581 to so honour Sir Francis Drake, the first British sailor to make the around-the-world trip (but with a full crew!)

Gipsy Moth IV, King William Walk, Greenwich SE10, 081-853 3589. Apr-Oct Mon-Sat 10 am-6 pm, Sun noon-6 pm. Adults 30p, children & OAPs 20p.

# Best Flight To Make You Appreciate Air Travel

## Concorde

If money is no object, the Concorde is one way to beat jet lag and the boredom of a long transatlantic flight. With two flights a day from New York and three flights a week from Washington, D.C., the 100-passenger aircraft cruises at about 1,350 m.p.h. (2,150 k.p.h.) and accomplishes the New York-London flight in a shade over three hours. At Kennedy, the Concorde has its own lounge, where you're cloistered from the clamour of the airport and where the cossetting begins with a breakfast buffet, open bottles of wines and spirits, and a wide selection of British and American newspapers. On board, the flight is the equivalent of a long, leisurely dining experience, starting with orders for aperitifs and culminating with the serving of dessert, excellent cheeses, 20-year-old port, and after-dinner liqueurs. Included are frequently proffered baskets with fine clarets, burgundies, bordeaux, and champagnes, and a meal that might include fresh fruits, Scottish salmon, prime grilled fillet of Angus beef, and lobster. Other pampering touches include a gift pair of opera glasses and a fresh carnation with a pin—so that you arrive in London wearing the cachet of the Concorde. But the tab? One-way from New York, $4,167, from Washington, $3,713.

British Airways sales offices, 800/AIRWAYS.

# Best Upperdeck Tours

The Original London Transport Sightseeing Tour

One of the best introductions to the major sights and to the geography of London—and one of its best sightseeing values—is a 1½-hour tour aboard one of the traditional red double-decker buses. With more than 90 tours a day during the peak season, you won't need a reservation. Climb aboard at any of four departure points and pay your fare (although there is a discount for advance purchase). In good weather, it is pleasant on the open top deck, high above traffic snarling narrow city streets. A lively, sometimes subjective, commentary is provided by guides knowledgeable in London history and ready to colour the commentary with personal observations and opinions. You'll travel London's famous streets, such as Fleet Street, the Strand, and Park Lane, and pass such major sights as the Tower Bridge and Tower of London, Trafalgar Square, Westminster Abbey, St. Paul's Cathedral, and Downing Street. Your guide will point out landmarks that you might otherwise miss, such as the statues of griffins, the mythical winged lion, that mark the City boundaries, and the camels and sphinxes that decorate the iron seats along The Embankment.

London Coaches Limited, Jews Row, London SW18, 071-227 3456. Departures from Victoria, Piccadilly Circus, Baker St, Marble Arch, summer 9 am-7 pm, spring-autumn 10 am-5 pm, winter 10 am-4 pm. Adults £8, under 16 £4.

# Best Locations For Movies And TV

The Movie Map

If you're a fan of the big screen or addicted to the small screen, there is intriguing adventure to be found visiting movie and television locations in London and beyond. The British Tourist Authority has produced a handy map-brochure that pinpoints about 80 locations that were used as settings for famous productions from the past five decades, ranging from *Brideshead Revisited* to *Coronation Street*. In London, it will steer you to Lincoln's Inn and the Old Bailey, featured in *Rumpole of the Bailey*, to 165 Eaton Place familiar to followers of the popular series *Upstairs, Downstairs*, to Hampton Court used as a setting for the movie *A Man For All Seasons*, and to Covent Garden and Ascot, locations for *My Fair Lady*. In nearby Kent is Penshurst Place, featured in *The Prince and the Pauper*, while in Cambridgeshire and

Berkshire are numerous locations used in *Chariots of Fire*. Included are suggested itineraries for "Film Trails with a Theme"—romantic, historical, the classics, and murder, mystery, and suspense. The Movie Map is available free and makes interesting reading even if you are just an armchair traveller.

British Tourist Authority, Thames Tower, Blacks Rd, London W6, 071-846 9000. Convenient locations also at Victoria Station, Heathrow Airport, Harrods, and Selfridges.

## Best Ripping-Good Trips
Tragical History Tours

Who was Jack the Ripper? His identity remains unknown, as you'll learn during this evening bus tour. Tour guides, "Ripperologists" all, point out the site of each of the murderer's atrocities and elaborate on theories about the identity of the notorious 19th-century slasher who brought a reign of terror to the night streets of London. The tour also visits a Jacobean mansion, built in 1607, claimed to have been haunted by its former owner for more than 250 years. Also included are lore and legend relating to Sweeney Todd and to The Man in Grey. Refreshments are available at a pair of pubs chosen for their sinister pasts. Operated by the same company, The Ghost Bus offers a full-day 130-mile tour through the pretty Kent countryside. In Chislehurst Caves, by lantern light, visitors are introduced to the homes of at least five authenticated ghosts. Also on the itinerary is awesome Hever Castle, childhood home of Anne Boleyn, the "Pirate's Grave" at Goudhurst, and Pluckley, "England's most haunted village," where two exorcisms have been performed in the graveyard. Officially listed ghosts include a hooded monk, a highwayman, a mad miller, and the hanged schoolmaster. The tour includes a lunch stop at a country pub.

Tragical History Tours, The Business Centre, Sunnymead, 1 Bromley Ln, Chislehurst, Kent BR7 6LH, 081-467 3318. Bus Trip To Murder: Departs 7:15 pm daily from Temple Underground station (Embankment station Sun & hols). Adults £12.50, students £10, children £8.50. The Ghost Bus: Fri 9:45 am Temple station. Adults £23.50, children £17.

# ENVIRONS

## Best Palace Besides Buckingham

Windsor Castle

From a distance, the silhouette of the Queen's second home looks like an entire ancient city, its far-flung buildings studded with off-white towers and battlements. An even more impressive up-close look reveals that the visit is worth the 20-mile (32 kilometers) journey from London. Start your tour with a walk down the royal-blue-carpeted halls of The State Apartments. Used only for official entertaining and Ceremonies of State, these rooms are a textbook of architecture and design. Visitors admire the intricate gold moulding and ceiling designs, the distinctive chairs covered in red and green velvet, and the awesome works of art from the Royal Collection that seem to pop up at every turn. Peek inside a smaller but no less glamourous palace—the Dolls' House, designed by Sir Edwin Lutyens and given to Queen Mary by her subjects in 1923. This 1/12-scale palace is ornate in its own right, and is full of detailed touches, such as working plumbing and electricity, and a full library of miniature books. After a longish hike to the far end of the compound, you'll come upon St. George's Chapel, the burial place of 10 sovereigns, and the Shrine of the Order of the Garter. One of the finest examples of late medieval perpendicular architecture, started by King Edward IV in 1475, the chapel is an appropriate place to rest and reflect.

Windsor Castle, Windsor, 0753 831118. (Hours & admission fee vary for each attraction.)

## Most Amazing Maze
The gardens of Hampton Court Palace

This might be Henry VIII's Tudor palace, but it was William III who created the enchanting maze that stands as the centerpiece of the grounds of this grand country residence begun in 1514 by Thomas Wolsey. The twists and turns of the maze's neatly trimmed hedges have confounded visitors for centuries and are a delight to be lost in. (When getting lost becomes more frustrating than fun, there usually is someone around to help steer you out; without ruining the secret, there is a set combination of right and left turns that are supposed to lead to an exit from anywhere within the maze.) In any event, be sure to emerge in time to see the free-running deer graze the lawns around countless beds of vibrant yellow, red, and pink flowers. After walking through the gardens, which include the Great Vine, King's Privy Garden, Great Fountain Gardens, the Tudor and Elizabethan Knot Gardens, and Wilderness, you can take lunch or tea at the palace's Tiltyard Restaurant and Garden Café.

Hampton Court Palace, East Molesey, Surrey KT8 9AU, 081-977 7227. Mid-Mar-mid-Oct 9:30 am-6 pm; Mid-Oct-mid-Mar 9:30 am-4:30 pm. Adults & OAPs £1, children under 16 75p, children under 5 free.

## Most Famous Public School In England
Eton College, Eton

First, for those from outside the U.K., a primer in terms is necessary: In England, the phrase "public school" means a very *private*, exclusive school. And this famous boys' school, located about 25 miles (40 kilometers) from London, is the most prestigious of its type in the country. Founded by Henry VI in 1440, Eton has long been a training ground for English political, military, and literary leaders. On guided tours of the historic grounds, you are likely to see young schoolboys wearing smart tailcoats. Tours include a stroll through the school's oldest portion (a quadrangle called The Cloisters), a visit to its striking 15th-century chapel, and a stop at a museum chronicling the school's history, including a display showing the 21 British Prime Ministers the school has produced. The laid-back town of Eton offers some nice additional diversions. Eton High Street is crammed with antique shops, craft stores, and other small boutiques; it also has a few nice, upmarket pubs, wine bars, and cafés. Eton is adjacent to Windsor, making it a nice side trip to an outing to this area to see Windsor Castle, the world's oldest and largest inhabited castle (see separate listing).

Eton College, Eton, Buckinghamshire, 0753 863593. Apr-Sep daily 10:30 am-5 pm; limited days and hours during school term.


# Most Poetic Little Church In England

Stoke Poges

Perhaps no greater poetic appreciation of England's rock-solid commonfolk was ever written than Thomas Gray's *Elegy Written in a Country Churchyard*. First published around 1750, Gray's poem of tribute to the nameless denizens of a churchyard cemetery gained its author nearly universal acclaim. This lyrical piece became the most famous and best-loved English poem of its era— perhaps of all time. To visit the source of Gray's inspiration, journey about 10 miles north of Windsor and Eton, toward the town of Stoke Poges. On the main road into town, just before the village itself, you'll find Stoke Poges Church, the site of the churchyard depicted in the poem. Much has changed in the nearly 250 years since Gray surveyed this scene, but, nonetheless, the churchyard still presents a tranquil, poetic setting. Its gothic serenity is further enlivened by a beautiful modern garden nearby (including a lake, fountain, and rose garden), erected as a tribute to Gray in the 1920s. The poet will not only always be remembered in this churchyard—he will also always *be* here: Upon his death in 1771, Thomas Gray was buried in the famous yard of Stoke Poges Church.

Stoke Poges Church, Stoke Poges Ln, Stoke Poges, Buckinghamshire.


# England's Best-Kept Furnishings

Ham House

Bordering the Thames and surrounded by beautiful terraced gardens and meadowland, this 17th-century mansion and its gardens have been remarkably preserved. Originally built around 1610, the H-shaped building was extended and refurnished in the 1680s (by Elizabeth Dysart, wife of a minister to Charles II) in the Baroque style of the period—which is how it looks today, showcasing some of the best-preserved late-Stuart furnishings in all of England. Highlights include Corinthian pillars, a massive carved staircase with exquisite reliefs that date to the 1630s, chairs and couches covered in fine silk, rich wall hangings, marble fireplaces, and collections of textiles, costumes, and miniatures, including a portrait of Queen Elizabeth I by Hilliard. There are exceptional tapestries in a room originally created as a bed chamber for Queen Catherine, consort of Charles II. This lavish country house offers a gift shop, a cafeteria in the Orangery (both open Easter-October), and guided tours on Thursdays.

Ham House, Ham St, Petersham, Richmond, Surrey, 081-940 1950. Tue-Sun 11 am-5 pm. Adults £2, children & students £1.

## Best Place To See What Became Of A Famous Ship

Jourdans

Visitors from the United States—especially those few who can trace their family's arrival in the New World to the famous Pilgrim voyage from England in 1620—will find a certain barn in this village very interesting. Located some 30 miles out of London, Jourdans is home to the 1688 Friends Meeting House, a Quaker (Society of Friends) hall erected by William Penn. The village's other Quaker farm buildings include one known as the "Mayflower Barn," the timbers of which are said to include wood from the ship of the same name which carried the Pilgrims to Plymouth Rock, Massachusetts, in 1620 (and then returned to England). The barn is open daily as part of the town's Quaker exhibits and artefacts. Penn, founder of the U.S. state of Pennsylvania, and much of his family (both wives and many of their children) are buried in the town's churchyard. Nearby, in Chalfont St. Giles, is the cottage to which writer John Milton fled in 1665 to avoid London's plague; it is here that the blind, aged poet finished *Paradise Lost* and wrote all of *Paradise Regained.* The cottage contains personal memorabilia that belonged to Milton and valuable editions of his timeless works of literature.

Friends Meeting House, Jourdans, Mon, Wed-Sat hours vary by season; Mayflower Barn, daily 7 am-10 pm. Free. Milton's Cottage, Chalfont St. Giles, Mar-Oct Tue-Sat 10 am-6 pm. Adults £1, children 40p.

## Best Stately Home Where The Kids Won't Get Bored

Woburn Abbey

Kids tend to get fidgety at museum-like stately homes as parents examine period furnishings and other items of Historic Significance. At this splendid stately mansion, ancestral home of the Dukes of Bedford for more than 300 years, there is diversion aplenty. Parts of the 3,000-acre grounds have been converted into a park with free-ranging deer descended from the Imperial herd of China and into Britain's largest drive-through wildlife park. Wild Animal Kingdom is home to lions, tigers, elephants, monkeys, and wolves, and also offers amusement rides, a petting zoo, and sea-lion shows. The mansion itself, built to the plan of a medieval monastery, contains 18th-century English and French furniture, silver crafted by Huguenot silversmiths, and porcelain from the Continent and from China. Art lovers admire works by Gainsborough, Rembrandt, Reynolds, Van Dyck, and other old masters in what is acknowledged as one of the world's finest private art collections. For antique collectors, there is a cluster of more than three dozen shops with silver, glass, crystal, porcelain, artworks, and various other antiques and collectibles. You'll find set lunches and dinners at the timbered 19th-century Paris House in Woburn Park and good pub food at the Black Horse, an old coaching inn.

Woburn Abbey, Woburn, Bedfordshire MK43 0TP, 0525 290666. (Hours vary according to season, as well as for house, park, and shops.)

## Best English Town To Say, "When In Rome..."

### St. Albans

Visit this ancient market town on a Wednesday or Saturday and stroll down St. Peter's Street, where a lively street market, crowded with stalls of fruit and vegetables, haberdashery, men's and women's clothing, and a variety of household goods, dates back to Saxon times. Established under Roman rule 2,000 years ago as Verulamium, the town received its present name from a Roman soldier named Alban who became Britain's first Christian martyr when he was killed for defending a priest. At the Verulamium Museum, you can inspect superbly preserved Roman artifacts, including mosaic tiles, pottery, jewelry, glassware, and various implements. You can also view a Roman heating system and an excavated Roman theatre. St. Albans' Romanesque-Gothic cathedral, with a long, distinctive narrow nave, was founded in the 8th century and constructed with bricks salvaged from a Roman building. Part of the Magna Carta was prepared here at a time when the cathedral was a major Benedictine abbey. Other historical sites around town include a tall clock tower built at the beginning of the 15th century. It is located at French Row, named for foreign mercenaries imported in 1215 by Barons opposed to King John.

Tourist Information Centre, Town Hall, Market Place, St. Albans, Hertfordshire AL3 5DJ, 0727 64511.

## Best "Fairy Tale Castle"

Leeds Castle

Set on two small islands in a lake surrounded by 500 acres of rolling parkland near Maidstone, Kent, this 11th-century palace once was described by Lord Conway as "the loveliest castle in the world." If you make the hour or so drive from London to tour Leeds Castle or stay in one of its 20 exquisitely appointed rooms (available for groups or conferences only), there's a good chance you'll concur with Conway's generous assessment. Within the cream-coloured stone walls of the castle reside odd attractions such as a remarkable collection of ornamental dog collars dating back to the Middle Ages. Less eccentric touches of grace include a collection of medieval furnishings and French and English tapestries, fabrics, and paintings. Newer additions—such as a maze made from yew trees and an aviary that houses black swans, rare geese, and peacocks, and several endangered species of birds—complement the ancient castle, which was transformed from a Norman fortress to a royal palace by King Henry VIII. The Castle's lodgings include 10 principal rooms, furnished in a sumptuously royal manner (with antiques and fine art) as well as 10 smaller, more modern (yet no less luxurious) rooms.

Leeds Castle, Maidstone, Kent ME17 1PL, 0622 765400. Mar 16–Oct 31 Mon-Sun 11 am-6 pm; Nov-Mar 15 Sat & Sun 11 am-5 pm. Adults £5.60, students & OAPs £4.60, children £3.90.

## Best Very Dickens Of A Cathedral Town

Rochester

Because the famous cathedral at Canterbury is such a magnet, many visitors bypass another ancient Kentish town, Rochester. As a result, they miss a delightful town with medieval walls that dates to pre-Roman times and has the second oldest cathedral in England, built in 1077 (shortly after the Norman conquest), on a site consecrated in 604. Strategically placed on the River Medway across from the Royal Navy Yards at Chatham, Rochester has a brace of fine castles. Rochester Castle, dating from 1087, is a nonpareil example of Norman military architecture and has the tallest keep in England (with a great panoramic view of the countryside). Upnor Castle, an Elizabethan fortification built in 1559, has displays chronicling a naval engagement on the river in 1667 against marauding Dutch vessels. Rochester also is a Dickensian town. The author lived for many years at nearby Gad's Hill Place and used Rochester locales in many of his books. The Bull, an 18th-century inn on High Street, is said to be the pub of the same name in *Pickwick Papers*. At the Charles Dickens Centre, housed in an Elizabethan building, visitors are whisked back to Victorian times to witness the grim reality of squalid slums and meet Dickens' characters. Before leaving Rochester, be sure to stroll High Street, full of restored Victorian architecture and lots of tea rooms, inns, and shops with antiques, china, and crafts.

Tourist Information Centre, Eastgate Cottage, High St, Kent ME1 1EW, 0634 43666.

## Top Spot For Tellers Of Tales

Canterbury

Make a modern-day pilgrimage from London to this ancient town with medieval walls, England's most famous cathedral, and an exhibit that uses modern technology to recreate Geoffrey Chaucer's tales of 14th-century pilgrims journeying from London to Canterbury. The pilgrims were on their way to the shrine of Thomas-à-Becket, slain by four knights who acted upon Henry II's plea to "be rid of this turbulent priest." At Canterbury Cathedral, built soon after the Norman conquest, you can visit Becket's shrine, inspect an ancient Norman crypt and the tombs of Henry IV and Edward the Black Prince, and attend the lovely choral evensong. Other historic sites around Canterbury include the Museum of Arms and Armour in the city's only surviving gatehouse, 16th-century Huguenot weaving houses, the shell of a Roman townhouse with a mosaic floor, and Greyfriars, a 13th-century Franciscan friary with gardens sweeping down to the River Stour. At The Canterbury Tales (St. Margaret's Street), Chaucer's colourful stories of his immortal band of pilgrims come to life through creative audio-visual techniques.

Tourist Information Centre, 34 St. Margaret's St, Canterbury, Kent CT1 2TG, 0227 766567.

## Best Limey Coney Island

Southend-on-Sea

This quintessential East Enders' seaside resort is

almost a stereotype of Cockney culture. It is to London what Coney Island is to New York. In season, virtually every available centimeter of the pebbly beach is crammed with holidaymakers, faces turned to the sun, knotted handkerchieves covering bald pates, trouser legs rolled up for paddling. Flanking the beach along the front are more sunworshippers sprawled in hired deckchairs, shutting their ears to the cries of barkers trying to fill excursion boats for trips out onto the bay—literally, "Anymore for the *Skylark*." Across the street are rows of video arcades, vendors of cockles and whelks, storefront eateries dishing up stolid London fare—sausage-and-mash and fish and chips— and outlets for Rossi's whipped ice cream (*no one* goes to Southend without sampling a Rossi's!). The mile-long pier (longest in England) provides a breezy walk—or you can ride out on a train, to peer at the anglers or across the open sea toward Belgium. Southend's greatest asset is perhaps its proximity to London; drive about 35 miles (56 kilometers) from Piccadilly Circus and you can sniff the briny.

Southend-on-Sea, Civic Centre, Victoria Ave, Essex SS2 6ER. 0702 355122.

## Best "London-by-the-Sea"
Brighton

Its beach isn't much—pebbly, often impossibly crowded, and fronting the gunmetal waters of the Channel that usually are teeth-chatteringly cold, even for paddling. But Brighton does have appeal across a broad range of society. It is at once chirpy Max Bygraves and distinguished Yehudi Menuhin. Brighton is everyman's resort, gaudy and a little seedy, with a tacky amusement pier, cockle stalls, ice-cream vendors, and take-away fish-and-chip shops along the front, plus inexpensive seafood restaurants, bingo halls, movie houses, and row-upon-row of bed-and-breakfast lodgings. But it also has culture, with excellent art deco and art nouveau at the Brighton Art Gallery and Museum, West End tryouts at the Theatre Royal, and the Brighton Festival, held in May, which assembles some of the world's top classical-music talent. Don't miss exploring The Lanes, a labyrinth of alleys crammed with antique, jewelry, clothing, and book shops, and sprinkled liberally with cafés, pubs, and teashops (try The Mock Turtle for afternoon tea). Be sure to visit the Royal Pavilion. This summer palace, built in 1823 for the Prince Regent and recently restored, is an odd architectural hybrid of Islamic domes and Indian, Oriental, and Gothic styling. In Regency times, Brighton was a chic, fashionable resort. Although it now is more of a family resort, many of its ornamental Regency buildings remain. Dubbed "London-by-the-Sea," Brighton is only 55 minutes by express train from Victoria Station.

Tourist Information Centre, Marlborough House, 54 Old Steine, East Sussex BN1 1EQ, 0273 23755.

# Best Spot To Spot Red Sails In The Sunset

Maldon, Essex

In AD 991, Viking longboats sailed up the Black-water River to attack a Saxon fort built by King Edward the Elder. Today, these waters are plied by Thames sailing barges chartered by holidaymakers to explore the coastal waters of East Anglia. This town, only about 50 miles (80 kilometers) from central London, is a great spot to arrange a sailing holiday—or simply to spend a few hours soaking up the atmosphere. There are quayside pubs, a small maritime museum, a stand with fresh cock-les, whelks, mussels, and oysters, and moored barges and sailboats that at low tide become mired in the mud. You may also find an Old Salt demon-strating the nautical art of knot-tying and selling a variety of bracelets, pendants, bookmarks, and key chains. A riverside park (with a large adjacent car park) offers swimming, paddleboats, tennis courts, and kiddie amusements. Diversions include the High Street shops, a market on Thursdays and Saturdays, and Thames sailing barge races annu-ally in early June.

Tourist Information Centre, Maritime Centre, Hythe Quay, Maldon, Essex, 0621 856503.

# INDEX

# NOTES

# NOTES

# NOTES

# NOTES

# NOTES